The American Dictionary of Campaigns and Elections

Michael L. Young, Ph.D.

Hamilton Press

Lanham • New York • London

Abt Books

Hamilton Press

4720 Boston Way
Lanham, MD 20706

3 Henrietta Street
London WC2E 8LU England

Printed in the United States of America

British Cataloging in Publication Information Available

Co-published by arrangement with Abt Books.

Library of Congress Cataloging-in-Publication Data

Young, Michael L.
The American dictionary of campaigns and elections.

Bibliography: p.
Includes index.
1. Electioneering—United States—Dictionaries.
2. Campaign management—United States —Dictionaries.
3. Elections—United States—Dictionaries.
4. Politics, Practical—Dictionaries. I. Title.
JK1971.Y68 1987 324.7'0973 87-14828
ISBN 0-8191-5446-6 (alk. paper)

All Hamilton Press books are produced on acid-free
paper which exceeds the minimum standards set by the National
Historical Publication and Records Commission.

Hamilton Press

To JoAnne,
my political sponsor

CONTENTS

ACKNOWLEDGEMENTS

I owe a great deal to the many colleagues, friends and students who gave so much to this book. As every author comes to know, scores of people ultimately contribute to a manuscript, not all of whom can adequately be acknowledged in a brief space.

There are, however, certain people who were so instrumental to the completion of this book that they must be thanked individually.

Dr. Christopher McKenna, my colleague at Penn State/Harrisburg, supported my efforts generously and was always ready with help and encouragement. Dr. Robert Bresler, also a Penn State colleague, was a constant source of good ideas and a reliable sounding board for uncovering ideas that were not so good.

Louise Morgan, my secretary and friend, ably and efficiently typed earlier versions of the manuscript and helped in so many other ways.

My old comrades in arms from the 1976 Heinz campaign originally inspired this book, especially Pat Killian, Ron Maiorana and Don Raymond.

Also helpful in so many ways was my friend and former business partner pollster, Bill Cromer; Debbie Boyd, probably the best politician I know; Mark Keisling, a friend and student who has taught me much more about politics than I have taught him; and Joe O'Conner, writer and political savant who graciously reviewed earlier drafts of the manuscript and gave me many, many good ideas.

The students in my campaign and election courses endured endless earlier versions of the manuscript and inspired many improvements (about which they will be happy).

My editor at ABT books, Kay Hardy, provided much appreciated early encouragement and helpful suggestions for improvements in the text. Many books must die for lack of a sympathetic editor.

My editor at Hamilton Books, Beth Carnes, made the birthing process almost painless. Along the way I learned a little about the book business and a lot about why authors need editors.

Finally, I want to thank all of the friends I have made in political life. This book is really about you and your exciting world.

Michael Young
Hershey, Pennsylvania
December 1, 1986

PREFACE

The *American Dictionary of Campaigns and Elections* is the product of an exhaustive search and review of the professional and scholarly literature on campaigns and elections. The Dictionary has been written for those who work in or follow politics, who are fascinated by the political process and interested in the specialized language that derives from it. In particular (but in no particular order) the book has been written for the following audiences: students and professors for use as a supplementary text in courses in American Government, Political Parties, Political Behavior, and Campaigns and Elections; political journalists; libraries and reference departments; campaign professionals and workers; political action committees (PAC's) and staff; national, state, county and municipal political party committees and staffs; and federal, state, and local elected officials and staff.

The work is an encyclopedic dictionary approach to defining and describing the major notions, concepts, tools and terms associated with the contemporary American political campaign. It includes approximately 725 entries arranged alphabetically within seven chapters. Each main entry is developed in enough detail to give readers a working knowledge of the term and the context in which it is used. The Dictionary is interdisciplinary in scope and method. It incorporates the contributions of political science, sociology, statistics, advertising, public relations, public opinion research, and journalism to the language of political campaigning.

About three terms were considered for every one term finally included. A given term was either included or excluded on the bases of two related criterion: one was the author's professional knowledge of the term's usage and importance; the other criterion relied on documented usage of the term among other scholars or professionals active in the field.

A word about chapter organization is needed. The seven chapters are arranged according to the subfields and major subject areas of campaigns and elections—as they occur to the author. In designating chapters I have been guided more by my own sense of the language and its usage than by any rigid conceptual or theoretical assumptions. Others may disagree about what are and are not the proper specialized areas about which the language and study of campaigns and elections should be organized. A vigorous dialogue on these matters would be a valuable contribution to the development of this new field.

Michael Young
The Pennsylvania State University
December, 1986

HOW TO USE THIS BOOK

The *American Dictionary of Campaigns and Elections* classifies and documents the language of an emerging field of professional and academic activity. The book is designed to be used in two ways.

Readers may find a term arranged alphabetically within each of the volume's seven chapters. The seven chapters themselves represent major subjects and subfields within the campaigns and elections area —such as "media and politics," "polling and public opinion," and so on. A reading of any of the chapters will give the reader the basic notions, concepts and terminology used in that particular subject area.

A second way to use the *American Dictionary of Campaigns and Elections* is as an alphabetical listing of the key terms and concepts in the field. Any of the over 725 entries can be accessed directly by consulting the Index at the end of the book. The Index is arranged alphabetically A through Z. The respective chapter in which the entry appears is shown in parentheses.

1

CAMPAIGN PROCESSES

ADVANCE logistical planning and preparation for a campaign event. Advance or advancing is carried out by the advanceman or woman whose task it is to insure that campaign events unfold smoothly.

To make sure that the inevitable hitches and glitches that snarl campaign schedules are avoided, the advanceman or woman usually visits the site of the scheduled campaign appearance at least once before the candidate arrives. There he or she confers with campaign officials and others involved in the campaign schedule to work out the details of the candidate's arrival, appearance, and departure. Frequently, the advanceman or woman will walk or drive the actual route that the candidate will later travel in order to ensure that all arrangements are in order and the event will occur as planned.

Advance is a critical function in the modern campaign, almost invisible when competently executed, and all too visible when bungled. *See also: SCHEDULING*

ADVANCEMAN *See ADVANCE*

ADVISORY BALLOT non-binding referendums designed to determine the electorate's opinions or preferences on some issue or candidacy. Advisory ballots are in effect a kind of massive poll, intended to reveal voters' feelings and attitudes without compelling direct action on them.

There are several types of advisory ballots in use in the United States today. Usually these deal with major public policy questions or issues. They generally appear on the ballot in terms of a referendum question to which a voter may vote yes or no.

A few states use a special form of the advisory ballot for their presidential primary elections. These elections are also referred to as "beauty contests" and "preferential primaries." Their outcomes are not linked to the selection of convention delegates. Voters participating in them are given the op-

portunity to express their candidate preferences so that delegates chosen by a separate process will be aware of the public's choice.
Presidential beauty contests can and have resulted in elections in which one candidate wins the advisory vote while another wins the delegate race. *See also: BLIND PRIMARIES; INITIATIVE AND REFERENDUM*

ALMANAC OF AMERICAN POLITICS a biennial chronicle of American politics and politicians. First published in 1972, the Almanac of American Politics has become the authoritative field guide to American politics and the standard reference to the goings and comings of American politicians. The heart of the Almanac is the state by state, Arizona to Wyoming, two year chronology of political events. The recent political history of each state is reviewed; the latest contests for major statewide office are discussed; and an overview of each of the state's congressional districts is presented. The key to the Almanac's great popularity is probably the authors' well honed sense of the basic thrusts and themes that underlie the diversity in American politics. Beyond this the Almanac offers a great deal of useful and reliable information packaged in a concise and easy to read format. This formula has made the Almanac an almost essential resource for those serious about their politics. *See also: CAMPAIGNS AND ELECTIONS (C&E); PUBLIC OPINION QUARTERLY*

AMERICAN ASSOCIATION OF POLITICAL CONSULTANTS (AAPC) a professional association whose membership is generally open to the more renowned political consultants. Founded in 1969 by Joseph Napolitan, the AAPC now has about 200 full members and another 200 associate members.
Full membership is limited to full-time political consultants who manage campaigns for a living. Other professionals who provide specialized services, such as polling or media production, are eligible for associate membership. For those political consultants who enjoy travel, there is also the International Association of Political Consultants (IAPC). The IAPC holds a three day convention every year in a different European city. Every fourth year it convenes in the United States to coincide with the American presidential election. *See also: POLITICAL CONSULTANTS*

APPOINTMENTS *See VACANCY*

APPORTIONMENT the process whereby the 50 states establish election districts from which members of the U.S. House of Representatives are elected. Since the one man, one vote judicial decisions of the 1960s and 1970s, the 50 states have also been required to use the decennial census data to reapportion their state legislatures.
In effect, the states must reapportion every 10 years if they have either lost population, gained population, or if the population has been redistributed within the state. The standard for apportionment is straightforward enough. The United States Supreme Court has ruled that all election districts be

equal in population to all others of that same class or district. For example, if a state senate district in the largest most densely populated city in the state contains 200,000 persons, all other senate districts in that state, including those in sparsely populated rural areas, must contain 200,000 people.

Despite the simpleness of the apportionment criterion, the reapportionment process is intensely political and usually controversial. The fundamental reason for this is that the existing configuration of voting districts in any state represents the status quo for the distribution of political power within that state. When voters and the communities in which they live are moved from one district to another, become part of a larger or smaller area, or are split into multiple districts, that status quo is disturbed.

The exact political consequences of reapportionment are sometimes hard to document. But there are sure to be winners and losers in the process. Even more important perhaps, most politicians assume that their careers may be at stake when voting districts are rearranged. *See also: GERRYMANDERING; ONE MAN, ONE VOTE; ROTTEN BOROUGHS*

AT LARGE ELECTION elections in which a member of a legislative body is chosen by all the voters of the electing municipality, county, or state. The alternative to at large elections is election by subdivision or district. At large elections are not used extensively in the United States. United States Senators are elected at large, but United States House members may not be except where there is only one Representative to be elected or where the state legislature fails to reapportion after the decennial census. No states elect their legislatures at large, although the practice is still somewhat common at the local level of American government. There, counties and municipalities sometimes elect all or part of their legislative bodies at large rather than from wards or other district units.

The use of at large elections is supported by some but criticized by others. Those who favor the practice argue that it produces a more capable elected official by drawing on all the available political talent. Advocates also believe that at large elections reduce parochialism and over concern with narrow local interests. Opponents of at large elections claim that they tend to reduce minority group representation by diluting their voting strength across the entire jurisdiction. Critics aslo charge that legislators tend to be less responsive and accountable to the voters when elected at large.

The courts have recently heard several challenges to the use of at large elections at the local level. Where judges have found that the system was intended to minimize the voting strength of minority groups, they have generally required the adoption of single member voting districts. This trend seems likely to decrease the number of at large elections in American politics. *See also: SINGLE MEMBER DISTRICT*

AVOCATIONALIST *See VOCATIONALIST*

BAKER v. CARR *See ONE MAN, ONE VOTE*

BALLOT ACCESS qualifying for a position on the general election ballot. Ballot access is not a problem for candidates for the Democratic or Republican parties who are insured of a position when they win their primary election. But for third party and Independent candidates, ballot access can be a major chore.

The individual states establish their own laws governing who will and will not be on the ballot. In general the Democrats and Republicans (who control the state legislatures who make these laws) have made it as difficult as possible for parties other than their own to gain access to the ballot. While Democratic and Republican candidates have been provided automatic ballot access, third party and Independent candidates usually must petition to be listed.

The process is particularly burdensome for third party presidential candidates who must research and comply with 51 bewildering sets of laws regarding filing deadlines, the circulation of petitions, petition formats, and the number of signatures required.

Ironically, ballot access has only become a problem for third party and Independent candidates since the introduction of the Australian (secret) ballot in the 1890's. Before then there was no official ballot; parties and candidates simply prepared and distributed their own ballots (or "party strips") on election day. The "stickers" sometimes used today by write in campaigns are the last residue of this once common practice. *See also: AUSTRALIAN BALLOT; ELECTORAL LAW; ELECTORAL SYSTEM; THIRD PARTIES*

BALLOT PROPOSITIONS issues that are placed on the ballot to be voted on at the same time that a scheduled primary or general election is held. Ballot propositions are usually in the form of a question upon which voters are able to vote yes or no.

Ballot propositions are widely used in the United States. In a typical general election, about 4 out of 5 states will decide statewide ballot issues. All together perhaps 400 to 500 propositions will be voted upon and thousands more will have appeared on local ballots.

There are two main ways of getting ballot propositions on the ballot. The most common of these is the "referendum" in which state or local legislatures may submit statutes or constitutional amendments to the electorate; or voters may request a referendum on legislation already passed by the legislature. Less frequently used, but available in about half the states is the "initiative" under which voters may initiate statutes or constitutional amendments by petitioning that they be placed on the ballot.

Ballot propositions are sometimes dull stuff, legislative minutiae encased in stifling legalese. But more often today they deal with issues that generate intense feeling and excitement among the electorate—taxes, smoking, the environment, right to work laws, nuclear power plants, bond issues, and so on. It is not unusual for more money to be spent in campaigns for and against these issues than on any of the candidate races. In fact, ballot propositions sometimes attract more voters than do the contests for elective office that appear on the same ballot. *See also: BALLOT TITLES; INITIATIVE AND REFERENDUM*

BALLOT TITLES a sentence or two that summarizes the contents of a ballot proposition in simple straightforward language. Ballot propositions themselves are frequently lengthy, complex, and written in formalistic legal language. Since they are often difficult to understand, ballot titles are used to indicate to voters the general scope of the issue before them.

Ballot titles are what most voters probably understand they are voting on. There is some controversy about ballot titles themselves being sometimes misleading and confusing. Public opinion polls have indicated that voters do not always understand clearly what they are voting upon or the implications of the side of the issue they have chosen. In recognition of this, campaigns for and against ballot propositions often adopt simple thematic advertising strategies or just invoke voters to vote yes or no. *See also: BALLOT PROPOSITIONS*

BOILER ROOM *See TELEPHONE BANKS*

BOOTLEG the obtaining of political intelligence, and other information of interest concerning the other side. Bootleg ranges in importance from the acquisition of an unauthorized copy of the opposition's travel schedule to the procurement of an opponent's polls or media plans.

Voluntarily offered bootleg has been considered fair sport in campaigns until recently—and it is thought to be fairly common. But the reactions to the bootlegging of President Carter's briefing book in 1980 may bring about new ethical standards in these matters—much as the Watergate disclosures did for the more blatant dirty tricks of an earlier political era. *See also: CAMPAIGN SPY; DIRTY TRICKS*

BRIEFING BOOK looseleaf notebooks of facts and data compiled by campaigns. Briefing books can serve several functions, however, their main purpose is the preparation of appropriate answers to issues or questions to which a candidate might have to respond.

For example, if the issue of tax reform had been raised during the campaign, the briefing book might suggest how that issue should be handled—perhaps even offering appropriate phraseology.

Briefing books are also used to prepare candidates for public appearances . Often they serve as scripts during rehearsals for press conferences or debates. It was a briefing book that was acquired from the Carter campaign by the Reagan campaign in 1980. The keen interest in these documents by the other side underlines the strategic importance briefing books are accorded in political campaigns. *See also: BOOTLEG; CAMPAIGN SPY; DIRTY TRICKS*

BUCKLIN PLAN *See PREFERENTIAL VOTING*

CAMPAIGNS AND ELECTIONS (C&E) the first serious journal exclusively devoted to the field of political campaigns and elections. CAMPAIGNS AND ELECTIONS (C&E) bills itself as the "journal of political action" and that is a pretty fair description of the editorial product.

C&E publishes articles on the principles and techniques of practical politics. Early articles (the first volume appeared in Spring 1980) were mostly nuts and bolts, but more recently the journal has included a good mix of the academic and the applied.

Recent editions have included pieces on targeting, polling, using computers, writing press releases, absentee ballots and election day management. Regularly appearing are features on the Federal Elections Commission (FEC), the Federal Communications Commission (FCC) and PAC's. Each issue also includes a book review column which critiques recent books about campaigning and elections.

C&E's contributor list includes both scholars and practicing political professionals. Articles have been written by Herbert Alexander, Robert Agranoff, Hank Parkenson, Larry Sabato, Linda Lee Kaid, Murray Fisher, and Jean Westwood.

Other publications which regularly provide coverage in the field are the *Congressional Quarterly Weekly*, *The National Journal* and the *Washington Post Weekly*. Besides these there are dozens of subscription newsletters which monitor and analyze the political scene. Among the best known of these are the *Baron Report*, the *Evans Novak Political Report* and the *Garth Report*.
See also: PUBLIC OPINION QUARTERLY

CAMPAIGN SPY the campaign mole, the agent provoceteur that penetrates every campaign—or at least the imagination of every campaign manager. Campaign spies are an enduring tradition in American politics. Almost every campaign has one, or assumes that it does.

Elaborate measures are sometimes taken to detect and counter spying in campaigns. Larger campaigns establish complex security measures and install sophisticated electronic equipment designed to thwart bugging and eavesdropping.

Campaign spying is probably not as prevalent as it once was. The post-Watergate atmosphere has emphasized the risks inherent in political espionage—while it has diminished any glamour spying may have held. Accumulating information about the other side is still legitimate and standard practice, but use of a planted spy is not. If someone hands you information voluntarily that's probably acceptable; but if you encourage and help someone steal it—then its not acceptable.

The efficacy of campaign spying is dubious. Occasionally a spy may have made the difference between winning and losing, but more often the information they provide isn't very important. Most spies are low level personnel such as clerks, messengers, and secretaries, who only have access to low level information. Even when they do uncover something, the frantic pace of campaigning means that the intelligence is rapidly outdated.

Then too there are only a few items of information that are really potentially harmful in the opposition's hands. These include the poll—particularly its analysis—and the media plan. But they are usually tightly held by a few senior campaign personnel, none of whom are likely to be the campaign spy.

For all the attention given to the threat of spying most leaks come in other ways. Veteran campaigners say that the most common source on intelligence about the other side comes from disgruntled employees and the covering press. University of Virginia political scientist Larry Saboto reports that one political consultant told him: "I don't need spies, I have the press" (1983:24). *See also: BOOTLEG; DIRTY TRICKS; LEAKS*

CANDIDATE any man or woman who seeks one of the approximately 500,000 elective offices filled at local, state and federal levels. Candidates are said to stand for office in England; in the United States they run for office.

Candidacy confers a psychological status as well as a legal status. The word derives from the Latin candidatus which means the wearer of the white robe. Roman candidates are said to have worn these as evidence of their good character. This ancient Latin symbolism is still expressed in the generally high standards of integrity the American electorate demands of the modern politician.

Within the political campaign itself, candidacy often bestows a kind of exalted status. A candidate becomes "the candidate", the symbol of the campaign, loved and honored by supporters and the motivation for the strenuous and intensive work undertaken during the campaign.

Candidacy also triggers legal status. Usually some overt act such as announcing or filing begins candidate status. For federal elections, candidate status is created when someone has raised or spent more than $5000. In state elections, filing or authorizing the formation of campaign committees are typical triggers.

Legal status has different consequences depending on the jurisdiction involved and the office sought. For federal elections, legal candidacy means that the provisions of the Federal Elections Campaign Act (FECA) must be fulfilled. It also invokes various Federal Communication Commission (FCC) rules regarding access to the electronic media. In state elections many of the same FCC rules apply. In addition some states have specific disclosure and reporting requirements for legal candidates. *See also: ANNOUNCING; FILING; PROXY CANDIDATE*

CANDIDATE SERVICES jargon for the specialized goods and services available to political candidates and others involved in professional political life. Candidate services fall into three broad classifications: organization and management services; polling and research services; and media and advertising services.

Within these categories are dozens of specific consulting specialties. The more common among them include: fund raising; demographic analysis;

speech writing; time buying; radio and television production; polling; public relations; direct mail; and press relations.

Today campaigns may contract with a single firm to organize and manage the campaign, or they may purchase candidate services from several specialized firms. For example, a candidate might contract with firm A to produce media, firm B to do direct mail, firm C to conduct the polling, and so on.

Specialization has been the trend among political consultants in the past several years. Along with this has been a steady increase in the cost of these services. This pattern is a familiar one in evolving professions. Candidate services in the future will probably be offered more and more by the specialists and less and less by the generalists. *See also: POLITICAL CONSULTANT*

CANVASSING a survey of the voters in an election district—carried out door to door or by telephone. Canvassing is undertaken by political parties and candidate organizations in order to locate prospective voters and determine their voting intentions. This vital information is then available for subsequent campaign operations—in particular GOTV efforts, telephone banks and election day activities.

A canvass is more like a population census than a poll (with which it is often confused). Its purpose is to contact as many voters as possible. Usually campaign workers equipped with street lists visit registered voters, drop off some literature, offer to answer questions, and solicit that voter's support on election day.

Canvassers classify those they contact according to their professed voting intentions. Voters are identified as strong supporters, weak supporters, undecideds or opposed. Undecideds and weak supporters must be recontacted several times to solicit their vote. Strong supporters will be called on election day to remind them to vote, while opposed voters will usually not be contacted again.

Traditionally, political parties or campaigns canvass their electorates near the end of the campaign—often the final weekend before election day. Lately, however, many professional politicians are emphasizing earlier canvassing. Some campaigns in fact now carry on some level of canvassing throughout the entire election season. *See also: ELECTION DAY ACTIVITIES; VOTER CONTACT*

CANVASSING BOARDS commissions established under election law for the purpose of collecting ballots and certifying election results. Canvassing Boards are usually established at both county and state levels. Some larger municipalities also set up their own canvassing boards.

The procedures under which ballots are officially counted varies among electoral jurisdictions. In general however the "official returns" are collected from the local polling places on election night and taken to a designated central storage area for safekeeping. Subsequently these ballots are forwarded to municipal, county and state boards who consolidate them, certify the results and issue a certificate of election to the winners. Canvassing boards often take several weeks or longer to count the vote. As a result the official returns are not certified until a month or so after the election. Except for very close elections involving the possibility of a recount—all of this is anti-climactic. In most cases the voting results have been known for weeks already because the unofficial returns are reported on election night or the following day. *See Also: ELECTION JUDGES; POLLWATCHERS; UNOFFICIAL RETURNS*

CARPETBAGGERS elected officials or candidates who do not live in the constituency they represent or aspire to represent. Politicians who live in but were not born in their districts are also sometimes called carpetbaggers. The term has a number of widely used synonyms including "parachutist", "outsider", and "foreigner". It is of post-Civil War reconstruction era vintage when carpetbaggers were Northerners who went south to exploit the natives and enrich themselves.

Today many local residency rules do not require a candidate to even live in the jurisdiction they represent—let alone to have always lived there. Still strong local ties continue to be highly valued in candidates.

Other things at all equal, the local boy or girl has an important advantage with most electorates. There are some obvious reasons for this. Locals are likely to be better known, perhaps with family roots deep in the community. Consequently they are likely to be more trusted and to know and care more about the district, its traditions, values, and needs. And a local is more likely to have worked in and contributed to the community—to have paid his dues and kept them current.

Regardless of the advantages of being local, carpetbagging is not uncommon. Politicians do move into legislative districts and even across states to run for office. Robert Kennedy did it to win a U.S. Senate seat and Jay Rockefeller did it to win the governorship of West Virginia. Several recent instances of carpetbagging have occurred in connection with congressional races and state legislative races.

The carpetbagger label is still a serious charge in American politics, but it no longer carries the electoral handicap it once did. *See also: LOCAL RESIDENCY RULES*

CASEWORK political jargon for the process of helping constituents who are dealing with the government. Casework—also known as constituent services—runs the gamut from picking up licence plates or running down lost government checks to ironing out problems with the IRS or arranging a high level meeting with a government official.

Political scientist Richard F. Fenno, Jr. described the nature of case work in his study of the "home style" of congressmen:

> The core activity is providing help to individuals, groups and localities in coping with the federal government. Individuals need someone to intercede with the

> bureaucracies handling their . . . benefits . . . checks . . . pensions . . . military status . . . and the like. Private groups and local governments need assistance in pursuing federal funds for . . . highways, dams, buildings, small business loans, and so forth. (1978:01)

Many incumbents put a lot of effort into providing constituent service because they believe they can be re-elected on the basis of it. And in fact, incumbents who ignore or avoid casework probably do so at their political peril. When a congressman or state legislator does lose it is usually not for any policy position they took or failed to take. More likely it was because of the impression that the incumbent lost touch with their constituency. Casework is the traditional way elected officials maintain that contact. *See also: CONSTITUENCY; INCUMBENT*

CONSTITUENCY the people who live within a voting district represented by an elected official. The constituency of the Governor of New Mexico is the population of New Mexico. The constituency of the Congressional district which includes Brooklyn are the people of Brooklyn. The constituency of the Mayor of Miami are the people who live in Miami.

A geographic area itself may also be considered a constituency. With some exceptions constituencies in the United States are single member districts which elect one official.

The notion of constituency includes the idea that an elected official is the personal representative of the people who elected him—someone who should be an advocate and a intermediary for constituents dealing with government. In fact many legislators do devote considerable time to constituent casework: answering mail, interceding with the bureaucracy, and even running errands.

Sometimes a politician's constituency grows beyond its original geographic boundaries. These so called "second constituences" might include a national ethnic group, a particular economic interest or even a distinct philosophical point of view. Second constituencies are in effect a kind of functional representation that has informally developed in American politics. *See also: CASEWORK; POLITICAL BASE*

CONSTITUENT SERVICE *See CASEWORK*

CONTESTED ELECTION a disputed election in which one or more of the candidates challenge the official returns. Contested elections usually involve allegations of voting fraud of some kind—although there are a number of other legal grounds on which an election can be questioned.

Most electoral systems provide for a recount which may be requested by the complaining candidate(s). The cost of the recount—which is usually considerable—is borne by the petitioning candidate(s). If that candidate is subsequently declared the winner the electoral jurisdiction bears the cost.

When recounts are inconclusive or other issues are raised, contested elections are resolved by either the legislature or the courts. In most states and in the U.S. Congress, the respective legislative chambers are empowered to finally decide who will be seated. Contested elections involving non-legislative offices are normally resolved by the courts. *See also: UNOFFICIAL RETURNS*

DEBATES stylized political affairs which feature joint appearances by opposing candidates, who submit to formal questioning from a panel. Debates have become major media events during presidential campaigns. They are also often scheduled in congressional and state level races.

Political debates have a long tradition in American campaigns. Common during much of the 19th Century they were memorialized in the lore that grew out of the legendary Lincoln—Douglas debates. The modern era of political debating began in 1960 when Richard Nixon debated John Kennedy on national television. Subsequently presidential and vice presidential debates were held in 1976, 1980 and 1984. The debating format has also become a common feature of presidential primary elections.

Contemporary debates bear faint resemblance to the political debates of earlier eras. Today's debates are more accurately described as "dual simultaneous press conferences"—the candidates meet the press and all do it at the same time and in the same place. The similarity to a press conference is actually striking; each candidate makes a statement and then is asked in turn a series of questions. The focus of the exchange is much more on the question and answer process than on any direct clash of issues or personality between opposing candidates.

Sometimes campaigns include an interlude before a debate that has been referred to as the "meta-debate"—a debate about the debate. Meta-debates include all the wrangling among opposing candidates: where will the debate be held; when; what will the format be; who will moderate; who will be on the panel; how will the questions be chosen; who will be in the audience; what are the ground rules; and on and on and on. The meta-debate itself often becomes a tool of campaign strategy with one side trying to put another at some tactical disadvantage.

All of this underscores the considerable importance campaigners assign to debates. Whether voters always do is another so far unsettled question. *See also: NAME IDENTIFICATION; TWO STEP FLOW; WHATISNAME*

DECOMPRESSION the feelings of anxiety, depression and acute ennui associated with the ending of a political campaign. Known as "pack withdrawal" among journalists, decompression is the post campaign letdown brought on by the frantic pace of electoral politics.

Washington D.C. therapist Isaiah Zimmerman diagnosed decompression for the WASHINGTON POST after the 1984 election:

> anyone who is close to the center of the campaign is faced with an abrupt stop . . . for the losers, they are pushing until the last minute, only to find it didn't work. They go kind of numb, get spacey. There is also a desire to scramble, to go into what's next, but their heart is not in it . . . The winners also feel depressed because

the campaign is such a turn-on. It's the equivalent of war. They are experiencing an intense terrific team spirit and it's all dismantled very quickly.

Decompression seems almost inevitable given the nature of modern politics. Campaigns build up a tremendous amount of momentum and intensity, then end explosively on election day. Yesterday there would be no tomorrow. It was around the clock, push, push, push, adrenalin pumping, frenetic furious all out effort—today it is over.

The best cure for decompression is rest and relaxation. The really difficult cases respond only to the anticipation and excitement that comes with planning the next campaign. *See also: MOMENTUM; PEAKING*

DIRECT DEMOCRACY *See INITIATIVE AND REFERENDUM*

DOOR TO DOOR CAMPAIGNING *See CANVASSING*

DROP BYS brief appearances by a candidate at a cocktail party, kaffeeklatsch, fund raiser, or other campaign event. Drop bys allow a busy candidate to meet the people in attendance, perhaps make a short talk and then depart for other scheduled campaign stops.

The logistics of the drop by are appealing to harried campaign schedulers who often are inundated with requests for the candidate's time. In the course of a evening a candidate might appear at a half dozen or more social affairs—with perhaps time left over for a late campaign meeting, an interview, or even a much needed good night's sleep.

The term drop by may have been borrowed from Washington, D.C. cocktail party usage. There, a drop by is a party guest expected to stay 20 to 30 minutes, have a drink, say hello to everyone and then depart for another party. *See also: KAFFEEKLATSCH; SCHEDULING*

EARLY RETURNS *See FLASH RETURNS*

ELECTION BOARDS *See CANVASSING BOARDS*

ELECTION DAY the climax to the weeks, months and sometimes years that precedes the casting of ballots. Election day is a long day. Polling places are typically open from 7:00 a.m. to 8:00 p.m., or even later. The date for election day varies according to the type of election, the year in the election cycle and the particular state, or locality involved.

General elections are traditionally held on the 1st Tuesday after the 1st Monday in November. Some localities, however, use this day only in presidential election years, opting for an earlier date in off year elections. Primary elections are usually held in the Spring or Summer from as early as February to as late as September. April or May dates are typical. Special elections called to fill vacancies may be held at any time depending on the laws of the jurisdiction.

Several proposals have been made recently regarding the scheduling of election day. Most of them are designed to increase voting by making it more convenient. Among these suggestions have been recommendations to open the polls for twenty-four hours, schedule elections over more than one day and hold elections on Sunday.

Election day occurs at least twice a year in most jurisdictions, but may happen three, four, five or more times under some circumstances. Voters in runoff primary states have at least three election days in each election year and special elections can add one or more dates to the election calendar.

The frequency of elections in the United States may increase voter apathy and contribute to low turnout. Many political observers believe this is the case arguing that voters are bored and exhausted by the long succession of elections. The premise that too many elections dull voter interest seems plausible, but so far there is no solid evidence to support it. *See also: ELECTION DAY ACTIVITIES*

ELECTION DAY ACTIVITIES traditional labors carried out on the final day of political campaigns. Election day activities are the nitty gritty of organizational politics: manning the polls; distributing literature; setting up GOTV operations; canvassing; running telephone banks; and allocating street money. These chores are performed by the election day organization which includes precinct and ward leaders, poll watchers, runners, election judges, and volunteers.

In general election day activities are designed to persuade undecideds while making sure that one's own supporters turnout and vote. A campaign might identify undecideds with pre-election canvassing, then target them for election day literature drops, telephone calls, or personal visits. Campaigns use similar tactics to get their own supporters to the polls. Favorable voters are identified with pre-election canvassing, then re-contacted on election day to insure that they have gotten out to vote.

Election day operations include ballot security programs in some jurisdictions. These emphasize the detection and prevention of voting fraud such as ballot box stuffing, short counting, and vote buying. Most ballot security efforts concentrate on staffing polling places with pollwatchers and other election officials who can monitor actual voting.

Many professional politicians believe that election day activities can determine the outcome of close elections. Experts disagree but some suggest that a good election day organization can make a difference of 5 to 15 percent in final voting results. *See also: CANVASSING; ELECTION DAY; GOTV; PEAKING; POLLWATCHERS; STREET MONEY; VOTER CONTACT; WHOLESALE POLITICS*

ELECTORAL SYSTEM the framework of laws, customs, practices, and traditions within which elections are conducted. Electoral systems comprise all of the formal and informal arrangements that prevail in a given jurisdiction with regard to the filling of public offices. These include registration laws, ballot forms, filing regulations, ballot access laws, and all of the rules and regulations that determine how elections are administered.

Two major characteristics mark the American electoral system. One is diversity. Despite the increased federal influence on state election laws, there is still great variety in the practices found across the country. Some of these differences are probably not of great consequence, such as the hours the polls are open, filing fees, and how candidate names are designated on the official ballot. Other differences are more substantial, such as registration procedures, the conditions established for a political party to qualify for the ballot, or the strictness of campaign finance laws.

The second distinctive feature of the American electoral system is the bias in it. Electoral systems are not neutral in their impacts—that is they favor certain kinds of candidates, parties and conditions in the competition for voter support. Evidence of this is abundant. Political scientists have found for example that the party column ballot (Indiana ballot) is more likely to produce straight ticket voting than the office block ballot (Massachusetts ballot).

The latter, on the other hand is believed to promote ticket splitting.

Other research has revealed that long ballots discourage voters with less education from voting for offices listed toward the bottom of the ballot. Scholars have also discovered that ballot position—the order in which a party or candidate's name appears on the ballot—can also alter the outcome of an election. Even different ballot titles on ballot propositions can produce widely different voting results. Ballot access laws, registration laws, and campaign finance laws have also been shown to have various kinds of influences on elections.

Reviewing all of this, cynics sometimes conclude that the electoral system is rigged to maintain the status quo. Election laws, they charge, are designed by incumbents to discourage change while perpetuating themselves in power. Others regard this view of things to be naive. They point out that it is the winners and not the losers who write election laws. If these laws favor those who make them it should not be surprising. That, afterall, is what politics is all about. *See also: BALLOT ACCESS; BALLOT POSITION; BALLOTS; REGISTRATION; SINGLE MEMBER DISTRICT*

FAIR CAMPAIGN PRACTICES carrying on a political campaign without resort to illegal or unethical practices—that is dirty tricks. Fair campaign practices are sometimes monitored by groups of (usually) leading citizens organized into fair campaign practices committees.

These committees are mostly local, voluntary, and often impermanent. The more active of them scrutinize campaigns for evidence of dirty tricks, investigate complaints, and publicize their findings.

Frequently fair campaign practices committees press candidates to sign agreements promising to run fair campaigns. These pledges probably do have some influence on the subsequent conduct of the campaign. They put candidates on record as supporting a high standard and they encourage the public and the press to hold campaigns to that standard. *See also: CAMPAIGN SPY; DIRTY TRICKS*

FAITHLESS ELECTOR a member of the Electoral College who casts a presidential ballot for someone other than the winner of their state's popular vote. Faithless electors are kind of quadrennial political boogey-men, hauled out every four years by critics of the Electoral College System. But in fact faithless electors are rare.

Electors are required by law in most states—and by strong tradition in all states—to vote for the candidate to whom they were pledged. The pressures to do so—social, political and even economic—are considerable. Furthermore presidential candidates in most states control the selection of electors pledged to them. Almost always those chosen are long time loyalists, party leaders or trusted supporters, who have every reason to vote for the candidate to whom they are pledged.

Nevertheless electors do sometimes defect. These are usually secret supporters of a third party candidate or mere eccentrics. They never amount to more than one or two votes and they have yet to influence the outcome of a presidential election. But they are powerful symbols to critics of the Electoral College as well as to others who believe that presidents should be elected by direct popular vote. *See also: BATTLEGROUND STATES*

FILING a formal declaration that a candidate is seeking an elective office. Filing normally follows the announcing of candidacy. It is the legal procedure by which a candidate secures a position on the ballot.

Individual states vary in their filing regulations. In some states candidates must only indicate their intention to run, and pay a nominal filing fee (these fees are as little as 50 or 100 dollars to run for Governor, U.S. Senator or even President.)

In other states, however, the filing requirements are more rigorous. Many states require candidates to circulate and return nominating petitions. These petitions must include a specified minimum number of signatures of registered voters who indicate their support for the prospective candidacy.

Candidates running as Independents face even stiffer filing rules—as do candidates of third parties that have not previously qualified for the ballot. Typically these candidates must gather a substantial number of signatures on their nominating petition.

Usually the required number of signatures is measured in terms of the number of voters who cast ballots in a recent election. Pennsylvania law for example stipulates that Independent candidates must have secured signatures at least equal to 2% of the highest vote received by any candidate during the last election.

The standard argument for filing requirements is that they discourage frivolous or pointless candidacies. The evidence is that they do achieve this to some extent. Their influence on the number of candidates running in Democratic or Republican party primaries is probably slight. But it is likely that filing requirements do reduce the incidence of third party and Independent candidacies. *See also: ANNOUNCEMENT; BALLOT ACCESS; CROSSFILING*

FIRE IN THE BELLY having the energy, determination, and zeal for a tough undertaking. Fire in the belly is to be all fired up, full of zest, enthusiasm and zeal. To lack fire in the belly is to be flat, tired, burned out, and cooled off.

Fire in the belly is strong feelings, passionate commitments, the energy for one more charge, one more effort, one more time! Young politicians and idealogical zealots are more likely to have fire in the belly. Older politicians and less intense ones might lack it.

In late 1983, a newspaper inquired "whether President Reagan has the fire in the belly needed to take on the rigors of another campaign." Another noted about the same time the difference between Walter Mondale now and 8 years earlier when he "lacked the fire in the belly" to sustain a long campaign.

Fire in the belly is not synonymous with guts or backbone. The former implies drive, determination, enthusiasm, zeal and competitiveness; the latter mean courage, daring, fortitude, and bravery. Almost every politician would take umbrage at the charge that they lacked guts; the more candid might admit to a little less fire in the belly than they once had.

FIRST PAST THE POST the oldest and simplest rule for determining electoral winners. First past the post systems require only simple pluralities of the total vote cast.

Known also as winner take all systems, the first past the post rule predominates in United States elections. Under it each voter usually has a single vote to cast in a single member district. The candidate who is first past the post—that is gets the most votes—wins the election.

The principal exceptions to first past the post in American elections are run off primaries and proportional representation (PR). Run offs require the two highest vote getters in an earlier primary to run against each other to produce a majority winner. Conversely PR allocates legislative seats according to the total vote won even if that is as little as 10 or 20%.

Political scientists believe that first past the post systems reinforce the prevailing two party system. Third parties or Independent candidates rarely win pluralities and their cooperation is not needed to knit majority coalitions together either. First past the post also encourages major parties to become broad based in order to appeal to middle of the road voters who often hold the balance of electoral power. *See also: MAJORITY; PLURALITY*

FLASH RETURNS early quick and informal counts of voting results. Flash returns are reported on election night shortly after the polls close.

Sometimes these early returns are simply tear sheets taken from voting machines. Other times they may be handwritten slips of paper based on a summary tabulation of the balloting.

Flash returns are actually the "unofficial" unofficial returns. They are compiled only for top of the ticket contests-those that generate the most attention from the public and media.

The balance of the unofficial returns are gathered from each polling place and taken to some central location. From there they are released to the media who report them to the public. Usually there is a lag of several hours between the first flash returns and the later unofficial returns. *See also: UNOFFICIAL RETURNS*

GRASS ROOTS the people, the common voter in the electorate, the rank and file. Metaphorically, the grass roots are the source of all political power. Politicians are fond of demonstrating their grass roots support and claiming to run grass roots campaigns.

When the term is used rhetorically it implies broad based support for a candidate or issue. When it is used more literally, it often refers to an emphasis on campaign organizational strategies—like voter contact, canvassing, and telephone banks—in contrast to a heavy reliance on media.

HIRED GUN political consultants or other paid political professionals—especially those whose commitment is to financial gain rather than to causes or candidates. Hired gun is a western frontier metaphor that evokes the mercenary image some have of political consultants. The term is usually one of contempt and disdain, although political professionals themselves and other political insiders do use it sometimes to express esteem and admiration.

Hired guns may also be "political whores". Unlike hired guns, however, the term political whore is always one of disgust and derision. One political entrepreneur recently explained to a PHILADELPHIA INQUIRER'S feature writer why he was a political whore.

> The reason I'm a political whore is that I'll work for two camps, three camps, four camps—all of whom might be running for the same office. They get the same smile and the same thank you for the same dollar. . .a whore doesn't need to know about your background. . .who would I be not to take an order.

A political whore is not necessarily someone who commits illegal or even unethical acts. Instead, it is someone who will do deals with or work for anyone who can reward them. Politicians who change sides easily or who are known for yielding to political expediency are often called political whores. *See also: POLITICAL CONSULTANTS*

HORSE RACE a metaphor for the election contest which stresses the drama and excitement of the campaign rather than issues or other matters of substance. The horse race emphasizes the competitive and theatrical—the media events, the strategies being used, the latest poll results, and so on. Journalists are often criticized for the disproportionate amount of attention they give to the horse race.

Candidates too are prone to place great importance on the horse race, particularly in assessing their own polls. They do this with some justification since a campaign's fund raising success is at least partly dependent on favorable poll showings. But an obsession with the horse race in a poll can obscure the more important strategic information that will ultimately determine winning and losing. *See also: HANDICAPPING; HORSE RACE JOURNALIAM; NEWS HOOKS*

HUSTINGS the campaign trail. Hustings is literally a place for making campaign speeches. In current usage, it refers to the locations where the public parts of the political campaign are carried on—"Senator Smith returned to the hustings yesterday, stopping and speaking in five towns and cities." Hustings is journalese—used mostly by reporters writing about campaigns and elections. It is archaic for most other uses. *See also: SCHEDULING*

IDENTIFYING AND PULLING *See CANVASSING*

IN THE LOOP insider jargon for being a political insider. In the loop is to be informed, in touch, and inner circle. People in the loop are "plugged in" to all the major issues and participate in all the important decisions. Being in the loop brings status and information—being out of the loop brings anxiety and frustration.

Actually most political campaigns have several loops. While not everyone "is in the loop", almost everyone is in a loop. Its less a question then of being in the loop than which loop one is in.

Little systematic research has been done on communication patterns in campaigns. Experience suggests however that the several loops in most campaigns are differentiated mostly by level and exclusivity of membership. The upper loops include only very senior people and few of them. Lower loops include more people and are less exclusive.

The upper loop in political campaigns usually consists of the candidate, the campaign manager, the pollster, the media consultant, the senior fund raiser and one or two other advisors. Interestingly enough press secretaries are often out of this loop. Stephen Hess a scholar and author at the Brookings Institute, estimates that only about one in five government agency press secretaries are ever in the upper loop (1984). The same proportion probably holds for campaigns. Apparently it is the fear of leaks that leads to this ostracism.

INITIATIVE AND REFERENDUM electoral mechanisms which permit voters to commit what is referred to as direct democracy. The initiative allows supporters of legislation to place it on the ballot for a vote, bypassing the legislature. The referendum lets the legislature itself put a measure on the ballot for voter approval or rejection.

In practice initiatives usually deal with issues like tax cuts, regulation of nuclear wastes, and establishment of the death penalty. Referendums are generally used to determine the fate of bond issues or constitutional amendments. Initiatives make up about 20% of the ballot propositions placed before voters on election day, while the other 80% are referendum measures. The two devices reach the ballot in different ways. Referendums are simpler since they are usually placed on the ballot by a vote of the legislature. Initiatives however require several steps before a measure can actually be voted on. Supporters must submit a proposal for review to the state's chief legal officer. Subsequently, the state's chief election officer provides all registered voters with information about the proposal—sometimes including the arguments that have been made for and against it.

Proponents of the initiative measure then have a specified period of time to qualify it for the ballot by securing a designated number of signatures from registered voters. Nationally about 15% of all initiative petitions actually qualify for the ballot and approximately 40% of these are approved by the voters.

Both the initiative and referendum are widely available in the United States. Almost 50% of the states have the initiative and about 80% provide some form of the referendum. In recent years there has been a substantial increase in the use of both. Neither the initiative nor the referendum are used in federal elections. Congress however has considered legislation that would adopt a version of the initiative. *See also: BALLOT PROPOSITIONS; RECALL*

INSIDER *See IN THE LOOP*

INVISIBLE PRIMARY the informal, behind the scenes and mostly obscure politicking that precedes the early presidential primaries and caucuses. The invisible primary begins after the election of the last president—and continues until the first nomination contests over three years later held to choose the next president.

The term was invented by journalist Arthur Hadley. He argues that the eventual major party nominee is actually determined during this interval. According to Hadley the subsequent caucuses and primaries are mostly rituals that confirm the decisions reached in the pre-primary period.

The invisible primary includes all the political events that lead up to the Iowa and New Hampshire contests: the straw polls, the trial heats, the announcements, the cattle shows and the sometimes frenetic efforts to attract the attention of great mentioners. Candidates use this time to raise money, recruit supporters, set up organizations, make local contacts, and generate wide and favorable press coverage.

The invisible primary is not limited to presidential contests. Hundreds of thousands of state and local elections are preceded by similar maneuvering that can greatly influence election outcomes. *See also: CATTLE SHOWS; GREAT MENTIONERS; STRAW POLLS*

KAFFEEKLATSCH a traditional campaign social event designed to bring a candidate into personal contact with small groups of voters. Kaffeeklatsches (or coffees as they are also called) are hosted by a campaign supporter in their own home. The host invites the registered voters in the neighborhood to meet the candidate and hear him speak. Afterwards hosts ask for campaign contributions and try to sign up volunteers.

Kaffeeklatsches can be scheduled so that the candidate can drop by briefly, meet the people in attendance, make a short talk, and depart for other scheduled campaign stops. Coffees are widely used in urban and suburban areas where large concentrations of voters live. The equivalent function in rural areas and small towns is the firehall party and the church social. *See also: DROP BYS; SPECIAL EVENTS*

LAME DUCK an elected official whose term of office is coming to an end. Lame ducks are usually politicians who are not running or have been defeated for re-election. Politicians volunteer for lame duck status much more often than it is imposed on them—incumbents at all levels in the United States are usually re-elected.

Whether voluntary or involuntary, lame ducks inevitably lose power and influence as their final day in office approaches. William Safire in Safire's *Political Dictionary* (1978) reports that the term originally referred to a bankrupt businessman. A political lame duck is someone who has lost not his money, but his power.

LANDSLIDE an election in which the winner's margin of victory is at least 20% of the vote. Normally this requires 60% or more of the vote for the winning candidate. Landslides are regularly declared, however, in presidential elections when the winner receives at least 55% of the vote. Presidential victories of this magnitude often translate into Electoral College margins of overwhelming proportion.

Political analysts look to landslides as expressions of mandates from the people. But linking voters' policy preferences to electoral results is chancey business in nonparliamentary systems like that of the United States. On the other hand, there is no doubt that a large margin of victory in an election can substantially increase the power and influence of the winner. *See also: MANDATE*

LAST HURRAH a usually sentimental expression which refers to the last campaign of a veteran politician. It was coined by the author Edwin O'Connor who used it as the title in his book about the legendary Boston mayor James Curley.

Last hurrahs may be maudlin and melancholy times for supporters and friends, but they can be happy and cheerful times for opponents and enemies. Last hurrahs are sometimes used tactically to hold off would be opponents for one last term. A politician who has had his last hurrah may still be in office, but he has become a lame duck. *See also: LAME DUCK*

LATERAL ENTRY getting into elective politics without first serving in lower level office. The technology of the new politics and the general decline of political parties has made it possible for candidates to enter competition for high public office without serving the traditional apprenticeship in lower offices. Lateral entry candidates substitute heavy media use for the personal networks and public exposure that are the fruits of long time public service. Lateral entry is seen among wealthy businessmen and entrepreneurs—like George Romney, Milton Shapp, John Y. Brown, and Lew Lehrman. It also occurs among well known performers who have had successful careers in sports or entertainment—examples include Bill Bradey, George Murphy, and Ronald Reagan.

Political scientists fret some about the quality and durability of lateral entry candidates. So far there is little evidence that suggests they perform any better or any worse than their more traditional colleagues. *See also: NEW POLITICS*

LEAGUE OF WOMEN VOTERS a widely respected nonpartisan organization whose activities are oriented to raising the level of public interest and knowledge of the electoral process. The League, which was founded in 1920, grew out of the women's suffrage movement. It is a national organization with state and local chapters.

The national office is probably best known for its sponsorship of presidential debates. State and local chapters also sponsor debates, as well as candidate forums in which candidates appear and discuss issues or answer questions. The League also disseminates informational literature about campaigns and elections, and local chapters regularly publish "voter guides" based on candidates' answers to League questions. The League and its chapters put a good deal of effort into maintaining their image of strict nonpartisanship. *See also: DEBATES*

LOSING the eventual fate of most candidates for public office. More than 75% of all candidates lose in either their primary or general elections. These odds of more than 3 to 1 are heavily weighted against candidates who are running for the first time, who are running underfinanced campaigns, or who are running against an incumbent.

Incumbency is an especially important factor in winning or losing. As a class, incumbents win over 90% of the time. They are usually better known than their opponents and better financed. More often than not, incumbents also have a party registration edge among voters. Experienced political handicappers understand these facts about winning and losing and typically will concentrate their energy and resources on open seat races rather than contests which include an incumbent. *See also: HANDICAPPING; INCUMBENT*

MAJORITY the proportion of votes required to win an election. The share of the vote that constitutes winning is a critical issue in any electoral system. There are four basic types of majorities used in American elections: extraordinary majorities; absolute majorities; simple majorities; and pluralities.

Extraordinary majorities usually specify some proportion of the vote substantially greater than 50%. A common extraordinary majority is two-thirds of the votes cast. Absolute majorities require a voting total of one more than half of the number of voters qualified to vote or registered to vote. Simple majorities are less rigorous than either extraordinary majorities or absolute majorities. They require a vote of one more than half of the total votes actually cast.

Pluralities are the least demanding of all. They require only that the voting total be greater than the number of votes received by any other candidate. Most elections in the United States require only a plurality to win. Two important exceptions to this are run off primaries and most ballot issues. *See also BALLOT ISSUES; PLURALITY; RUN OFF PRIMARY*

MANDATE a popular charge from the electorate to carry out a particular program or policy. Mandates bestow a kind of moral suasion and political legitimacy on the politicians who receive them. They are usually associated with impressive victories or stunning defeats. Electoral wins of 60% or greater are widely interpreted as mandates.

The notion of mandates is loose when applied to American politics. The original concept was developed in the context of European parliamentary systems—where elections can express clear voter intentions, and well disciplined political parties exist to carry out the popular will.

Most scholars think it is specious to interpret American electoral wins as mandates to carry out specific policies or programs. They argue that the vagueness of party platforms and candidate positions make it uncertain just what a politician is advocating. Even when that is clear, voters themselves will usually possess a low degree of knowledge and understanding about specific policy issues.

This scholary view does not prevail everywhere. Victorious American politicians regularly uncover mandates to pursue this policy objective or enact that special program. Indeed the finding of mandates among the election returns is now almost an inevitable ritual after every presidential election. The fiction that voters really know or care about these discoveries is an established, perhaps necessary, American political tradition.

MOLE *See CAMPAIGN SPY*

MULTI-MEMBER DISTRICT *See SINGLE MEMBER DISTRICT*

NEW POLITICS popular shorthand for the changes that distinguish modern electoral politics from the politics of earlier times. The new politics contrasts with the "old politics" in three fundamental ways. All of these are linked to the decline of the political parties that has gradually occurred over the past several decades.

First, the new politics is candidate centered rather than party centered. No longer do political parties dominate nominations and elections. Now it is candidates who raise money, put organizations together and campaign, all more or less independent of party aid or counsel. This shift from party to candidate focus has produced a style of electoral politics in which parties are increasingly irrelevant to the outcome of elections.

Second, the new politics is media oriented rather than organization oriented. Under the old "retail politics" the parties controlled the flow of information to voters. Political organizations were the intermediaries through which candidates communicated with the electorate. Today the wholesale politics of television, radio, and direct mail have eroded this party function. Now candidates can communicate directly with the electorate, and they do.

Third, the new politics is technology driven. Technology has changed the management style of campaigns as well as the managers. Political professionals are more expert in public relations, advertising, polling, direct mail and sophisticated computer research. No longer are campaigns mainly run by party workers and volunteers. These have been replaced by media consultants, direct mail specialists, pollsters, professional fund raisers, and many others.

Trends toward the new politics are widespread. Yet not everywhere has the old politics been supplanted. Political parties still run many local campaigns—and they still perform many traditional functions like canvassing, distribution of literature, fund raising, recruiting volunteers, and pollwatching. The old politics still works well in some places at sometimes and the political parties can still be good at practicing it. *See also: WHOLESALE POLITICS*

OFF YEAR ELECTION any election held in other than a presidential election year. Off year elections held two years after a presidential election are labeled "mid-term elections". Those off year elections held one year or three years after a presidential election are referred to as "odd year" elections or "off-off year" elections.

For example, 1984 and 1988, are presidential election years; 1986 and 1990 are mid-term election years; and 1985, 1987, and 1989 are odd year or off—off year elections. These various election cycles produce some reoccurring political patterns.

Presidential elections usually record the highest turnout of any election year. These elections normally produce significant electoral gains for the party of the winning presidential candidate. The winning party can expect to gain seats in the House of Representatives and often the Senate. Gains in state offices are also typical.

Mid-term off year elections on the other hand stimulate less voter turnout than in presidential election years. Almost invariably mid-terms produce losses for the incumbent president's party.

Odd year elections witness lower voter turnout than either mid-term elections or presidential elections. These contests feature local elections—mayor, council, county officials, etc.—although several states elect governors and other state officials during odd years. Many states in fact schedule their local or state elections in odd years to separate them from the influence of national issues and trends. *See also: ELECTION DAY*

OFFICIAL RETURNS *See UNOFFICIAL RETURNS*

OLD POLITICS *See NEW POLITICS*

OPEN SEATS election campaigns in which there is no incumbent. Open seats occur when the incumbent has retired, died or lost an earlier primary. Legislative redistricting can also create an open seat. About 12% of all congressional seats fall open every two years. State and local legislatures have a higher rate of races in which both candidates are non-incumbents. Open seat races are more fiercely contested than contests featuring incumbents. One measure of the competitiveness of these contests is the spending. On average, open seat challengers raise and spend almost three times more than challengers of incumbents.

Since incumbents usually win and challengers usually lose, the minority party views an open seat as their best chance to oust the entrenched majority party. And the majority party itself takes seriously the possibility they might lose without the advantage of incumbency.

Both ins and outs tend to see open seats as their best opportunity to win and hold on to a seat. Statistics bear this out. About 75% of all Congressmen initially won their offices in open seat contests. *See also: INCUMBENTS; MARGINAL SEATS*

OPPOSITION RESEARCH research into the public record of an electoral opponent. Opposition research or "O" research is a systematic examination and compilation of what an opponent has said and done in public life.

In the post-Watergate era some sharp lines have been drawn between what is proper and legitimate opposition research and what crosses over into the realm of dirty tricks and campaigns spies. Proper and legitimate is information that is on the public record, such as speeches, interviews, news stories, voting and attendence records. Improper and not legitimate is the use of any illegal means to collect information or the use of confidential information not readily accessible to others.

Most opposition research done in campaigns is routine. It might include any or all of the following products:

1. "Roll call analysis"—a listing by subject, vote number, and date of the yes or no positions taken by an opponent during legislative voting.
2. "Quote books"—a chronological record of an opponent's public statements organized by issue or topic.
3. "Interest Group Ratings"—a compilation of the ratings or report cards given to an opponent by organized lobby groups.
4. "Financial Reports Analysis"—analysis of an opponent's financial filings and disclosures. These include listings of major contributors as well as a record of campaign expenditures.

The most heavily used "O" research is likely to reveal one (or more) of the following opponent actions:

1) Opponent voted for a pay raise, or
2) Opponent missed a large number of legislative roll calls, or
3) Opponent went on a junket, or
4) Opponent voted to raise taxes, or
5) Opponent was charged with financial irregularities, such as failure to pay taxes.

Candidates of course are aware of the danger presented by these issues—and they put effort into avoiding being trapped in them. *See also: NEGATIVE ADVERTISING; REPORT CARDS*

OUT OF THE LOOP *See IN THE LOOP*

PACK WITHDRAWAL *See DECOMPRESSION*

PARACHUTIST *See CARPETBAGGER*

PETITION *See FILING*

PHONEBANK *See BOILER ROOM*

PLURALITY a voting total larger than that received by any opponent but less than a 50% majority. The candidate who has won more votes than any other candidate is said to have a plurality. Pluralities constitute winning for most American elections. The major exception is runoff primaries which require a simple majority to win.

Here's an example that illustrates the difference between pluralities and majorities. Imagine a race in which there are three candidates: A, B, and C. After the votes are counted "A" is found to have 51%, "B" 45% and "C" 4%. "A" has won with a majority of the vote.

Now imagine another race with the same three candidates. This time after the votes are counted "A" has 45%, "B" 40% and "C" 15%. "A" has also won this election, but with a plurality rather than a majority.

Primary elections are regularly won by pluralities since more than two candidates often compete. Pluralities are also not unusual in general elections especially where there is a tradition of third party or Independent candidate participation. *See also: MAJORITY; MINORITY PRESIDENT*

PLURAL VOTING a system of voting in which some elite voters are given the right to cast more than one ballot. Plural voting assigns weights to voter characteristics, then assigns votes on that basis. Multiple votes can be awarded for property ownership, family position, education, wealth, or occupation. For example a head of household might be given two votes, a large tax payer might be given three votes and so on.

Plural voting is not used in the United States. Moreover it is very hard to imagine it ever being introduced given the strong national tradition of egalitarianism and ever expanding suffrage. Nevertheless there are certain election practices and patterns in the United States which may have the same effect as would plural voting.

Before implementation of the Supreme Court's one man, one vote rule, many state legislatures were elected by de-facto plural voting. Even today some voting districts remain unequal in population.

The manner by which U.S. Senators are elected is also a form of plural voting since residents of small states elect the same number of Senators as do residents of larger states. A voter in Wyoming casts the equivalent of about 90 votes for U.S. Senator for every vote cast by a voter in California.

Finally prevailing patterns of voter turnout can also constitute plural voting. Even in presidential elections about 50% of the eligible electorate don't vote—giving those 50% who do the equivalent of two votes. Off year elections and primary elections produce even more striking comparisons. When turnout goes down to say 25%—not unusual in local and primary elections—every voter who does vote counts for four votes.

POLITICAL CONSULTANTS professional campaign specialists who provide a range of candidate services to politicians and political organizations.

Political consultants are relatively new on the political scene. Before the early 1960's they hardly existed outside of California and a few large cities. Up to that time most campaign operations were handled by local party workers or volunteers recruited for specific campaigns.

By the mid 1960's however this all began to change. The continuing deterioration of the political parties left a growing vacuum in American politics. Into it stepped the political consultant equipped with new technology and specialized training in media, polling and other skill areas.

Early consultants were often "full service". They would come into a campaign and oversee most operations—sometimes even serving as campaign managers. As the profession developed, however, specialization has evolved. Most political consultants now market themselves as experts in one or two areas such as media, polling or direct mail.

The candidate services offered by today's consultants fall into three broad classifications: management services; polling services; and media services. Within these categories are dozens of specific consulting specialties such as direct mail, fund raising, time buying, public relations, and speech writing.

Most political consultants work only within one of the two major political parties—they will work just for Democratic candidates or just for Republican candidates. Some do this because they are committed ideologues or at least loyal partisans. But many political consultants are actually apathetic or even hostile to parties. They stay within one camp because the political parties themselves express discomfort at consultants who jump back and forth. *See also: AMERICAN ASSOCIATION OF POLITICAL CONSULTANTS; CANDIDATE SERVICES; NEW POLITICS*

POLITICAL WHORE *See HIRED GUN*

PROPORTIONAL REPRESENTATION (PR) a general method of allocating legislative or convention delegate seats according to the proportion of the total vote won by a candidate or political party. Proportional Representation (PR) can be used in multi-seat districts where more than one seat is up. Its objective is to give to each major political faction the legislative representation equivalent to that faction's support in the overall population.

PR works this way: Imagine five slots were up for election. Each political party puts up a list of candidates, as many as five since five seats are available. After balloting the total vote for each party is counted. If party "A" received 40% of the vote, that party would win 40% or two of the five seats; if party "B" wins 20% of the total vote that party would win 20% or one of the seats.

Actual winning candidates are selected by starting with the highest vote getter on each party's list and working down. In the example above party "A" would elect their top two candidates (with 40% of the vote) while party "B" would elect only their top candidate (with 20% of the vote).

PR is common in European multi-party parliamentary systems, but unusual in America. Single member districts and winner take all plurality systems predominate in U.S. elections.

Today most American debate about PR centers on its use by the national political parties to choose convention delegates during presidential caucuses and primaries. The Democratic Party particularly has encouraged its state parties to use PR in selecting delegates to presidential conventions. *See also: SINGLE MEMBER DISTRICT*

QUOTE BOOK *See OPPOSITION RESEARCH*

REAPPORTIONMENT *See APPORTIONMENT*

RECALL an electoral procedure which enables voters to remove an official from office before the scheduled expiration of his term. Recall is not authorized by the federal government, however 14 states and hundreds of municipalities do allow it.

The procedures required to implement a recall vary from state to state. Usually an elected official is guaranteed a minimum term; after that, aggrieved voters may request a recall election by circulating a petition among qualified voters.

When a petition drive is successful (a typical requirement is that 25% of those who voted in the last election sign the petition) the public official must stand for a special election. Usually voters are asked to vote yes or no on the question should (x) remain in the office of (mayor, judge, state senator, etc.) Sometimes rival candidates are permitted to file and run in the same special election.

The recall device is controversial. Supporters argue that it gives voters a direct check on the behavior and policy choices of incumbents. Along with other tools of direct democracy like the initiative and referendum, the recall makes representative democracy work better by increasing public official accountability.

Critics of the recall counter that it is unfair to elected officials who have been given a set term to accomplish their goals. Opponents also argue that the recall works against the formulation of sound public policy because it encourages officials to pander to the short term passions of the electorate.

In practice the recall is not heavily used in American politics. During the past several years there have been some highly publicized attempts to remove mayors in Seattle, San Francisco, Cleveland and Philadelphia. But most recall efforts are drives to remove local officials like county judges and school board members. Occasionally a judge is recalled or a local official removed, but recall campaigns are generally not successful. *See also: INITIATIVE AND REFERENDUM*

RECOUNT *See CONTESTED ELECTION*

ROLL CALL ANALYSIS *See OPPOSITION RESEARCH*

ROTTEN BOROUGHS voting districts that give disproportionately heavy representation to thinly populated areas. Rotten boroughs result from a failure to reapportion in response to shifts in the population. The expression is borrowed from English usage where rotten boroughs were once large towns that had declined—but had not lost their original legislative representation.

The term rotten borough has been used in two contexts in the United States. The first and most significant referred to the huge disparities in per capita representation that developed in most states as the nation urbanized. The one man, one vote court decisions of the 1960's—which required the reapportionment of congressional and state legislative districts after each decennial census—largely eliminated this kind of rotten borough.

The epithet rotten borough was also used to disparage the system once employed by the National Republican Party to allocate convention delegates to the eleven states of the old confederacy. From the end of Reconstruction until about 1920, southern delegates were given convention voting representation that ignored the political reality that the Republican Party had almost ceased to exist in the Old South. The Republicans themselves reformed these southern delegate rotten boroughs after losses in 1912 and 1916. *See also: APPORTIONMENT; ONE MAN, ONE VOTE*

SCHEDULING the process of planning, organizing and monitoring a candidate's campaign appearances. Scheduling stategists treat the candidate's time as a scarce resource to be allocated to the uses that will yield the most votes.

Procedure in most campaigns is to accept requests from inviting organizations or from field staff people, then set up working "block schedules" for the month. The closer one gets to the day or week, the more details are worked in—such as the time and place of events, the travel time required, the names of key people who will be meeting the candidate and telephone numbers of contact personnel.

Schedulers are staff who administer the scheduling operation. They are key people in campaigns. All requests for candidate appearances are cleared through them and they often initiate or plan other events attended by the candidate. In larger campaigns particularly, this is a nerve wracking job that positions the scheduler squarely in the midst of conflicting forces—candidate, field staff, campaign management, party people, and the covering media. The scheduler's task is to keep everyone as happy as possible while providing the candidate the opportunity to campaign in settings that will yield votes.

Scheduling decisions are influenced by the particular strategic objectives of a given campaign. In general though, schedulers evaluate a possible appearance in terms of its potential to attract media attention. The fund raising potential of an appearance may also be important. And in smaller campaigns such things as crowd size and prestige of the sponsoring organization are considered. *See also: ADVANCE*

SECOND CONSTITUENCY *See CONSTITUENCY*

SINGLE ISSUE POLITICS a style of political combat characterized by almost total emphasis on achievement of one particular goal. Single issue politics is practiced by "single issue groups" organized to concentrate on one burning issue, such as nuclear freeze, abortion, gun control or school prayer.

Single issue politics are not new. There have always been organizations in American life committed to a single objective—abolitionists, prohibitionists, suffragettes and the like. But today there are many more of them and their influence on the political system is much greater.

Modern single issue politics emerged during the 1970's. The reasons for its development are complex. Political scientists however usually cite the continuing decline of political parties and the growth of PAC's as major contributing factors.

Both politicians and political scientists worry about the trend to single issue politics. Politicians frequently find themselves in vicious cross fires between these groups and their opponents. Group members are often zealots who tie their support to a politician's behavior on that single issue. When the single issue groups are also well financed, they can withhold contributions to a politician's campaign or even support an opponent.

Political scientists also express reservations about single issue politics. Their most basic concern is that the groups destabilize the political system. American politics is based on bargaining, compromise, and coalition building. Single interest groups by contrast eschew compromise and promote conflict. *See also: ISSUE VOTING; PAC's*

SINGLE MEMBER DISTRICT a legislative territory which may elect only one legislator. Single member districts differ from multi-member districts in which two or more legislators are elected at the same time. The single member district predominates in the United States. Congress and most state legislatures are single member.

Multi-member districts however are found. A handful of states have adopted this form for elections to the lower house of their legislatures and substantial number of municipalities use multi-member districts for their local legislative bodies.

The typical multi-member district system allows voters to cast as many votes as there are positions to be filled. For example if a district has three seats, each voter gets three votes and the three highest vote getters are elected.

Single member districts are a major barrier to the development of viable third parties in the United States. Elections in them are usually determined by a pluarity system in which the candidate with the largest vote wins the seat, even though other candidates may have received almost as many votes.

Third parties rarely win these "winner take all" contests which would allow them to share in political power with the two major political parties. *See also: AT LARGE ELECTIONS; ELECTORAL SYSTEM; PROPORTIONAL REPRESENTATION; THIRD PARTIES; TWO PARTY SYSTEM*

SPECIAL ELECTION an election held in the interval between regularly scheduled primary and general elections. Special elections are usually called to fill vacancies caused by death, resignation, or removal of the incumbent.

States and municipalities have adopted a more or less uniform set of procedures which they use when the need for a special election arises. A specified public official such as governor, presiding officer of the legislature, mayor, or judge, declares that a vacancy exists. The same official eventually issues a "writ of election" setting the date and other conditions for the election.

State law usually requires special elections to be held at least 60 to 90 days after the last regular election. In practice most are held during late Winter (January to March) or Summer (July to September). Normal nominating methods such as primary elections and conventions are not used. Instead candidates get on the ballot by petition or by being selected in special party meetings.

Political observers watch special elections as barometers of current voter sentiment or a test of the popularity of the party in power. Well known political figures sometimes encourage this speculation by becoming visibly involved in the campaign on behalf of their party's candidate. Special elections often attract larger than average campaign contributions as well as media attention. Not infrequently these elections are called because the balance of power in a legislative body is at stake. Even when this is not the case, heavy interest focuses on them because they are the "only show in town". *See also: FILING; VACANCY*

STOREFRONTS downtown or neighborhood campaign offices. Storefronts are highly visible well located facilities situated especially to facilitate public awareness and access. Typically they include a public reception area staffed by workers who distribute literature, answer questions and perform other campaign tasks.

Storefronts are often the hub of local campaign activity—where volunteers congregate, mailings are produced and telephone banks are operated. In earlier times most serious campaigns maintained storefronts. These were places where voters could come in, pick up literature, talk to campaign officials and perhaps even meet the candidate.

Today storefronts are becoming scarce. They are a "retail" strategy and modern politics has shifted away from retail politics toward wholesale politics. Instead of concentrating on personal campaigning and direct voter contact, campaigns now stress the use of mass media to attract votes.

Neither retail politics nor storefronts have disappeared entirely, nor are they likely to do so. Many local campaigns operate storefronts and occasionally large state and even national campaigns still use them. *See also: WHOLESALE POLITICS*

STREET LISTS names of voters compiled by election officials or campaign workers. Street lists are usually assembled from the rolls of registered voters. Formats vary but most street lists include the name of the voter, his address, political party registration, and perhaps a phone number. Names are arranged in long columns and organized by precinct, ward or other political subdivision. Sometimes these lists are typed or even hand written, but, more and more today they are computer produced.

Street lists are important in organizing canvassing operations. Campaign workers equipped with them can locate registered voters, drop off literature, answer questions, and ask for that voter's support.

Street lists are also used in GOTV operations. Here campaigns—perhaps aided by telephone banks and direct mail—use street lists to call or visit favorable voters, remind them to vote and even take them to the polling place. *See also: CANVASSING; ELECTION DAY ACTIVITY; GOTV; VOTER CONTACT ACTIVITIES*

SURROGATES official stand-ins for political candidates. Surrogates are usually prestigious supporters who substitute for a candidate unable to make a particular campaign appearance.

Presidential campaigns are the heaviest users of surrogates. For incumbent presidents there is a rich source of surrogates always available: cabinet officers, legislative leaders, senior staffers, and other notable supporters. Gubernatorial, congressional and even local candidates also regularly use surrogates. The practice allows some "personal" campaigning even when the candidates themselves cannot appear.

Surrogate scheduling is also an effective way to draw prominent people into the campaign giving them highly visible roles that many find gratifying. In some campaigns surrogates are provided with elaborate staff help, scheduling assistance and advance work. But in other campaigns surrogates don't receive much more than an address and some brochures.

Sometimes surrogates can get a candidate in serious trouble as Louis Farrakhan did to Jesse Jackson in 1984. Reverend Jackson eventually had to disavow Farrakhan's controversial rhetoric by saying that he couldn't "control the actions of a surrogate".

More often however surrogates conduct themselves with both decorum and discretion. Their objective is to represent their candidate as artfully as possible while attracting media coverage to the campaign. *See also: CANDIDATE*

TELEPHONE BANK canvassing operations which rely on organized callers to call and talk with voters. Telephone banks are also known as "boiler rooms" after the early practice of locating many of them in basements or boiler rooms.

Telephone banks are widely used in modern campaigns. They have two main purposes: fund raising—to solicit contributions for the campaign; and voter canvassing—to identify supporters and turn them out on election day.

The typical phone bank operation might have from 10 to 50 callers in a single large room, each equipped with a telephone, a list of names with telephone numbers, and a "script". The caller dials a number, identifies himself and reads the script, all in as little as two minutes time.

Campaigns that carry on voter contact and GOTV efforts rely heavily on their boiler room operations. So do those campaigns that emphasize organizational strategies and tactics rather than media. *See also: CANVASSING; GOTV; VOTER CONTACT*

UNOFFICIAL RETURNS the voting returns reported on election night or early the following morning and commonly but mistakenly understood to be the final returns. After the polls close in each precinct, two sets of voting results are actually prepared. The first set, the official returns, are placed in a sealed envelope and taken to a designated storage area for safekeeping.

The second set, the unofficial returns, are collected by election officials who take them to a central location such as a courthouse where other unofficial returns have been collected. From there the unofficial returns are disseminated to the covering media who report them to the public. A count of the first set of returns—the official returns—will not begin for several days after the election—and will not be certified until a month or more after the election. *See also: FLASH RETURNS*

VACANCY a public office left unfilled because the incumbent has died, resigned, been removed, or disqualified. Thousand's of vacancies occur in the United States every year. Death or resignation causes most of these. Only a handful of public officials are ever impeached or subjected to recall.

Vacancies are filled in one of three ways: appointment, special election; and legal succession. Appointment is used to fill the vast majority of vacancies, including some of the highest offices in government. For example, state governors fill United States Senate vacancies by appointment until the next scheduled election.

Special elections are used however to fill some vacancies, including many legislative seats. Usually, the law requires that a designated official, such as the state's chief election official, call a special election within a prescribed duration of time. Legal succession is the third method of filling vacancies. The law specifies the successor who is usually an incumbent appointed, or elected official. Legal succession is used to fill vacancies in many executive offices, including the presidency, gubernatorial vacancies in most states and mayoral vacancies in many cities. *See also: SPECIAL ELECTION*

VOCATIONALISTS a term developed by political scientist Xandra Kayden to describe the people who staff and run campaigns. According to Kayden, campaigns include both vocationalists and avocationalists (1978:41-60). Vocationalists are professionals for whom campaigning is a career. These include three types of campaign workers: organizers, apprentices, and seekers:

> (organizers) are political workers who participate on a paid basis in several campaigns. . . .. and on the staffs of elected or appointed officials. . . ..
> apprentices were college students on leave for the summer to participate in the campaign. . . ..
> seekers were older members of the campaign organization who used the campaign as a forum to evaluate their careers and professions.

Avocationalists unlike the career oriented vocationalist, are amateurs for whom campaigning is more hobby than vocation. These also include three types of campaign worker: believers, materialists, and joiners:

> Believers hold traditional values, believe in the system and felt good about meeting their civic responsibility (most believers are middle aged women). . . ..
> Materialists (are) men who made up the volunteer field organization in the campaign, (and looked for a reward of a job or prestige). . . ..
> Joiners are similar to believers except that they did not express their motivation in terms of civic responsibility (but rather in terms of meeting people and social relationships).

Kayden's typology of campaign professionals and amateurs provides important insights about the motivations and perspectives of people who work in political campaigns. It is particularly valuable because only a few empirical studies of campaign organizations have been reported. *See also: AMATEURS AND REGULARS*

VOTER CONTACT a general reference to campaign activities that put the candidate or a campaign worker in direct contact with potential voters. Voter contact activities include telephone banks, door to door canvassing, registration drives, and election day activities. These are all examples of retail politics rather than the wholesale politics that characterizes media campaigns.

There is often tension in the modern campaign between those who put a greater stress on voter contact and organization, and those who prefer to emphasize media. Many political professionals feel strongly one way or the other about the issue.

Some small local campaigns rely entirely on voter contact to communicate with voters, while a few large campaigns depend exclusively on media. Most campaigns, however, opt for a blend of the two.

Studies indicate that voter contact can be highly effective in mobilizing turnout on election day. Some research has shown that up to 85% of those who were contacted do vote in the election. And a good election day organization can make a difference of 5 to 15% in the voting results. *See also: CANVASSING; ELECTION DAY ACTIVITIES; GOTV; TELEPHONE BANKS*

WEST OF THE POTOMAC a metaphor for the American heartland, the people, the public, and especially the electorate. The common wisdom in Washington, D.C. is that there is a kind of insulation that grows up in the capital that makes it hard for those who live in Washington to really know and understand what is happening in the rest of the country.

Some reporters and public officials pride themselves on making regular pilgrimages West of the Potomac to keep in touch with the feelings and attitudes of the people. Polls and public opinion research—which are avidly consumed in Washington—accomplish much the same thing for others. Indeed, it is almost axiomatic among politicians that those who lose touch with their constituency are in danger of also losing their office.

At one time there was an informal rule observed among reporters: anything that happens East of the Potomac, i.e., in a politician's personal life in Washington, doesn't get reported West of the Potomac, i.e., in the home district. In general that rule no longer holds and reporters treat just about everything not off the record as fair game. *See also: OFF THE RECORD; ON THE RECORD*

WIMP a whining weakling, someone without backbone who is a pushover, a political pansy. Wimp surfaced as a widely used invective in the early 1980's. It was used in the 1982 Illinois gubernatoral which featured incumbent Republican James Thompson opposed by Democratic Adlai Stevenson. Stevenson drew the taunt and it stuck. He also lost the election after a very close race not settled until after a recount.

Democrat Walter Mondale was tagged with the term during the 1984 presidential election—as were several other candidates for state and local offices. Wimp is an expression that will probably survive. It describes the antithesis of the macho image that some candidates try to project and many voters seem to expect.

So far wimps have been exclusively male candidates. A female politician with wimp characteristics has no established nomenclature. Among the terms suggested to describe a female wimp are wimpess, wimpette, wamp, simp, and mouse.

WINNER TAKE ALL *See UNIT RULE*

WINNING *See LOSING*

WORKING THE FENCE in the argot of advance, candidates who are engaged in direct or people to people campaigning are working the fence. "Working the crowd" and "working the gate" have much the same meaning. Many politicians genuinely appear to enjoy "pressing the flesh", while there are certainly some who do not. However, in the modern campaign, candidates who work the fence are often doing so for the benefit of the television camera there to record it. *See also: ADVANCE; WHOLESALE POLITICS*

2

MEDIA AND POLITICS

ACTUALITIES audio or video tapes prepared by a political campaign and "fed" to radio and television stations for pickup in their newscasts and campaign coverages. Actualities are designed to look and sound like actual news stories. They usually feature the candidate reacting to a recent event, making a statement about a current issue, or in an excerpt from a speech. Radio actualities are more common than television actualities. They are easier to produce and to transmit. For radio the tape is "cut" by the candidate and offered free to any station that wishes to use it. The radio station simply dials an advertised number and records the actuality on the phone. It is then ready to be rotated into broadcast coverage whenever the station chooses to use it.

A newer form of actuality is the so called "informercial", described as an electronic press release. Informercials are video tapes produced to resemble on-the-air news coverage. They usually feature what appears to be reporters interviewing people, narrating footage, or providing commentary. In fact, these are performers appearing in a slick promotion sponsored by a candidate or other client.

Actualities are mildly controversial, informercials somewhat more so. Campaigns use them to increase the amount of unpaid media coverage they receive. Some segments of the media disparage them as "canned" and managed news, while others welcome them as important elements of their campaign coverage. This latter attitude is more common at smaller stations with limited news budgets. *See also: NEWS RELEASE; UNPAID MEDIA*

ADJACENCIES *See SPOTS*

ADVANCE TEXT copies of a candidate's or public official's scheduled speech or remarks—provided to the media in advance of the actual delivery.

The practice of providing advance text is one that benefits both coverage media and the campaign. It is in fact common for reporters to skip a routine speech and to write their story on the event from the advance text. The dissemination of advance text is especially important to radio and television reporters who must plan in advance which portions of a speech they will film or tape.

The campaigns also benefit by distribution of advance text. Doing so can enhance the campaign's relationship with the media—and it increases the likelihood that an event will be covered and that the coverage will be accurate. *See also: NEWS RELEASE*

AGENCY COMMISSION the compensation paid to an advertising agency or to the producer of political advertising. Agency commissions are usually paid by the publisher, radio, or television stations with which the advertising is placed. They are frequently the major form of payment received by the producer of political advertising.

The standard commission rate to an agency or producer is 15% payable on the gross amount of advertising purchased. For example a "buy" of $5,000 would yield a commission of $750.

In modern politics a specialization known as political time buying has developed to meet the particular needs of campaigns in placing advertising on radio and television. Time buyers are often compensated with a share of the agency commission. *See also: POLITICAL ADVERTISING; TIME BUYING*

ARBITRON the trade name for the electronic system used by the American Research Bureau (ARB) to collect the data upon which program ratings are based. The Arbitron system consists of recording devices placed in a scientific sample of American homes.

These recording devices are wired to a central computer which tabulates data about program choices and set usage. This system supplemented by diary records is the basis for the widely used Arbitron rating system.

Since the cost of advertising time on the electronic media is based on program ratings, the function of broadcast rating services is similar to that of the audit bureaus which certify circulation figures for magazines and newspapers. *See also: AUDIT BUREAUS; NIELSON RATING*

AUDIMETER *See NIELSON RATING*

AUDIT BUREAUS service bureaus which review and verify the circulation figures of newspapers and magazines. Since the cost of advertising space in the print media is based on circulation figures, the function of the audit bureaus is similar to that of the broadcast rating services such as Arbitron which measure the delivered audience for radio and television programs.

The largest and best known of the audit bureaus is the Audit Bureau of Circulation (ABC) which validates the circulation statements of newspapers and magazines that have 70% or more paid circulation. *See also: ARBITRON; NIELSON RATINGS*

B WIRE one of the two main news reporting circuits provided by the national wire service—and known respectively as the A wire and the B wire. The B wire is the state and regional wire. It covers stories oriented to a local region or particular state.

The A wire is the national wire. It provides nationally oriented news to subscribers all over the country.

Wire services provide a daily flow of news stories and features for their subscribers who include virtually all daily newspapers and a substantial number of broadcast outlets. The largest of the wire services and the most widely used are the Associated Press (AP) and United Press International (UPI).

Wire service influence is especially strong among the smaller print and electronic media which rely on them heavily for news that originates anywhere outside the local area. *See also: WIRE SERVICES*

BACKGROUNDERS press conferences or other interview settings in which a campaign official or candidate speaks to reporters with the understanding that the "source" will not be directly identified. Backgrounders provide information that may be used but is "not for attribution". They should not be confused with off the record interviews or statements which are not reported in any form.

Backgrounders are strictly on-the-record meetings between reporter and source. Usually, reporters attending backgrounders understand that they may use any information gained as long as its source is only vaguely identified. News stories that cite "highly placed sources," "usually reliable sources," or "sources close to the candidate" are usually the product of backgrounders.

One version of the backgrounder is the "deep backgrounder." When news sources specify that they are speaking for deep background, they are stipulating that they be identified in the vaguest terms or not at all.

Campaign officials like backgrounders because they provide an opportunity to suggest a favorable story or disclose information without publicly being identified with it. Reporters are generally willing to accept the restrictions imposed by backgrounders as long as the precise identification of a source is not critical to a story. *See also: OFF THE RECORD; ON THE RECORD*

BASIC INVESTMENT CONCEPT a popular direct mail strategy used to raise money in political campaigns. The basic investment concept involves the repetition of two basic steps over and over until fund raising goals have been met. In the first step investment "seed money" is raised; in the second step this capital is invested in a mass "prospecting" mailing that solicits contributions for the campaign.

During subsequent repetitions of this cycle the proceeds are taken from one mailing and reinvested in another mailing; along the way a house list of proven donors is accumulated. These contributors are mailed to again and again along with other prospective givers.

The unique feature of the basic investment concept is that it reinvests all of the profits from a mailing in a followup mailing. The logic is very similar to that of plowing back profits into a growing business: by delaying rewards and incurring additional risk, the eventual payoffs will be greater.

The basic investment concept can be enormously profitable. Direct mailers can return up to $10 for every $1 initial investment. But not all direct mail operations use the basic investment concept. Another strategy known as the "dual investment concept" invests profits less aggressively in followup mailings. This approach relies less on prospecitng lists and more on established house lists. *See also: COMPILED LISTS; DIRECT MAIL; HOUSE LIST*

BASIC PIECE the campaign brochure or literature. Almost every serious political campaign has some kind of basic piece designed to be widely distributed. These are produced on high grade paper and feature photographs of the candidate in settings calculated to appeal to voters. Usually, they include a few paragraphs on the issues of the campaign or the themes that are being promoted.

The basic piece serves some major functions in the campaign. It gives the campaign visibility and provides a tangible link for volunteers and others working in the field. It also lends a certain credibility to the campaign and demonstrates to campaign workers that the campaign is viable.

The distribution of brochures and other forms of campaign literature may also have some influence on the electorate, but there is no convincing evidence of this. Most political professionals believe that printed campaign material has negligible impact on actual voting. *See also: VERTICAL MEDIA*

BASIC SPEECH the stock or stump speech given by a candidate. Basic speeches are the all occasion talk for rallies, dinners, fund raising events, press tours, and so on.

For most candidates the basic speech evolves over weeks and even months of campaigning. It might originate as a formal written address but over time it is adapted, adjusted and honed to express the particular personality and emphasis of the candidate.

Good basic speeches sound the themes of the campaign, let the candidate express his more attractive qualities and establish a positive candidate image. Perhaps most important of all the effective basic speech includes key sections and phrases that allow local broadcast media to take 30 or 60 second "sound bites" which will be played on the six o'clock news.

Basic speeches are usually modular so that sections can be added or deleted to fit local circumstances or the particular occasion. Invariably they include mention of well known community figures and allusion to important local traditions or pressing local issues.

Reporters covering campaigns hear the basic speech dozens of times. This is one reason the press often ignores formal candidate remarks entirely in their coverage—to dwell on this or that incident seemingly far removed from the day's campaigning.

Candidates simply don't do that many different things from stop to stop and so reporters look for novel story lines and news angles. This same search for variety also leads campaigns to put on media events which maintain press interest.

BEAT SYSTEM the traditional approach to monitoring and gathering news, used by both print and electronic media. Beats are regular journalistic assignments where newsworthy events are most likely to occur. News stories from established beats probably outnumber other stories by two to one or better.

There are two main types of beats, geographic or place beats and functional or subject beats. Geographic beats include sites like city hall, the state capitol, Washington, a particular region of the country, or a foreign nation. Functional beats are assignments to important policy areas, such as education, the economy, defense, health, or foreign affairs.

The major media in the United States all tend to cover the same beats. This results in considerable uniformity in news coverage. It also provides political professionals with the opportunity to plan media events and anticipate unpaid media coverage. *See also: MEDIA EVENTS; NEWS VALUES; PACK JOURNALISM; UNPAID MEDIA*

BLITZ a tactical approach to voter contact characterized by highly concentrated intense activity. Blitz was originally a military term which described any sudden swift strategic attacks designed to overwhelm an opponent's defense. In politics, the blitz is especially applied to certain aspects of media campaigns and to canvassing.

Media blitzes are saturation time buying over a few days or weeks. Canvassing blitzes involve heavy telephone or door-to-door solicitation of voters carried out over a few days or over a weekend. Literature drops by volunteers who stuff mailboxes with campaign literature are often part of the canvass.

The essence of the blitz strategy both the media version and the canvassing version—is to employ overwhelming numbers or resources over a short period of time, in order to overcome resistance from the opponent. *See also: CANVASSING; MEDIA BLITZ*

BOARDS outdoor advertising, especially billboards. Boards have long been a fixture in political campaigns. They are thought to be especially effective in raising the name recognition of a candidate.

Boards are rated for their effectiveness on the basis of their showing or the percentage of the traveling public that is exposed to them. A "50 showing" for example means that 50% of the public will see the billboard message over a 30 day period.

Most political professionals believe that large expenditures for billboards are wasteful. The conventional wisdom is that billboards should be used at the start of a campaign to raise awareness of the campaign itself. They can also be used when a candidate's name recognition is low, or where other forms of advertising are not available (such as in many rural areas).

Beyond these applications, other forms of political advertising are probably more effective. *See also: SHOWING; TWENTY-FOUR SHEET*

BRAG SHEETS brief candidate biographies that are used in media kits, news releases, and other press functions. Brag sheets are one to two page vitaes which highlight a candidate's political experience, personal history, occupation, and education.

They are often brazenly promotional and sometimes fast and loose with proferred facts. The media has learned to be skeptical of brag sheets, and more than a few candidates have been embarrassed by inaccuracies in their campaign biographies.

BROADCASTING *See NARROWCASTING*

BROCHURE *See BASIC PIECE*

BUYING THE MARKET a classic strategy used by political time buyers. Buying the market involves the scheduling of saturation advertising on all or most of the local radio and television outlets available. The saturation schedule is maintained for a period ranging from several days to a couple of weeks.

The strategy of buying the market is normally employed in situations in which a candidate is not well known, and therefore, does not have high name recognition. Sometimes campaigns also buy the market to reach the largest number of voters possible. This latter practice can be an inefficient use of campaign resources if it is not tied to the overall campaign plan. *See also: FLAT BUY; MEDIA BLITZ; ORCHESTRATED FINISH; SPURT SCHEDULE; TIME BUYING*

CAMPAIGN BUTTONS probably the oldest form of political advertising. Campaign buttons belong to a large class of gadgets and gimmicks like key rings, hats, horns, pens, ashtrays, etc.

These flotsam and jetsam of politics are ubiquitous in the modern campaign. Yet most political professionals consider them to be inefficient expenditures, having high unit costs and dubious influence on voters.

Even though they are widely thought to be a waste of money, buttons and other gadgets are used in almost every campaign. They probably do have some limited value in raising name recognition and in giving a kind of legitimacy to the unfolding campaign.

But the major benefit of using buttons and related paraphernalia is the sense of purpose and involvement they give workers and supporters within the campaign. Campaign buttons allow those involved to identify with the campaign, to feel it is important, and to communicate their feelings about the campaign and their role in it. *See also: VERTICAL MEDIA*

CAMPAIGN LITERATURE See BASIC PIECE

CHARACTERIZATION media jargon for an election night forecast that merely hints at the results without flatly predicting them. Characterizations are used by reporters to indicate trends and suggest outcomes. They stop short of identifying actual winners and losers, but usually leave little doubt about the way things are going.

In 1984 for example one network reported at 6:02 pm (while virtually all the polls in the country were still open)

> There are no indicators so far—including the results from a national poll of voters—that would contradict the expectation that President Reagan will win tonight's election.

Another network reported a few minutes later:

> Voters across the country today in overwhelming numbers appear to be voting for Ronald Reagan. Our (exit poll) indicates the president is leading his opponent with every major voter group except blacks and the poor.

Such characterizations are usually based on key precinct analysis and exit polls completed earlier in the day. Networks and their local affiliates use these rather than actual prediction to avoid calling elections before the polls close. Characterizations also allow the networks to hedge until enough actual voting results come in to indicate a firm trend.

Characterizations and actual election night predictions are controversial. Some believe they may discourage voter turnout or otherwise affect the results of elections in those areas where the polls remain open. Others discount the influence of these forecasts on voters. The existing evidence suggests that network forecasts or characterizations may depress slightly the turnout for "down ticket" races. Some western Democratic candidates in 1980 for example pinned their defeats on the early forecasts of Republican victory made in the east. *See also: EXIT POLLS; KEY PRECINCTS*

CLIPPING SERVICES private businesses—usually small and local—employed by political campaigns to monitor and report press coverage. Clipping services subscribe to newspapers and magazines, read them, and clip and copy pieces published on the campaign. Sometimes they also follow radio and television and provide transcripts of broadcast stories or editorial comment.

Clipping services are very popular in modern campaigning and they do supply important feedback. Clipped articles are used to brief candidates and are circulated among campaign staff. But the commercial services are often slow and always expensive. Consequently smaller campaigns and those with limited budgets frequently use volunteers instead of paid clippers.

Monitoring of press coverage furnsihes an astonishing amount of the political intelligence that is gathered on the opposition—much more than all of the cloak and dagger hi-jinks associated with dirty tricks and campaign spies. Most campaigns probably learn most of what they know about their opponents from public press accounts provided by clipping services.

COMPILED LISTS one of the five basic types of mailing lists used in connection with direct mail fund raising. Compiled lists include the names of people who belong to specific organizations or who follow a particular occupation. The other types of widely used mailing lists are: house lists; "outside contributors lists"; "commercial lists"; and "universal" lists.

House lists include the names of contributors who have responded to a previous fund raising appeal from the campaign. Outside contributors lists are made up of individuals and organizations who have contributed to similar candidates or causes. Commercial lists are lists of people who have purchased certain goods or services. Universal lists are composed of persons who share some very general characteristics like all having telephones or drivers licenses or living in the same town.

Mailing lists have several sources. Some of them—particularly house lists—are maintained by candidates and political organizations from campaign to campaign. Others are obtained from political parties, other candidates who share theirs, and friendly organizations. Mailing lists are also available from list brokers who make a business of renting and selling them.

The selection and use of mailing lists is increasingly being linked to polling and to geodemographics: polls suggest which voters would favor a particular candidate; geodemographics indicate where these voters live; and mailing lists provide the voters names and addresses. *See also: BASIC INVESTMENT CONCEPT; DIRECT MAIL; HOUSE LIST*

COMPLEMENTARITY an important theory in political advertising. The notion of complementarity holds that the effectiveness of a campaign message is increased when it is delivered through more than one kind of media. Using multiple forms of media—television, radio, newspapers, magazines, etc.—produces repetition and reinforcement. This in turn leads to higher recall of the message.

Complementarity doesn't require that identical advertising be used in the different media or that advertising strategy consist of lifts from television spots. Instead it emphasizes repetition and reinforcement of the same basic theme. If a campaign for example is stressing the candidate's experience, the experience theme should be employed in all campaign advertising. But it should be adapted to the unique nature of the particular medium used.

The corollary of the notion of complementarity is that a campaign message should be delivered through unpaid media as well as paid media. Getting press coverage that harmonizes with campaign advertising themes achieves repetition and reinforcement of the basic message—just as does using several different kinds of media. Moreover the unpaid media coverage is usually more credible to voters than is political advertising. *See also: LIFT; RADIO; TELEVISION*

CONTRAST SPOTS political commercials that emphasize the differences between the candidates—especially those differences which hinge on policy and issue positions. Contrast spots are negative advertising that attack an opponent by directly and unfavorably comparing that opponent's record or positions with those of the sponsoring candidate.

Many political consultants believe that contrast spots which run near the end of a campaign can be decisive. Research in fact has shown that Independents and undecideds—two very important voter groups—much prefer contrast spots to other forms of negative advertising.

Apparently the high information factual nature of these spots makes these voters feel more confident about the decision that they are trying to make. *See also: MAN IN THE STREET; NEGATIVE ADVERTISING; SPOTS; TALKING HEADS; WEATHERVANE SPOTS*

CONTROLLED MEDIA *See UNPAID MEDIA*

COOL MEDIUM the famous phrase used by the late Marshall McLuhan to describe the nature of television. A cool medium—television is the best example—provides little detail and a low degree of information. It presents only general images and incomplete impressions. Viewers have to involve themselves in the message in order to complete the partial picture. And viewers fill in these images by projecting their own hopes, wishes and expectations onto them.

McLuhan drew a sharp distinction between a cool medium and a hot medium. In a cool medium the image is vague and the audience finishes it with their own feelings and attitudes. But in a hot medium like newspapers, books, and radio, the information level is so rich and detailed that the audience is left with very little to complete.

These differences mean that candidates must approach the two media types with different strategies. In television the emphasis is on style and image creation rather than on detailed discussion of issues. Candidates may be advised to use rhetoric that is vague enough to be interpreted in several different ways—or to avoid taking distinctive positions while giving the impression that they are in fact doing so.

With a hot medium the strategies are different. Candidates may be advised to emphasize detail and substance. With newspapers or radio, issues can be discussed fully and a great deal more information can be presented.

Candidates also may be cool or hot personalities in the sense that they do better in one type of medium than they do in the other. John Kennedy, Ronald Reagan and Jimmy Carter were cool, but Richard Nixon, Lyndon Johnson and Walter Mondale were hot. Since television has come to dominate electoral politics, those politicians who do well with it tend to be more successful than those who do not. *See also: CANDIDATE IMAGE; RADIO; TELEVISION*

COPY the words used in political advertising. Copy is the written or spoken script designed to run in spots or print ads. The general usage of the term has been extended to include all of the creative elements of an advertisement—the visual as well as the verbal.

Some of the copy in political advertising is written or designed by political consultants who specialize in media production. A good deal of copy however is produced by regular advertising agencies which may take on one or two political campaigns a year.

There is a long running and not too serious argument between political consultants and advertising professionals about their shared responsibilities. Some political consultants allege that advertising agencies should not work for political campaigns because they don't understand politics. While some advertising professionals claim that political consultants shouldn't do advertising because all they do understand is politics. *See also: POLITICAL ADVERTISING*

COST PER THOUSAND (CPM) a widely used measure of the efficiency of newspapers, radio or television in delivering advertising audiences. Cost Per Thousand (CPM) is the cost of a unit of advertising air time or newspaper space per one thousand people exposed to the message.

The CPM criterion is most useful when the media compared are all of the same type, with very similar audiences. For example, three television stations which have similar sized audiences and market demographics can be evaluated. Or two newspapers can be analyzed if they both have similar circulations and readerships.

CPM considerations do not weigh as heavily in the placing of political advertising as they do for some other kinds of advertising. This is because of the unique time factor that distinguishes political advertising: the closer the spot or ad is run to election day the more valuable it is.

"Cost per voter" is an analogous concept used by political strategists in allocating campaign expenditures. Most political professionals believe that television produces the lowest cost per voter. *See also: NARROWCASTING; TIME BUYING*

DAISY SPOT the best known and possibly the most effective political commercial ever shown. The daisy spot was produced for the 1964 Lyndon Johnson campaign against Barry Goldwater.

Tony Schwartz the creator of the daisy spot later described it in the Responsive Chord (1973):

> The spot shows a little girl in a field counting petals on a daisy. As her count reaches ten the visual motion is frozen and the viewer hears a countdown. When the countdown reaches zero we see a nuclear explosion and hear President Johnson say, 'These are the stakes, to make a world in which all God's children can grow, or go into the darkness. Either we must love each other or we must die.' As the screen goes to black at the end, white lettering appears stating 'on November 3rd, vote for President Johnson'.

The daisy spot was so controversial that the Johnson campaign pulled it after only one showing. Nevertheless it provoked enough interest and debate that it was shown countless more times as part of news coverage and commentary. Even today over two decades later the daisy spot is occasionally aired as an example of political advertising. The impact of the spot has been widely discussed and analyzed. The general consensus is that it, and commercials like it, are effective because they surface feelings that voters already have. Rather than try to pursuade or change minds about something, these spots bring out the fears, beliefs, and biases that are already there. For example if research shows that a candidate is perceived as a big spender, soft on crime, a friend of the rich, or dishonest, a political spot can be designed to remind the viewer of those feelings already present.

These notions about political advertising are really specific applications of positioning—the strategy that candidates can be marketed by building political advertising around what voters already feel and believe. *See also: COOL MEDIUM; NEGATIVE ADVERTISING; POLITICAL ADVERTISING; POSITIONING; TELEVISION*

DIRECT MAIL a specialization among political consultants that involves producing and sending mass mailings to carefully selected lists of "prospects." Direct mail is used for both fund raising and political advertising. There are several different approaches employed in direct mail operations. Most of them combine some mixture of house lists and "prospecting lists". House lists are composed of the names and addresses of contributors or supporters who have responded to an earlier direct mailing. People who respond to prospecting list mailings are placed on the house list. Prospecting lists themselves come from several sources. Some of them are supplied by "list brokers" who sell or rent them to the campaign. Others come from previous campaigns, other candidates and the membership records of friendly organizations.

The major advantage of direct mail over other advertising or fund raising methods is that it allows a campaign to tailor individual appeals to very specialized audiences. The electorate or potential contributors can be cut in many different ways so that the particular concerns of each group may be addressed. Direct mailers refer to this as "rifle shooting", which they contrast with the "shotgunning" approach of other forms of mass media.

Candidates of both parties are increasingly likely to use direct mail. Inexpensive computers and high speed printers have brought the technology within reach of smaller campaigns, while the costs of competing media have continued to rise. Voters also are becoming more accustomed to receiving direct mail because of its wide use in private sector marketing.

These trends seem certain to make direct mail as much of a staple in the modern campaign as were campaign buttons and billboards in earlier times. *See also: BASIC INVESTMENT CONCEPT; COMPILED LISTS; HOUSE LISTS; NARROWCASTING; POLITICAL ADVERTISING*

DISCLAIMER tag lines or "authorization notices" found at the end of political advertising. Disclaimers are usually short and concise. For advertising financed and authorized by a candidate's own campaign, the usual format is:

Paid for by the Jack Smith for Congress Committee, Bob Brown, Treasurer.

For advertising that represents an independent expenditure, the disclaimer identifies the sponsor and states that it was not authorized by any candidate. The usual format for these is:

Paid for by the XYZ committee, and not authorized by any candidate

Most campaigns use some version of these basic tags. Some however, try to gain some additional advertising exposure by appending inventive disclaimers such as:

This ad was paid for by a whole bunch of people who want to see Jack Smith in Congress, Bob Brown Treasurer.

The argument for requiring disclaimers is similar to the reasoning advanced for requiring disclosure in campaign finance laws. According to their advocates both provide the information needed to permit voters to better evaluate candidates and make choices.

Disclaimers are required by the Federal Elections Commission (FEC) under provisions of the Federal Elections Campaign Act (FECA). Under FEC guidelines disclaimers must accompany all broadcast and print advertising. This includes radio, television, newspapers, outdoor advertising, posters, yard signs and direct mail.

Federal rules cover only federal campaigns for Congress and President. Individual state laws prescribe the disclaimer rules applied to state and local elections. *See also: FEDERAL ELECTION CAMPAIGN ACT (FECA); POLITICAL ADVERTISING*

EDITORIAL BOARDS meetings between political candidates and the editorial staffs of newspapers, news magazines, radio and television stations. Editorial boards are often held in relaxed informal settings that allow some easy give and take between staff and candidate.

A typical session might begin with introductions all around, a brief statement by the candidate and then followup questions from reporters and editors. In lieu of a formal presentation the campaign may simply distribute copies of position papers, major speeches, or other campaign literature.

Both candidates and news outlets benefit from editorial boards. Candidates have an opportunity to meet and establish a relationship with senior editors, reporters, and news-directors. These are the people who will be making policy decisions about campaign coverage and pre-election endorsements. Candidates can get acquainted, discuss their backgrounds, explain their positions, and generally clear up any confusion or misconceptions that may exist.

News outlets also gain from these meetings. Staff has the chance to meet candidates, learn their views, question them on their backgrounds or positions, and generally examine their qualifications for public office.

Editorial boards receive considerable prominence in campaign planning and scheduling. The emphasis placed on these meetings underscores the significance campaigns attach to press relations. Senior editorial staff in particular are viewed as important opinion makers—political gatekeepers, who can make or break a campaign by their decision to extend serious coverage or make an endorsement. *See also: ENDORSEMENTS; NEWS-VALUES*

EQUAL TIME RULE a well known provision in Section 315 of the Federal Communications Act (FCC) which provides certain "access rights" to political candidates and others who deal with the electronic media. The Equal Time Rule requires broadcasters who either sell or give free airtime to one candidate to make available equal opportunities for all competing candidates.

Under the Equal Time Rule a broadcaster does not have to sell time to any except federal candidates–however if they do so they must offer to sell equal time to opposing candidates. Moreover a broadcaster does not have to provide free time coverage to any candidate–but if they do so they must give equal time to all competing candidates.

The FCC exempts certain kinds of media coverage from the Equal Time Rule. The major exceptions are regularly scheduled newscasts, news programs and live coverage of news events. Debates and similar forums sponsored by someone other than a candidate or news organization are also exempted from the Equal Time Rule.

Some political analysts believe the Equal Time Rule actually reduces the air time available to campaigns. This happens, they say, because broadcasters simply limit all campaign coverage rather than provide time to minor candidates. Given the choice of all or none, many broadcasters choose none.

The Equal Time Rule is not the only FCC regulation that is accused of decreasing media coverage of political affairs. Critics also condemn the "Fairness Doctrine". This rule requires a broadcaster to present contrasting view points when they address "a controversial issue of public importance". Detractors charge that this policy discourages the coverage of many important and complex public issues because broadcasters are reluctant to invest the time and money necessary to present all sides. *See also: LOWEST UNIT RULE; POLITICAL PERIODS*

ETHNIC DICTIONARY a computer assisted listing of voters who are likely to belong to specific racial or ethnic groups. Ethnic dictionaries are one of many new techniques that tie the computer to voter contact activities. They are compiled by listing all of the surnames that are used in a particular constituency such as a state or large city–and then asking knowledgeable people to assign each of these surnames to an ethnic or racial grouping. This one is Polish, this one Jewish, this one is black, etc. Once this is done, all of the voters in that constituency can be assigned to the ethnic or racial group that includes their surname.

Ethnic dictionaries are mainly used to identify the ethnic or racial background of voters so that a campaign can target appeals to each type of voter. With an ethnic dictionary a campaign can fashion a direct mail package that sends different messages to each of the different ethnic groups in the electorate. *See also: DIRECT MAIL; ETHNIC GROUPS; GEO-DEMOGRAPHICS; TARGETING; VOTER CONTACT ACTIVITIES*

FAIRNESS DOCTRINE *See EQUAL TIME RULE*

FLAT BUY a strategy used in political time buying. The flat buy distributes the media budget evenly over the last three or four weeks of the campaign. A $100,000 flat buy for example might be allocated in four $25,000 increments.

The so called media blitz–an intense use of television and radio over a short period of time–is a version of the flat buy. A media blitz is saturation advertising–about 50 radio commercials a week per station or 25 television commercials.

The flat buy is one of several traditional approaches to placing political advertising. Others include buying the market, spurt schedules and orchestrated finishes. *See also: BUYING THE MARKET; ORCHESTRATED FINISH; PEAKING; SPURT SCHEDULE; TIME BUYING*

FLIP FLOPS *See WEATHERVANE SPOTS*

FREE MEDIA *See UNPAID MEDIA*

FREQUENCY *See REACH AND FREQUENCY*

(THE) FULL POSITION newspaper jargon used in the placement of political advertising. The full position is a preferred position that puts political advertising next to and following reading matter.

Space buyers often designate a preferred position when they reserve advertising space. Other preferred positions include the "island position" which is a political advertisement entirely surrounded by reading matter, the "N.R. position" which is political advertising situated next to reading matter, and the "well forward" position which is political advertising placed toward the front of the newspaper.

Space purchased without specification of a position is known as "run of the paper" or R.O.P. R.O.P. advertising is positioned at the discretion of the publisher.

FULL SHOWING *See SHOWING*

GATEKEEPERS *See GREAT MENTIONERS*

GENERATIVE MEDIA the more highly esteemed and respected news sources around the country. Generally, the term is understood to include the major national newspapers and magazines like the *New York Times*, the *Washington Post*, the *Wall Street Journal*, the *Los Angeles Times*, the *Christian Science Monitor*, *Newsweek*, and *Time* magazines.

Many believe that generative media shape and control the patterns of news coverage followed by most of the other news outlets in the country. The notion of a generative media is part of the popular idea that American journalism is dominated by a (largely) eastern elite. *See also: GREAT MENTIONERS*

GENERIC COMMERCIALS political advertising of a general and thematic orientation, produced and paid for by state or national party organizations rather than by local candidates or campaigns. Generic commercials are similar in function to "institutional" advertising in the private sector which is undertaken to support or promote a company or institution, rather than to sell a specific product or device.

Usually generics employ very broad themes or issues without referring to specific candidates. Sometimes, however, they are designed to be used by local candidates who may simply insert their name or other message at the end. Both major political parties are becoming more involved in the production of political advertising. As they do so, generic commercials are likely to become more common. *See also: POLITICAL ADVERTISING*

GHOST WRITER those shadowy political literati who make eloquent with their art the politicians who employ them. Ghost writers used to be anonymous figures or at least not widely known to the public. Today, there is hardly any secret about who they are and what they do. According to author and columnist William Safire (1978), there are seven categories of the genus ghost writer. These include: ghosts; speech writers; phrasemakers; wordsmiths; press secretaries; sloganeers; and research assistants.

Few major political figures today lack one or more of these literary surrogates who write speeches, draft position papers, issue press releases and author articles. Public awareness of them has become so high in fact that it has obscured the fact that many candidates and politicians insist on writing a considerable amount of their own material—albeit with some help from their ghost writer. *See also: WORDSMITH*

GLOSSY a black and white photograph with a shiny surface as opposed to one with a non-shiny matte finish. The shiny surface of the glossy reflects light away from the eye and, therefore, appears to be more dense than a matte finish.

Glossies of the candidate are included in the media kit, as well as in other material distributed to the media. They are favored over other forms for reproduction in newspapers and other print sources. *See also: MEDIA KIT*

GREAT MENTIONERS a newspaper reporter or columnist so influential that he or she can give the stature of credibility to presidential candidates simply by mentioning their names favorably in a column or two. The term may have been coined by the late Peter Lisagore of the *Chicago Daily News*. Great mentioners include no more than about two dozen widely read and respected journalists who write for newspapers like the *New York Times*, the *Washington Post*, the *Los Angeles Times*, the *Baltimore Sun*, and the *Wall Street Journal*.

They include writers like David Broder, Meg Greenfield, William Safire, Russell Baker, and George Will. These influentials make up a de facto screening committee that regularly analyzes the prospects of individuals running for president. The reputation and standing of these journalists among their peers have given them great weight in determining who will be considered a serious candidate and who will not be. Great mentioners are really political gatekeepers who control the press access to the public by deciding who will be reported on and what will be reported.

GRID SYSTEM *See ZONE COVERAGE*

GROSS RATING POINTS (GRPs) one of the standardized measures used by time buyers and media planners to gauge the impact of commercial media messages. Gross Rating Points or GRPs are the overall number of people in a target audience who are exposed to a message. It is calculated by multiplying reach and frequency.

Reach is simply the number of people who receive the message. Frequency is the number of times they are exposed to the message. Once reach and frequency are known, the calculation of GRPs is straightforward. For example, if the target group for a political commercial were persons aged 60 and over and 30% of them were exposed to the commercial an average of five times, the GRP would be 30% (reach) times 5 (frequency) or 150 gross rating points. *See also: RATING AND SHARE; REACH AND FREQUENCY*

HARD NEWS a reporting style used by both print and electronic media that emphasizes factual and objective information. Hard news is the product of straight news reporting—who, when, where, what, and how. A newspaper report of a campaign event, a press release, or the results of a recent poll is hard news—free of either analysis or interpretation.

The emphasis on hard news coverage of campaigns is criticized by those who believe the news should get beyond the objective facts, the hoopla, and the trivia of a campaign—to a focus on the substantive issues that confront the electorate. To be sure some media do quite a bit of this under the guise of interpretative reporting, news analysis, and so on. But hard news continues to make up the majority of news coverage given to campaigns and elections. *See also: NEWS VALUES*

HIGH EFFORT MEDIA in general, the print press. High effort media like magazines and newspapers are considered relatively hard to follow while low effort media like television and radio are considered relatively easy to follow.

Voters differ in their use of high effort and low effort media. The more informed and issue oriented voters regularly get their information from high effort media sources, particularly newspapers. Less informed and less issue oriented voters get their information from low effort media sources, particularly television.

There are also some demographic differences between users of high effort media and users of low effort media. High effort media users tend to be more affluent, have more education, and have higher socio-economic status. In contrast, low effort media users tend to be less affluent, have less education, and lower socio-economic status.

These differences between high effort and low effort media users encourage the development of separate media strategies—in order to reach both types of voter. *See also: COMPLEMENTARITY*

HORSE RACE JOURNALISM a style of campaign media coverage which emphasizes the competitive, dramatic, and suspenseful aspects of elections. Horse race journalism focuses on personalities, staff relations, media events, the latest poll results and so on–rather than substantive issues.

It is reporting that views politics as sporting affairs–horse races, in which the strategies and tactics, the theatrical and the hoopla are more important than either issues or policy choices. The race rather than the purpose for it becomes the story.

Many scholars and journalists criticize the practice of horse race journalism for ignoring the substantive issues of campaigns. They charge that the obsession with the horse race and its trivia obscures the really important issues confronting the electorate. Voters are titillated with twaddle rather than given the solid information needed to make electoral decisions.

Not everyone believes horse race journalism is a negative influence. Apologists for this style of reporting argue that it provides some positive benefits. Foremost among these the horse race style raises the public interest in politics–a subject that is boring and tedious to many people. By reporting news in a sports context, journalists encourage voters to learn about what they don't particularly like–which is politics–by hearing about it in terms of something they do like–which is sports. According to its defenders horse race journalism actually serves the democratic process–by presenting politics in a way that fosters voter interest and encourages voters to follow the campaign more closely. *See also: HORSE RACE; MEDIA EVENTS*

HOUSE LISTS names and addresses of political contributors who have responded to a previous direct mail appeal. House lists are used in political fund raising. They are compiled from larger mass mailings known as prospecting lists.

Contributors who first respond to prospecting lists are then placed on the house list which is used heavily during campaign fund raising. A proven house list is a valuable resource to a political campaign because people who donate once to a particular party or candidate are likely to do so again. *See also: BASIC INVESTMENT CONCEPT; COMPILED LIST; DIRECT MAIL*

INFORMERCIALS *See ACTUALITIES*

ISLAND POSITION *See FULL POSITION*

LEAD the opening sentences and paragraphs of a news story or news release. The lead is the slant or angle that is developed in the rest of the story. It is the most important part of a news story because it sets the tone for the rest of the piece.

Campaign press officials, who are well aware of this, often design their news releases to become the lead in subsequent media coverage. Campaigns which are consistently successful in doing this have a substantial advantage in their use of the unpaid media. *See also: NEWS PEGS; NEWS RELEASE; UNPAID MEDIA*

LEAKS the unauthorized or premature disclosure of information to the press. Leaks usually involve revelations that are either embarrassing or that compromise campaign strategy.

Political scientist Steven Hess has identified several kinds of leaks based on research he has done on government press offices (Hess, 1984). Many of these are also found in campaigning.

These include:

The "ego leak"–information disclosed by a staffer seeking a sense of self importance.

The "Goodwill leak"–information traded for future favors or favorable treatment from a reporter.

The "Policy leak"–information offered by an insider to attract press interest to a policy proposal.

The "Animus leak"–information given to settle a grudge or damage a reputation.

The "Trial Balloon leak"–information designed to assess public reaction before making a decision on some proposal under consideration.

There is one other kind of leak peculiar to campaigns. This is the so called "leaked poll" which shows surprising gains or an unexpected lead for the candidate whose poll has been leaked. In reality these leaks are usually contrived and carefully orchestrated by campaign strategists–who believe that the showing of favorable results will attract more attention and support to a candidate. *See also: BANDWAGON EFFECT; CAMPAIGN SPY*

LETTERSHOP a private business that handles most aspects of direct mail production and distribution. Lettershops offer an array of printing and specialty services that support campaign direct mail operations—creative work, addressing, labeling, imprinting, collating, binding, and so on. Lettershops have become staples of the modern campaign as the use of direct mail has increased. *See also: DIRECT MAIL*

LIBEL defamation of a person or reputation in writing and usually published. Slander constitutes the same act in oral form. Libelous statements usually impugn someone's honesty or competency. And they must be false. Normally, the judicial remedy for libel is civil suit.

Libel is a legal concept that has some special applications to political life. In general libel laws and remedies do not protect politicians or other "public persons" unless it is proven that the libel was made with malicious intent. Two United States Supreme Court cases have been important in delineating this area. One of these, *New York Times v. Sullivan*, 376 U.S. 254 (1964) held that a public official could not recover in court for libelous (i.e., false) criticisms of his conduct unless the libel was also malicious and reckless. The second influential case, *Monitor Patriot v. Roy*, 401 U.S. 265 (1971) held that a political candidate may not recover in court for libelous charges of criminal activity, unless malice is also proven.

These legal principles considerably reduced for public figures the normal protections available to other citizens. The logic for this restriction is that the public interest requires the widest possible freedom for criticism of public officials and public policy. Since public figures have voluntarily chosen their role in public life, they must accept the special responsibility of taking relatively unlimited criticism.

LIFT a condensed version of a radio or television spot which uses material from the original production. Lifts might be 15 second commercials using edited tape from an original 60 second commercial—or a lift might excerpt a radio spot from the original sound track of a television commercial.

The advantage of lifting is that it allows expensive footage to be reused. Lifts also permit the campaign to repeat its central themes and messages in multiple media formats. *See also: COMPLEMENTARITY*

LIST BROKERS *See COMPILED LISTS*

LITERATURE DROP *See STREET LISTS*

LOW EFFORT MEDIA *See HIGH EFFORT MEDIA*

LOWEST UNIT RULE (LUR) an administrative regulation adopted by the Federal Communication Commission in connection with time buying for political advertising. The Lowest Unit Rule (LUR) prohibits radio and television stations from charging political candidates more for their spots than the best commercial clients are charged. The LUR is in effect during political periods which run from 45 days preceding a primary election and from 60 days preceding a general election.

The rule was designed to make advertising time available to political candidates at a reasonable cost. In practice it has probably resulted in an overall decrease in the air time available to political campaigns. Both candidates and stations have found it unwieldy and cumbersome. Many campaigns in fact waive the LUR in order to avoid its complicated application. *See also: MAKE GOODS; POLITICAL PERIODS; TIME BUYING*

MAILING LIST *See COMPILED LISTS*

MAKE GOODS political spots run without charge by a radio or television station. Make goods are compensation for mistakes made in airing commercials.

Many things can go wrong after commercials are put into "rotation" or scheduled for regular play. A station may put the spot in the wrong time slot, or the play may be mechanically defective in some way. Sometimes broadcasters simply fail to run an ad that has been scheduled.

The frenetic pace of time buying in campaigns is responsible for much of the problem. Most political advertising is jammed into so called political periods–beginning 45 days before a primary election or 60 days before a general election. In fact half or more of all political "buys" occur in the ten days to 3 weeks before election day. Not surprisingly slips are sometimes made.

Some campaigns try to monitor the commercials they order. While workable in small local campaigns, monitoring becomes an awesome task in large campaigns that might buy thousands of time slots every week. Recently however some electronic equipment has been developed which may be able to automatically audit the playing of commercials. If successful it will permit documentation of any errors that do occur. *See also: LOWEST UNIT RULE (LUR); POLITICAL PERIOD; TIME BUYING*

MAN IN THE STREET a standard format used in political advertising to produce television spots. Man in the street commercials use actual interviews with ordinary people–the man in the street–to portray themes or attitudes favorable to a candidate. They are put together from many hours of shooting. The final product is a carefully edited piece that features several people offering their spontaneous view of a candidate.

The Ford campaign in 1976 used a man in the street spot of Georgians questioning the ability of Jimmy Carter. It left the impression that in all Georgia there was hardly anyone who believed Carter had been a good governor or would be a good president.

Political consultants use the format because they believe its naturalness is more credible than some other techniques. The style was used heavily in the early days of television and continues to be popular today with many media consultants.

The man in the street format accommodates some demographic targeting. If a candidate for example wants to create the impression that he is pro-labor, a man in the street spot can show obvious blue collar types in work settings making positive statements about the candidate's labor record.

Man in the street spots have high recall with likely voters who see them. There is also some evidence that they are particularly effective with liberal voters. *See also CONTRAST SPOTS; MONTAGE SPOTS; NEGATIVE ADVERTISING; SLICE OF LIFE; SPOTS; TALKING HEADS; WEATHERVANE SPOTS*

MAN TO MAN COVERAGE *See ZONE COVERAGE*

MEDIA BLITZ *See FLAT BUY*

MEDIA EVENTS activities designed and carried out by campaigns chiefly to attract wide media attention. Media events are elaboratley staged functions that have little or no intrinsic value beyond that given to them by media coverage.

Media events include walking tours, televised debates, press conferences, bill signings, and "photo opportunities". Even many traditional campaign operations like door to door canvassing, rallies, and parades have become media events. They are now planned and organized to facilitate media coverage rather than to allow candidates to campaign among voters.

The emphasis on media has altered the way campaigns operate. No longer are activities arranged to attract local crowds or expose candidates directly to voters. Now a scheduled event must provide good visuals, accommodate media deadlines, and fit the campaign media theme.

Pseudo-event is a close synonym for media event, but there is a useful distinction between the two terms. Pseudo-events are campaign activities that have no point whatsoever beyond the media attention they attract. "Photo opportunities" in which the candidate poses against interesting back drops are pseudo-events. So are such things as walking tours and other campaign gimmicks.

Media events however, such as rallies, press conferences, debates etc. usually have some secondary purpose beyond creating media interest. In the case of media events coverage is more important than the activity itself, but for pseudo-events there would be no activity at all if not for media coverage. *See also: WHOLESALE POLITICS*

MEDIA KITS packages of background information prepared by the campaign and distributed to newspapers, television and radio stations. Media kits–they are also sometimes called news kits or press kits–provide reporters, news directors, and editors with the facts, figures, and other material they need to cover the campaign.

Campaigners view media kits as an opportunity to encourage news coverage of the campaign–while guiding that coverage to the themes and issues that campaign strategy is emphasizing.

Kits are usually assembled in large manila folders with inside pockets for enclosures. Five standard items are included in most kits:

1) Glossies (black and white photographs) of the candidate
2) A candidate biography
3) "Fact sheets" and/or position papers
4) The campaign brochure or basic piece
5) Listing of key campaign personnel with phone numbers

Some kits are more elaborate. They might contain sample news releases, reprints of articles about the candidate, examples of campaign paraphernalia and even audio and video tapes. Media kits are mailed or hand delivered to news outlets. They are also distributed at news conferences, editorial board meetings, and other media events. *See also: MEDIA EVENT; NEWS VALUES*

MEDIA MARKET the geographic area reached by local television and radio broadcasts or newspaper circulations. Media markets are the people and places exposed to local programming and press coverage.

Across the entire United States there are 400 newspaper and 230 broadcast media markets. Some states and municipalities are almost wholly within a single media market, while others are split among several different markets. Almost 90% of Utah, for example is within the Salt Lake City market area. On the other hand Texas has 18 media markets spread across the state.

Within particular states there may be several markets of different sizes and geographic configurations. One example, Pennsylvania, a state of 12 million people, has seven major media markets. Combined these include a total of 31 television and 83 radio stations. They range in size from the huge Philadelphia market which has 34% of the state's voters to the tiny Erie Market with 3% of the state's voters.

The concept of media market has become a key influence in the modern political campaign. Once campaigns were staffed and run on the basis of political boundaries–precincts, wards, municipalities and counties. Strategies were developed and resources were allocated with respect to these traditional jurisdictional lines.

Today this is less and less the case. Larger more sophisticated campaigns are now planned and budgeted around media markets. Political advertising is especially created for targeted audiences while media events are designed to attract coverage in particular markets. And candidates are scheduled on the basis of market considerations. *See also: MEDIA EVENT*

MERGE AND PURGE a sophisticated procedure used in direct mail and other voter contact activities to compile new mailing lists from several different lists. Merging and purging is a technique that combines, refines, and edits multiple separate lists to create a best possible new list.

It is a method that has several variations. In all of them, two or more independent lists are merged, i.e. combined. Then one or more categories on this combined list are purged, i.e. deleted. This creates a new list which may be used directly or may be merged with one or more additional independent lists. Again one or more categories are purged from this new list. And the process of merging and purging goes on until a final blended list has been fashioned. *See also: DIRECT MAIL*

MONTAGE SPOTS a popular format used in political advertising to create televisions spots. The montage employs snippets of several pictures–usually still photographs–to tell a story about a candidate. Political consultants use the technique primarily to produce images rather than to provide information.

The montage spot presents viewers with a visual biographic sketch of the candidate. Photos used may be from the candidate's old family albums or from the scrapbooks and memorabilia of relatives or close friends. The spot usually depicts highlights of the candidate's life from childhood to the present.

The montage format has been used in a wide range of campaigns. Many political professionals believe it is effective for introducing candidates who are not well known or about whom the public holds fuzzy ideas. According to this view the montage format influences voters to think of candidates in human terms while becoming comfortable with them as persons. *See also CONTRAST SPOTS; MAN IN THE STREET; SLICE OF LIFE; SPOTS; TALKING HEADS; WEATHERVANE SPOTS*

NARROWCASTING media that is targeted to specific market segments rather than mass audiences. Narrowcasting is a departure from what is called broadcasting. The traditional electronic media–radio and television–are collectively referred to as broadcast media. Their major characteristic is the delivery of large undifferentiated audiences of listeners and viewers. Newer forms of electronic media such as cable television, low power TV and even FM radio are examples of narrowcast media. Their most prominent feature is the access they provide to particular market stratas. Political time buyers can choose among the two types according to the advantages and disadvantages of each. Essentially broadcasting differs from narrowcasting in the nature of the audiences provided and the cost effectiveness of the political advertising message.

Broadcast media deliver large audiences at low cost per thousand (CPM). But broadcasting also produces "wastage" if the political advertising is intended for only part of the larger audience–for example only voters who live in specific sections of the media market or only voters who belong to specific age, income or ethnic groups.

Narrowcasting can reduce the wastage. In fact the major advantage of narrowcasting is that it allows cost effective targeting of voter types identified as users of the particular media. The trend in modern campaigning has been toward more and more refined efforts to identify and reach voters in small well defined clusters. Should this continue, narrowcasting may transform political use of the electronic media in much the same way that direct mail changed political use of print media. *See also: COST PER THOUSAND; DIRECT MAIL; POLITICAL ADVERTISING; TELEVISION; TIME BUYING*

NATIONAL ELECTION SERVICE (NES) a vote tabulating service which monitors and reports the raw vote from most of the nation's 180,000 precincts. NES is a cooperative sponsored by the three major networks–ABC, CBS, and NBC–and by the two largest wire services–the AP and UPI.

The service was established in 1964 after the major news outlets chose cooperation over competition in the reporting of raw vote totals. The motivation was money. By 1964 the national media was spending millions to duplicate each other's frenzied efforts to count the votes cast in thousands of precincts across the country. As journalist Teddy White remembers it in AMERICA IN SEARCH OF ITSELF:

> Both of the dominant rival networks had adopted key–precincts analysis, but the raw counting of the actual vote was still the field of desperate competition. The networks would hire boy scouts, veteran groups, members of the League of Women Voters, to call in results from individual precincts on leased telephone wires at enormous cost, so that one or the other network could flash on its screen the latest count in a hotly contested race. (White, 1983: 176, 177)

Today NES spews out an impressive array of voting results throughout election night. Sponsoring news organizations receive updates on presidential voting every minute, state by state results every 5 minutes, U.S. Senate and Gubernatorial totals every 5 minutes, U.S. House races every 10 minutes, and county level returns every 15 minutes.

The system which produces this avalanche of voting results has a permanent staff of only 13 people–who spend most of their time planning and organizing an operation which does all its work in one day. On election day these 13 swell to about 85,000 who staff 4 regional offices and report remote from over 4,500 towns, cities, and counties across the nation. The day following the election nearly all of these employees are let go and most of the organization they worked for is shut down. *See also: FLASH RETURNS; UNOFFICIAL RETURNS*

NEGATIVE ADVERTISING political advertising which attacks an opponent. Negative advertising is a growing proportion of all political advertising. Experts estimate that today one of two political ads are negative; twenty years ago only about one in five were.

Even these figures understate the incidence of negative advertising. Some campaigns rely almost completely on it. So called independent expenditures–money spent by PAC's without coordination with a candidate–are about 80% negative.

The turn toward more negative advertising is attributed to several factors. One is the research finding that voters are more influenced by negatives. Some studies have revealed that voters pay more attention to spots that attack or criticize, recall those spots more accurately, and remember them longer.

Negative advertising is especially favored in certain types of campaigns. Candidates who are behind or slipping in the polls are particularly likely to "go negative". The reasoning here is that there is little to lose and much to gain from attacking an opponent who is pulling away. It is in fact usually a reliable indicator that one side is far ahead when the other side suddenly unleashes a barrage of negative spots.

Negatives are also heavily used by challengers and in low budget campaigns. Challengers employ them because they are effective against well known incumbents. Low budget campaigns find negatives attractive because they are often cheaper to produce and they can be aired on low cost radio.

Many observers worry about the growth of negative advertising. One concern is that negatives have increased the incidence of so called "negative voting"–ballots cast by voters who are voting against rather than for some candidate.

Even more serious perhaps is the suspicion that many negative ads are designed to chloroform voters, i.e. to suppress the turnout of an opponent's supporters by confusing or discouraging them. No one blames negative ads solely for declining voter turnout in the United States, but few doubt that negative advertising has contributed to that trend. *See also: CHLOROFORMING; CONTRAST SPOT; DAISY SPOT; POLITICAL ADVERTISING; TURNOUT; WEATHERVANE SPOTS*

NEWS BOYCOTT *See NEWS EMBARGO*

NEWS CONFERENCE a popular campaigning forum in which a candidate meets the local news media, issues a formal opening statement and then responds to reporters' questions. News conferences are traditionally scheduled to make major announcements or release important information. In theory, they are called when a candidate has something consequential to say. In practice they are sometimes staged to stimulate greater news coverage.

Location and scheduling are important logistics. Normally news conferences are held in locations that have traditionally hosted press functions—such as hotels or airports. Capitol buildings are favorite sites in state capitals, town halls serve the same purpose in many cities.

Often visually suggestive settings are chosen to symbolize the main purpose of the news conference. For example a candidate announcing a new study into rising health costs might schedule a conference at a local hospital—or a candidate proposing a new jobs program might meet the press in front of a state unemployment claims office.

Press conferences are generally scheduled early in the day between 9 a.m. and 2 p.m., with 10 a.m. the most popular. This timing permits the covering media to attend, ask some questions and still write their stories before deadline. *See also: MEDIA EVENTS; NEWS VALUES*

NEWS EMBARGO dated instructions on news releases. News embargoes or "boycotts" forbid publication before some future time.

Sometimes campaigns issue news releases which concern events yet to occur. For example, a release might be distributed concerning a press conference to be held the next day. The release would be embargoed until the time of the scheduled event.

Embargo instructions appear in the upper left hand corner of news releases—as in EMBARGOED UNTIL TUESDAY, APRIL 18, 10:00 A.M. In addition to embargoes, two other formats are also used to date news releases: HOLD FOR RELEASE (date, time) and ADVANCE FOR (date, time). Once distinctions were made among these three forms of dated instructions, but today all three are used interchangeably.

None of the dated instructions formats are used as frequently as are undated instructions. Campaigns are usually interested in getting out their news and having it used as soon as possible. Two undated release instruction formats are widely used: FOR IMMEDIATE RELEASE; and FOR RELEASE UPON RECEIPT. Both mean that there are no time conditions attached to the news release. *See also: NEWS RELEASE*

NEWS HOOKS *See NEWS PEGS*

NEWS KITS *See MEDIA KITS*

NEWS PEGS major events of the day, especially those prominently reported. News pegs are the big stories in the news—major government actions, important economic news, critical international events, or catastrophic disasters. These are the heavily covered news stories around which much of the remaining news is organized.

Competition for media attention encourages campaign officials to create "news hooks". These are news releases and other campaign events designed around the current news pegs. The assumption made is that news outlets are more likely to cover a campaign story if it is linked to the day's news. News hooks then depend on news pegs. Here is an example of this relationship: The week's top news story concerns heavy rain, high wind, and threats of flooding (the news peg). A campaign might issue a news release in which the candidate calls for improvements in flood insurance programs (the news hook).

Or another example: In the wake of new economic statistics showing rising unemployment and deepening recession, (the news peg) a candidate might schedule a news conference to announce sponsorship of an economic revitalization package (the news hook).

While news hooks are tied to news pegs, both are determined by the working definition of news used by reporters, editors, and other journalists. What constitutes news, governs not only what is reported in the media but also what is emphasized by candidates during political campaigns. *See also: LEAD; NEWS RELEASE; NEWS VALUES; STORY OF THE DAY*

NEWS RELEASE a formal written announcement, notification, or other news worthy information. News releases are produced and sent by campaigns to news outlets with the hope they will be used to write stories about the campaign.

News releases are prepared in a standardized format to accommodate the requirements of news organizations. Usually they are typed on a single page, double spaced, and 150 to 300 words long. Release instructions are placed in the upper left hand corner. The name and telephone number of the contact person (frequently the news secretary) appears in the right hand corner. Editorial headlines are centered about one-fourth down the sheet, followed by the news release itself which is written in the style of a news story.

Some news releases are simply ignored, but many are put to use in one way or another. Some media outlets print or read the release verbatim or with only minor changes. Smaller newspapers and broadcast media are more likely to do this. Other outlets—particularly larger ones—are more likely to use news releases as background information in writing their stories.

A variant form of the news release is the actuality. These are audio or videotapes designed to look and sound like actual news stories. They are prepared by campaigns and "fed" to radio and television stations for pickup in their newscasts and campaign coverages.

A newer form of actuality is the so called "informercial", described as an electronic news release. Informercials are video tapes produced to resemble on-the-air news coverage. They usually feature what appear to be reporters interviewing people, narrating footage, or providing commentary. In fact these are paid performers appearing in slick promotions paid for by a client or candidate. *See also: ACTUALITY; NEWS EMBARGO; NEWS PEGS; NEWS VALUES; UNPAID MEDIA*

NEWS VALUES the criteria used by reporters and editors to determine the "newsworthiness" of a story. News values are really implicit norms about what will interest a reader or listener. Scholars and journalists generally agree that news organizations look for the following six characteristics in a story:

1. Timeliness—news should have occurred recently.
2. Novelty—news should emphasize the unexpected or unordinary.
3. Titillation—news should be exciting and deal with controversy or conflict.
4. Proximity—news should involve local situations or people.
5. Relevance—news should concern events that affect peoples' lives.
6. Familiarity—news should feature well known people or widely followed events.

Journalists apply these standards to decide whether to cover a story. Few news stories have all of these elements. But the more of them a story does include, the more likely it will receive coverage.

Campaigners have discovered that the news values used by journalists mean that certain kinds of campaign activities are more likely to receive attention. Political consultant Hank Parkinson identifies the following as high news value events that usually attract coverage:

1. Announcing a candidacy
2. Filing for office
3. Scheduling of major appearances
4. Endorsements
5. Releasing of polls
6. Attacking an opponent or answering charges
7. Appointing key personnel to staff positions
8. Planning of a press conference
9. Disclosures on fund raising or other financial data
10. Introducing legislation (Parkinson, 1973: 18-28)

The ability to recognize and understand news values is vital to political campaigns. The media attention often crucial to electoral success is very influenced by them. *See also: NEWS PEGS; NEWS RELEASE; PACK JOURNALISM; STORY OF THE DAY*

NEWS WORTHINESS *See NEWS VALUES*

NIELSON RATING the widely followed broadcast ratings published by the A.C. Nielson Company. Nielson ratings are based upon data collected with an electronic device known as the "audimeter".
Audimeters are physically attached to monitored television sets in a 1700 household sample of American homes. Once activated these units automatically record decisions about program selection and duration of viewing. Broadcast rating services perform a function similar to the audit bureaus which certify circulation figures for newspapers and magazines. The cost of advertising time on the electronic media is based on these ratings just as the cost of advertising space in print media is based on circulation figures. *See also: AUDIT BUREAU; ARBITRON*

NOT FOR ATTRIBUTION *See OFF THE RECORD*

OFF THE RECORD information gained from a campaign official or other source that may not be reported in any form. Off the record conversations are often held in informal settings in which a source in effect says: I am going to give you some information, but you can't use it.
Ground rules stipulating that remarks are off the record are not actually invoked very often. Politicians find that talking off the record achieves very little and it can be embarrassing. An assumed off the record conversation involving presidential candidate Jesse Jackson generated heavy controversy in 1984, when an ethnic slur made by Jackson was later published. Reporters too are often hesitant to receive off the record information that they might later receive on the record and be able to use. Off the record should not be confused with backgrounders, which are on the record but not for attribution. *See also: BACKGROUNDER; ON THE RECORD*

ON THE RECORD anything that a candidate or campaign official says or does and any information that a journalist comes by—unless expressly understood otherwise in advance and agreed to by the journalist. Information that is on the record may be freely reported and the source may be quoted. When specified and agreed to in advance some information which is on the record may also be on background. This usually means that it may be used but it may not be attributed directly to its source.
Information that is not on the record is said to be off the record which means that it cannot be used or published. Both journalists and experienced politicians have a good working knowledge of the ground rules covering the disclosure of campaign information. In Washington, D.C. the protocols are so established that it is said that breakfast is on the record, lunch is

background, and dinner is off the record. *See also: BACKGROUNDER; OFF THE RECORD*

ORCHESTRATED FINISH a strategy used in political time buying to generate campaign momentum. Known also as the 10, 20, 30, 40 formula, the orchestrated finish distributes the media budget over the last four weeks of the campaign.

About 10% of advertising time is reserved four weeks from election day; 20% is purchased for 3 weeks away; 30% is allowed for two weeks out; and 40% is spent during the final week.

The orchestrated finish is one of several traditional approaches to placing political advertising. Some others include buying the market, flat buys, and spurt schedules. *See also: BUYING THE MARKET; FLAT BUY; PEAKING; SPURT SCHEDULE; TIME BUYING*

OUTDOOR ADVERTISING *See BOARDS*

PACK JOURNALISM the tendency of journalists covering a political campaign to all attend the same events, talk to the same people, emphasize the same facts and write the same kind of story. Pack journalism means that press coverage of the campaign doesn't vary much from reporter to reporter or among news outlets.

Thus the wire services, the major dailies and the television networks will all tend to report the same stories, recount the same events, emphasize the same themes and suggest the same meanings. This pattern of coverage in presidential campaigns was first revealed by Timothy Clover's BOYS ON THE BUS (1974) which criticized campaign news coverage during the 1972 presidential campaign.

Since then both journalists and political scientists have speculated on the causes (and cures) of pack journalism. Most believe there are three main explanations for it.

1. Journalists share a common professional socialization: they learn to write in the same way, to look for the same kind of stories and to share the same news values, or sense of what is and is not newsworthy.

2. Journalists socialize together a great deal. In major campaigns they travel together, stay at the same hotel and attend the same functions. They receive the same campaign handouts, go to the same campaign events, and have access to the same campaign officials. All of this encourages reporters to look at the campaign in the same way and to reflect that uniformity in their coverage.

3. Finally pack journalism serves the economic interests of news organizations. Assigning reporters to cover scheduled events or work established beats reduces the cost of gathering news. And it lessens the chance that any outlet will be "scooped" by a competitor. *See also: HORSE RACE JOURNALISM; NEWS VALUES; PRECISION JOURNALISM*

PAID MEDIA *See UNPAID MEDIA*

PARTICIPATIONS *See SPOTS*

PHOTO OPPORTUNITY *See MEDIA EVENT*

PICK UP *See NEWS RELEASE*

POLISPOTS *See SPOTS*

POLITICAL ADVERTISING includes all the types of advertising used to persuade and convince voters. Political advertising falls into four more or less distinct categories.

One of these is spots or "polispots". These are television and radio commercials which run from ten seconds to five minutes in length. A second form of political advertising is newspaper (and occasionally magazine) ads. These range from tiny classifieds in rural weeklies to full page displays in big city dailies.

Another classification is direct mail—which typically uses mass mailings of computer generated letters carefully targeted to prospective voters. The fourth type of political advertising is referred to as vertical media. This is campaign paraphernelia like bumper stickers, buttons, yard signs, banners, and key chains.

The types of political advertising used varies with the size and level of a campaign. Larger statewide or national campaigns emphasize spots and direct mail, but they produce few print ads or vertical media. Smaller local campaigns however are just the reverse. They are heavy users of newspapers and vertical media, like yard signs and billboards. But they rely much less on radio and television or even direct mail.

Political advertising goes through several recognizable stages in most campaigns. Strategists generally agree that three and sometime four distinct advertising phases are necessary to prepare voters to support specific candidates.

Phase one, early in the campaign employs advertising that stresses name identification. Phase two, with campaigning underway emphasizes advertising that establishes the candidate's position on the key issues. Phase three, well into the campaign uses negative advertising that attacks and criticizes an opponent. Phase four, during the final days and hours of the campaign relies on saturation advertising over a short period of time to deliver a media blitz. *See also: GENERIC COMMERCIALS; MEDIA BLITZ; NAME IDENTIFICATION; NEGATIVE ADVERTISING; VERTICAL MEDIA*

POLITICAL PERIODS jargon used by the Federal Communications Commission (FCC). Political periods designates the intervals beginning 45 days before a primary election and 60 days before a general election.

During these periods—roughly 6 weeks before the primary and 9 weeks before the general—broadcasters must charge the so-called "political rate" for political advertising. Under FCC's lowest unit rule the political rate may not be more than the rate a radio or television station charges their best commercial customers. However outside of political periods, candidates are treated as regular commercial customers and must pay full fare which is normally 50 to 75 percent higher.

Several other FCC rules are important to campaigns. One has do with who is entitled to buy time. Broadcasters are only required to sell time to federal candidates for president, vice-president, U.S. Senate, and U.S. House. FCC rules also dictate that stations which do sell time must make it available to all political candidates at the same rate—and they must offer every candidate as many spots as they have offered any opponents.

If a station sells fifty spots to a candidate in a primary, it must then be prepared to sell fifty spots to each of the opponents. In vigorously contested elections (or on sold out stations) this can mean suddenly making room in the broadcast schedule for candidates by turning down or cancelling more profitable commercial ads.

These FCC rules often mean that political campaigns are not as lucrative for stations as are commercial clients. Consequently many broadcasters limit the number of spots sold to candidates. Some radio and television stations in fact refuse to sell any advertising to non federal candidates. *See also: LOWEST UNIT RULE; MAKE GOODS; TIME BUYING*

POLITICAL PUNDIT any expert on political matters—an authority who holds forth publicly on the whys and wherefores of politics. Pundits specialize in forecasting political trends, analyzing political events, explaining elections, and generally elucidating upon the deeper meanings in political affairs.

Originally pundits were learned Indian Brahmins steeped in philosophy, history, and language. Today political pundits are usually journalists, commentators or academics, who exhibit their punditry on television, radio and in the editorial pages of newspapers.

Political punditry is widely practiced. Almost every local media market has several resident pundits who regularly ply their trade.

Still the national pundits receive most of the attention. These authorities include the principal on-air analysts for network television—people like Bill Moyers, Jeff Greenfield, and Hal Bruno—as well as the widely read columnists for the major national newspapers and news magazines—people like Michael Barone, William Safire, and George Will.

Because of their expert status and the wide dissemination of their views, political pundits exercise considerable influence on the direction and formation of public opinion. Punditry itself seems to be an expression of a deep drive in American culture to seek out and rely upon the opinion of experts. *See also: GREAT MENTIONERS; TWO STEP FLOW*

POLITICAL RATE *See LOWEST UNIT RULE*

PRECISION JOURNALISM news reporting which is based on quantitative analysis and social science data. Precision journalism in particular refers to the use of polling to research and write news stories.

Polling has become a major tool for American journalists. All three national commercial networks, ABC, CBS, and NBC, have formed joint ventures with (respectively) the *Washington Post*, the *New York Times*, and the Associated Press—to cooperatively produce national polls. In addition an estimated 500 print and electronic media outlets across the country now conduct polls with some regularity.

Precision journalism has influenced political reporting in a number of ways. Pre-election horse race polls continue to be popular and are probably still the single most frequent kind of media poll. Journalists also use polls to supplement coverage of recent news events, guide editorial commentary, report public opinion on current policy issues and even influence endorsements of political candidates.

The practice of precision journalism has provoked some disapproval both within and from outside the journalism profession. Among the charges made is the complaint that media polls are simplistic and lack methodological rigor. Other critics allege that conducting polls is a conflict of interest because it involves the press in manufacturing the news instead of impartially reporting it.

Precision journalism also has its supporters. They argue that the use of polls (and other social science data) in reporting serves the public because it substitutes objective information for guesses and speculation. There also is wide spread belief among editors and publishers that precision journalism builds circulation and ratings for media outlets that employ it. *See also: HORSE RACE JOURNALISM, POLLING*

PREFERRED POSITION *See FULL POSITION*

PRESS RELEASE *See NEWS RELEASE*

PSA'S public service announcements run free by broadcasters. PSA's are non-commercial spots produced by non-profits, civic groups and government agencies. They deal with such subjects as crime prevention, nutrition counseling, safety tips, health warnings, and shopping advice.

Generally PSA's are scheduled in "scraptime"—broadcasting hours either never reserved or very late at night. Once stations were required by the FCC to carry a certain number of PSA's. Recent changes in regulations have relieved this obligation, however most outlets continue to run them as community services.

Politicians sometimes use PSA's to improve their public exposure. They might appear in a spot designed to promote a popular program or service. A governor might do a PSA informing the elderly of a new housing assistance program or an Attorney General might appear in a commercial explaining how a new tough law on drunk driving works.

Opponents often bridle at this free media exposure, but there is little help for it unless the public official blatently abuses the opportunity. Incumbency has many many advantages. *See also: SPOTS*

PSEUDO EVENT *See MEDIA EVENT*

PUBLIC PERSONS *See LIBEL*

RADIO second in importance only to television as the most widely used political advertising medium. Political consultants list five important characteristics of radio that encourage them to include it in their media planning:

1. COST—Radio is much less expensive than television. Typically a radio spot costs only 15 to 20% of equal time on television. Radio is also more cost effective in dense urban television markets where TV station coverage extends far beyond a candidate's geographic district.
2. AUDIENCE—Radio allows audience segmentation. Unlike television which delivers heterogeneous mass audiences, radio stations attract specific demographic groups: ethnics, youth, college educated, blacks, upper income, etc., which can be identified by consulting audience rating services. These "strata" can be targeted for specific campaign appeals.
3. FLEXIBILITY—Radio spots are easier to produce than TV and can be placed into rotation faster. Because of this, radio adapts well to the fast pace, quick response atmosphere of many campaigns.
4. COMPATIBILITY—Radio spots can be used in conjunction with television or other forms of political advertising. This is the notion of complementarity—the theory that the effectiveness of any campaign message is enhanced when it is delivered through more than one kind of media.
5. SENSITIVITY—Radio accommodates controversial or sensitive topics. Many media specialists favor radio spots to criticize an opponent. Research has shown that voters are less offended by radio attacks than they are with TV attacks. A lot of radio spots are in fact one form or another of negative advertising.

Analysts estimate over 475 million radios are in use in the United States—about six sets per household. This pervasiveness alone would make radio appealing for political advertising. In fact radio is now the media tool of choice in most smaller campaigns and increasingly popular for larger campaigns. *See also: COMPLEMENTARITY; COOL MEDIUM; NEGATIVE ADVERTISING; POLITICAL ADVERTISING; TELEVISION; TIME BUYING*

RATE CARDS price lists used to calculate the costs of purchasing political advertising. Rate cards list the standard rates charged for space in newspapers and magazines or time on television or radio.

Newspaper and magazine rate cards list space rates as well as other technical information needed to plan print advertising. The costs of print advertising are generally quoted in terms of agate lines or column inches—the standard formula is 14 agate lines to a column inch and 8 column inches to a page. Within a particular publication, rates are based on the desirability of a particular section or the location on the page.

Television and radio rate cards list costs for the purchase of advertising time—sold in units, called spots, of 10, 20, 30 and 60 seconds. Spot prices vary according to the time of day, the length of the spot, and the number of time slots reserved.

Rate cards are normally available from individual media outlets. In addition, Standard Rate And Data Service also publishes the rate structures of most radio and television stations operating in the United States. *See also: FULL POSITION; LOWEST UNIT RULE; POLITICAL PERIODS; STANDARD RATE AND DATA SERVICE; TIME BUYING*

RATING AND SHARE one of the standardized measures used by time buyers and media planners to gauge the impact of commercial media messages. Ratings are the number of households in the audience of a program as a percentage of the total number of households with television sets. Share is the number of households in the audience of a program, as a percentage of the total number of households that actually have their sets on.

A program with a 20 rating might have a 31 share which means that 20% of all the households equipped with TV were tuned in and this was equal to 31% of all those households that actually had their sets on during the time that program was aired. *See also: GROSS RATING POINTS; REACH AND FREQUENCY*

RATING SERVICES *See NIELSON RATING*

REACH AND FREQUENCY one of the standardized measures used by time buyers and media planners to gauge the impact of commercial media messages. Reach is the number of people in a target group which receive a message. Frequency is the number of times they are exposed to it.

For example if 30% of a target group saw a political commercial an average of five times each, its reach would be 30 and its frequency would be 5. The reach of a message times its frequency is equal to its gross rating points (GRP). The latter yardstick is commonly used in the planning of media budgets. *See also: GROSS RATING POINTS; RATING AND SHARE*

RETAIL POLITICS *See WHOLESALE POLITICS*

ROAD BLOCKING scheduling the same spots or other programming at the same time on each of the three major broadcast networks—ABC, NBC, and CBS. Roadblocking tactics can also be applied to print media by purchasing advertising space in all of the newspapers which circulate in a targeted local area.

Roadblocking is the political media specialist's fantasy because it insures large audiences by reducing competing viewing opportunities. Prospective voters find it difficult or impossible to switch to another program. It is also one of the few techniques that accommodates the showing of longer commercials and political documentaries.

Despite its appeal roadblocking is unusual. Incumbents, especially presidents can sometime achieve it with major speeches, press conferences or other important news events. But lesser officials rarely command similar attention.

Even when campaigns are willing and financially able to pay for it, roadblocking is rarely undertaken. The growth of cable television and the availability of video cassette recorders have reduced the opportunities to capture audiences this way. *See also: NARROWCASTING; TIME BUYING*

ROTATION *See MAKE GOODS*

RUN OF PAPER (R.O.P.) *See FULL POSITION*

SALTING A LIST a technique used in direct mail to monitor the use of mailing lists. Salting a list is one way of determining whether a particular mailing went out on time and with the intended format.

Direct mailers salt lists by placing on them names of people (such as campaign staffers) who can report when they receive the mailed piece. Professionals distinguish between "decoy" names and "dummy" names. Decoys are names of real people added to a mailing list. Dummies are fictitious names with real addresses.

A related practice is known as "seeding a list". This involves placing real names on a mailing list so that any unauthorized or illegal use of the list can be detected. Both techniques—salting a list and seeding a list—are part of elaborate precautions sometimes used to insure the integrity and success of direct mail. *See also: COMPILED LISTS; DIRECT MAIL; HOUSE LISTS*

SATURATION CAMPAIGN *See FLAT BUY*

SECTION 315 *See EQUAL TIME RULE*

SHARE OF AUDIENCE *See RATING AND SHARE*

SHOOTING BOARD *See STORYBOARD*

SHOWING the proportion of the population within a specified marketing area that sees a billboard or other type of outdoor advertising. Most outdoor advertising is described and evaluated in terms of the exposure it gets from the mobile public.

A full showing—also referred to as a 100 showing—is an outdoor poster or series of outdoor posters that will expose the campaign message to almost every person in the marketing area over a 30 day period. A 50 showing or one half showing will expose the message to about 50% of the market area population and a 25 or quarter showing will expose the message to about 25% of the population. *See also: BOARDS; TWENTY-FOUR SHEET POSTER*

SLICE OF LIFE a standard format used in political advertising to create television spots. Slice of life features ordinary people doing everyday things: housewives shopping; workers commuting; people eating; etc.

Usually the scene shows the actors talking about some problem or discussing one of the candidates. The spot is designed to involve viewers in the slice of life they are seeing by identifying with the situation.

The slice of life format is not used in political advertising as heavily as are more popular formats like man in the street, weathervane spots, or even talking heads. Slice of life is more expensive than many other types of spot. Elaborate sets and paid performers can run the production expenses of a 30 second commercial to $20,000 or more.

Beyond cost considerations however many political consultants think that the slice of life mode is ineffective in political advertising. There are different opinions of why this might be so. But most critics simply believe the format is not credible in politics. Voters discount much of what they see and hear because they perceive the actors to be performers paid to promote a candidate. *See also: CONTRAST SPOTS; MAN IN THE STREET; MONTAGE SPOTS; TALKING HEADS; WEATHERVANE SPOTS*

SLOGAN *See THEME*

SPOTS political commercials on radio or television. Spots or "polispots" as they are sometimes called range in length from ten seconds to five minutes. Thirty second and sixty second spots are the most common. Television and radio outlets sell time to political campaigns who then run their spots in the purchased time intervals.

These spots sold by the networks are known as "participations," while those sold by affiliates are called "adjacencies". Adjacencies are time slots in which spots may be run at the half hour break during the network's prime time schedule. Usually there is a shortage of prime time adjacencies—about 65 to 75 are available each week—and political campaigns compete with each other and commercial advertisers for them.

Participations are more readily available than adjacencies. Nevertheless campaigns often have trouble reserving all of the air time that they would like to have. Stations frequently limit the number of spots that a campaign may purchase in order to minimize the disruption of their regular commercial schedules. *See also: CONTRAST SPOTS; MAN IN THE STREET; MONTAGE SPOTS; POLITICAL ADVERTISING; SLICE OF LIFE; TALKING HEAD; TIME BUYING*

SPURT SCHEDULE a technique used in political time buying. The spurt mixes short periods of heavy political advertising with longer periods of little or no advertising.

It begins with a burst of media saturation aired months or weeks before the election. After several days or even weeks the spurt ends. It may then be repeated or regular advertising may be started three or four weeks from election day.

This strategy of time buying exploits the absence of competition for early political advertising. It is believed to be effective in raising name identification for little known candidates, and in stimulating fund raising.

The spurt schedule is one of the traditional approaches to placing political advertising. Some others are buying the market, flat buys, and the orchestrated finish. *See also: BUYING THE MARKET; FLAT BUY; ORCHESTRATED FINISH; PEAKING; TIME BUYING*

STANDARD RATE AND DATA SERVICE (SRDS) a commercial reporting service which collects and publishes the advertising rates charged by print and broadcast media. Standard Rate and Data Service (SRDS) is the authoritative source for reliable information about the costs and conditions imposed by media outlets on their advertisers.

Political time buyers especially rely on SRDS, but the service is a basic tool for anyone planning or implementing a political advertising campaign. SRDS does not measure broadcast audience or verify circulation figures. The cost of advertising time and space are based on these figures. But rating services like Arbitron and Nielson, or audit bureaus like the Audit Bureau of Circulation do the actual research used to set these rates. *See also: POLITICAL ADVERTISING; TIME BUYING*

STORY OF THE DAY the news story that a campaign most wants the media to cover on a given day. The story of the day may be a campaign appearance, an important announcement, or even the advance text of a speech.

Campaigns focus attention on the event they want to be story of the day in order to emphasize important themes, project particular candidate images, or simply to lead with their strongest "news hook".

Efforts to channel and control campaign coverage are not always successful. Reporters simply may not cooperate, asking questions or pursuing story lines different from the one being promoted. Then too, uncontrolled external events may become the story of the day. The campaign may want to push coverage of the candidate's news conference, but if the candidate's former business partner is indicted, that instead could become the story of the day.

Sometimes campaigns ruin their own story of the day. Occasionally the candidate does this by making news with unrehearsed off the cuff answers to news queries. More often however campaigns inadvertently compete with themselves for news coverage by scheduling rival events or issuing news releases that deal with different issues. *See also: NEWS PEGS; NEWS RELEASE; NEWS VALUES*

STORYBOARDS layouts which illustrate a planned television spot using a sequence of comic strip like frames or panels. Storyboards are produced by artists who draw a series of individual panels which represent the flow of the commercial.

Six to twelve panels make up a storyboard. The panels are bound in a ringed binder so they can be flipped over during presentation.

Storyboards are developed by media consultants who use them during the planning and development of a spot. They are often used as visual aids when proposals are made to a candidate or campaign official.

Storyboards can also be used as the working blueprints from which the actual spot is produced. Both the audio narrative and video shooting instructions can be printed beneath each frame.

A more elaborate form of storyboard is the "shootingboard". These are sketches drawn one frame each for every second of the planned spot—30 frames for a 30 second spot, 60 frames for a 60 second spot, and so on. *See also: POLITICAL ADVERTISING; SPOTS*

STRAIGHT NEWS *See HARD NEWS*

SWEEPS four special rating periods each year in which the Arbitron and Nielson Rating services greatly expand their data collection. Sweeps occur in February, May, July, and November and last 28 days.

During sweeps the rating services (which do not cooperate) study audience levels in all of the 220 local media markets across the nation. To do this they supplement the electronic meters normally used with personal diaries. About 100,000 diaries are collected after sweep periods from viewers who wrote down what they watched. This combined use of diaries and electronic meters permits analysts to collect detailed demographics. Audiences can be identified by age, sex, income, education, occupation, and other important classifications.

The sweeps are important for three reasons: first networks and local stations react to them by scheduling prime programming designed to attract large audiences. Sweep periods are therefore good times to schedule political advertising.

Second, local advertising rates are established on the basis of sweep results. These rates are set by how many people watch a particular program or station. The larger the audience the more a station will charge. Finally the demographics collected during sweeps allow time buyers to target particular voter groups in specific local media markets. *See also: ARBITRON; NIELSON RATING; TIME BUYING*

TALKING HEADS a standard format used in political advertising to create television spots. The talking head features the candidate speaking directly into the camera. Usually he or she will be sitting at a desk or in a chair. The background might include a few props such as a bookcase or a flag—or there might be no props at all.

Political consultants use the talking head to provide information and to showcase their clients as knowledgeable and competent. The format was used heavily in the early days of televison. It is less popular today, now the trend is toward more visual formats that involve action and evoke images.

Many media consultants believe that voters find talking heads boring but this may be overly harsh. Some focus group research has indicated that talking head spots have a very high recall among likely voters. They may also be particularly effective with certain types of voters including undecideds and those who identify themselves as conservatives. *See also: CONTRAST SPOTS; MAN IN THE STREET; MONTAGE SPOTS; SLICE OF LIFE; SPOTS; WEATHERVANE SPOTS*

TELEPROMPTER electronic devices used during speeches, press conferences, and other kinds of media events. Teleprompters are glass screens mounted on podiums. The viewing audience can see through one side while the other side displays the text of a speech or prepared statement.

Dubbed "sincerity machines" in Great Britain—teleprompters are particularly well matched to the cool medium of television. They allow speakers to read their material without having to look down at a script in front of them. Instead they can look directly into the camera and establish "eye contact" with their audience.

Teleprompters are widely used in modern politics. The television networks all have them as do some large local stations and a few private studios. The machines however are expensive. Public officials who need them often rent them for fees ranging from $500 to $1000. *See also: COOL MEDIUM; TELEVISION*

TELEVISION the most influential medium used in modern campaigns. Television's role in electoral politics has gained steadily since its early uses in the 1952 presidential campaign. It began to be widely used in congressional and gubernatorial elections in the 1960's and 1970's. By the early 1980's television was being used regularly in state legislative races and even in local campaigns.

Today few major campaigns ignore television or fail to incorporate it into campaign strategy. Nevertheless, some experts believe that television's impact on elections may be exaggerated. Two political scientists, Thomas E. Patterson and Robert A. McClure, are among those who have challenged the vaunted power of television.

In their book, The Unseeing Eye, (1976) they argue that television news coverage (of presidential election campaigns) is probably no more influential than newspaper coverage in terms of altering voter attitudes. Moreover, McClure and Patterson concluded that political commercials had little effect on a voter's opinion of a candidate or party. They also found that 30 to 60 second spots, provide voters with much more information than generally believed.

Despite these findings, few political observers doubt the significance of television. The medium has an enormous presence in elections because it is heavily watched—TV is the major source of political news for about 65% of the electorate—and because it is trusted. Television is the most credible form of information for most voters. This pervasiveness and believability more than anything else has made television the single most important influence in modern American elections. *See also: COOL MEDIUM; NEGATIVE ADVERTISING; POLITICAL ADVERTISING; RADIO; TIME BUYING; UNPAID MEDIA*

TEN, TWENTY, THIRTY, FORTY FORMULA *See ORCHESTRATED FINISH*

TIME BUYING reserving television and radio time slots for political advertising. Time buying is a specialization that has grown up to meet the needs of campaigns to advertise in the electronic media.

Political time buyers work with polling data and demographic information about likely voters as well as with the published rating services like Standard Rate and Data and Arbitron. Their objective is always the same—provide the largest relevant audience of likely voters at the lowest cost. Skillful time buying is a critical function in modern politics because time buyers determine whether the intended audience actually sees the spots produced for them.

The standard time buying strategies include the flat buy, the orchestrated finish, and the spurt schedule. All are closely related to the ideas of momentum and peaking. Traditional campaign strategy is to build and sustain momentum so that a campaign peaks on or just before election day. The various approaches to time buying represent different theories about how to do this. *See also: BUYING THE MARKET; FLAT BUY; LOWEST UNIT RULE; NARROWCASTING; ORCHESTRATED FINISH; PEAKING; ROAD BLOCKING; SPURT SCHEDULE; STANDARD RATE AND DATA SERVICE (SRDS)*

TWENTY FOUR SHEET POSTER the standard size outdoor advertising poster or billboard. A twenty-four sheet poster is approximately 9 × 20 feet. Originally it required 24 individual sheets to produce the standard billboard. Modern printing presses have reduced this to 10 or less but the earlier nomenclature survives.

Thirty sheet posters, which are approximately 10 × 22 feet are also available, and are sometimes used for political accounts. *See also: BOARDS*

UNPAID MEDIA media coverage of a campaign—television, radio, or print—that is provided as normal news and is neither controlled nor paid for by the campaign. Unpaid media or free media as it is also called, includes the scope of general news coverage: press conferences, debates, newspaper and magazine stories, editorials, interviews, and talk shows. It is distinguished from paid media which includes all forms of political advertising: brochures, billboards, newspaper ads, signs, posters, radio and television spots.

Some studies of voting behavior suggest that the two forms of media affect voters quite differently. Unpaid media is apparently more credible than paid media; voters seem to put more stock in what they hear or read as news than what they see in political advertising. Unpaid media also seems to have more influence with ticket splitters and Independents—whereas, paid media is effectual in reinforcing voters who are already supporters or inclined to become supporters.

Political consultants try to use unpaid and paid media in coordination with each other. The basic strategy is to deliver the same message through multiple forms of media in order to achieve repetition and reinforcement. Consultants stress the importance of keeping unpaid and paid media messages consistent with each other. The two forms of media should not send out contradictory or conflicting messages. If they do, voters are likely to be cross pressured with the result that they may not vote at all or they may even vote for the opposition candidate. *See also: COMPLEMENTARITY; POLITICAL ADVERTISING*

VERTICAL MEDIA includes such campaign paraphernalia as bumper stickers, yard signs, key rings, campaign buttons, banners, and straw hats. Vertical media are the gimmicks and gadgets of political advertising. The term refers to just about any form of campaign advertising that doesn't use radio, television, or direct mail.

Political professionals disagree about the effectiveness of vertical media. Some believe it can increase name identification, as well as provide an important complement to more expensive kinds of advertising. Others concede that vertical media can motivate campaign workers and lend a sense of gathering momentum to the campaign, but doubt that it has much impact on voters. Many low budget campaigns are limited to vertical media for most or all of their political advertising. *See also: CAMPAIGN BUTTONS; COMPLEMENTARITY; POLITICAL ADVERTISING*

VOICE OVER a term used in the making of television commercials and films to describe production of the sound track narration. The voice over is produced by an announcer who reads a script while a print of the film or tape is being projected.

Media consultants consider the quality of the voice over to be critical in the success of their spots. A few particularly effective announcers have become specialists in doing the voice over for political advertising. They are called upon so often to produce their magic that their voices become familiar to electorates all over the country during political seasons. *See also: SPOTS*

WAVE OFF a gambit used by reporters to authenticate a story. Wave off is played with a source who will not directly confirm or deny a story. Columnist William Safire tells of using the wave off with Mayor Edward Koch of New York when Koch would not confirm a story that Safire was fairly certain had happened.

> Since columnists are often faced with that problem, I suggested a game of wave off—that the mayor need not publicly confirm the story if it were true, but that

he would privately wave me away from the story if it were not true. Mayor Koch said firmly, 'I'm not waving you off.' That was enough for me. I started to use the anecdote as the lead of a column about the fate of Israel in a Carter second term.

Wave offs and other techniques like backgrounders and off the record conversations are strategies used by the press to get stories without compromising a source or incurring a high risk that the account is not factual. These practices also benefit sources of stories who can have their version of events disclosed without being publicly named. *See also: BACKGROUNDER; OFF THE RECORD*

WEATHERVANE SPOTS a standard format used in negative advertising. Weathervane spots portray an opponent's record in a way that emphasizes inconsistencies or flipflops. The classic weathervane spot was one produced for Hubert Humphrey in 1968 during his race with Richard Nixon. It depicted Nixon as a kind of human weathervane: his right hand pointing North, his left hand pointing South, and his nose veering from East to West.

Weathervane spots have become a staple of political advertising. They are surprisingly easy to research and produce if an opponent has been in public life for some time. An established public record produces hundreds of speeches, interviews, votes, and statements. Virtually every politician has changed his public position on some issue. Usually, these changes are subtle and often they are justifiable. But when presented cleverly and out of their original context, they can be made to make an opponent look weak, vacillating, and even unethical. Not all weathervane spots are distortions of someone's record. Some politicians take an amazing variety of positions on public issues. Their records represent a bewildering patchwork of convenience and opportunism. This kind of pattern is ruthlessly revealed in well done weathervane spots. *See also: CONTRAST SPOTS; MAN IN THE STREET; NEGATIVE ADVERTISING; SPOTS*

WHOLESALE POLITICS electioneering that stresses the use of mass media—especially television—rather than meeting voters face to face or in small groups. Wholesale style politics pursues voters in large blocks by appealing to them through the electronic and print media.

Modern campaigns are more and more oriented to wholesale politics. This contrasts markedly with the "retail politics" of the pre-television period which emphasized lots of personal campaigning and direct voter contact. These earlier campaigns featured frequent public appearances by the candidate, rallies, social events, hand shaking tours, and door to door campaigning. Today this kind of activity is as likely to be staged as a media event or a "photo opportunity".

Wholesale style politics now dominate major elections in the United States. Retail politics has, however, not disappeared completely. Many local campaigns continue to rely on meeting voters and on personal campaigning by the candidate. In fact, most contemporary campaigns adopt a mixture of the two strategies. Even national campaigns and campaigns for major state offices employ some traditional retail tactics, such as canvassing and phone banks. And all but the tiniest local campaigns use some radio or television. *See also: DELIVERING; NEW POLITICS; MEDIA EVENTS; STOREFRONTS*

WIRE SERVICES news gathering organizations that provide news, features, and editorial comment to subscriber newspapers, radio, and television outlets. The major wire services are the Associated Press (AP) and the United Press International (UPI). Other widely used services include those provided by subsidiaries of the NEW YORK TIMES, the LOS ANGELES TIMES, the CHICAGO TRIBUNE, and by the Reuters Agency. Many of the larger newspaper chains also operate cooperating news services. These include Gannett, Copley, Newhouse, and Knight Ridder.

Wire services account for a large proportion of national news coverage. Virtually every daily newspaper in the United States subscribes to one or more of them as do hundreds of radio and television stations. Wire service feed is particularly influential with the small and medium sized dailies who rely on news services for almost all of their international and national news. In fact some local newspapers depend on the wires for their state and regional news as well.

Media outlets do vary considerably in the extent to which they use wire service products in their reporting. One expert estimates that the proportion of wire service feed used by subscribers ranges from as low as 10% to as high as 80%. Outlets also differ in their editing of wire stories. Some use material verbatim, while others will do extensive rewrites.

WORDSMITH a speechwriter who is especially good at translating complex ideas and proposals into simple, clear language. A wordsmith is a literary craftsman whose ability lies in forging the words and phrases that embody political speeches, position papers, and press releases. The term conveys approval, but it is often applied to a writer considered to be more of a skilled technician than a gifted author. *See also: GHOSTWRITER*

ZONE COVERAGE one of the strategies used by the print press in assigning reporters to campaigns. Zone coverage is now used by most newspapers and magazines. It requires them to rotate reporters among the candidates.

Once it was common practice to assign a reporter to a candidate for the duration of the campaign. This practice, known as "man-to-man", coverage is now less common. It has been abandoned altogether by most media outlets for their presidential campaign coverage.

Editors today believe that zone coverage produces better reporting than man-to-man coverage. Stories are fresher and reporters are less likely to become jaded or biased from too long exposure to a single candidate. *See also: NEWS VALUES*

ZOO the menagerie of assorted political animals—reporters, photographers, campaign staffers, television crews and other hanger ons—who follow major candidates on the hustings. Zoos are transported in a zoo bus or a zoo plane, neither of which ever exceeds minimum housekeeping standards.

Traveling zoos are informal, convivial atmospheres where a good deal of fellowship and camaraderie can develop. They are also busy, noisy, uncomfortable, and lacking in many basic creature comforts.

At least once during every campaign, zoo dwellers stage a revolt against their living conditions. The NEW YORK TIMES reported on the uprising in the 1984 Mondale campaign:

> This week, according to anguished reports from the road, the Mondale zoo plane is in revolt, complaining that its denizens, despite the high fares they pay, get meals that are not only different from the candidate's plane but also inedible. After consecutive servings between Iowa and Mississippi of cold, greasy chicken and soggy white bread sandwiches with potato chips, this group lodged an angry protest with the Mondale trip director, Peter Kyros, who said he would investigate what one reporter called 'a significant human rights violation.'

Despite the generally notorious reputation enjoyed by zoos, there is rarely any shortage of applicants for available vacancies on the bus or plane. In recent years presidential campaigns have successfully charged 150 percent of the first class airline fare for seats on the zoo plane.

3

POLLING AND PUBLIC OPINION

AMERICAN ASSOCIATION FOR PUBLIC OPINION RESEARCH (AAPOR) a professional association of pollsters and other researchers involved in the production and use of polls. The AAPOR, in cooperation with the National Council on Public Polls, has developed a code of ethics designed to cover the reporting of polling results.

In general the AAPOR code holds that all relevant facts be disclosed that could influence interpretation of the poll. These include the identity of the sponsor, the wording of the questions, the statistical characteristics of the sample, the kind of interviewing done, and the times and dates on which respondents were surveyed. The code suggests that the absence of this information should cause a poll to be viewed with healthy skepticism.

AAPOR also publishes the PUBLIC OPINION QUARTERLY which is generally considered to be the most prestigious and influencial journal in the polling field. *See also: POLLING; POLLS; PUBLIC OPINION QUARTERLY*

APPROVAL RATING *See JOB RATING*

BANDWAGON EFFECT the alleged influence that polls can have on the outcome of an election. The existence of a bandwagon effect is controversial. Those who subscribe to the notion believe that front runners benefit from polls showing them ahead since voters will want to "climb aboard the bandwagon" of the leading candidate. This view is challenged by others who discount the existence of any bandwagon effect and argue that polls are not a major influence on most voters.

Evidence for and against the bandwagon effect is mostly anecdotal. On balance it seems likely that the bandwagon effect operates most often among political activists who have a clear interest in being on the winning side.

Polls certainly influence the media coverage that a campaign receives, and they have a substantial impact on fund raising efforts. But it is doubtful if these effects extend to the electorate as a whole or if they significantly influence voters to vote for one candidate rather than another. *See also: MOMENTUM*

BASELINE POLL *See BENCHMARK POLL*

BELLWETHER DISTRICTS precincts, wards, or other voting districts that are believed to be barometers of public opinion and harbingers of electoral outcome. Bellwether districts are looked to by politicians, journalists, and even pollsters for early readings of how an election will turn out.

Usually, bellwethers are selected because they appear to be microcosms of much larger areas, or because their past voting patterns are very similar to the voting patterns of the larger area. For almost fifty years Maine was considered a national bellwether, until 1936 when it was one of only two states to back Landon over Roosevelt. Almost every state has one or more counties or municipalities that are considered bellwethers. And most local areas count a bellwether or two among their precincts and wards.

The belief in bellwethers is persistent political lore. But it is seriously challenged by political scientists and others who consider the past predictive accuracy of bellwethers to be a statistical fluke (or "artifact") that occurs by chance. Scholars reason that eventually, the bellwether will be wrong because it is only accidental that it has been right in the past. Since there is no way to know when this will happen, reliance on bellwethers as political augeries is risky. *See also: POCKETBOOK INDEX; PROBABILITY SAMPLING*

BENCHMARK POLL a baseline public opinion poll which serves as a basic reference point and planning tool for political campaigns. Benchmark polls are usually completed in the pre-campaign period, six to twelve months before the campaign begins. They involve long series of questions and large samples.

Benchmarks are designed to survey the attitudes and moods of the electorate to produce the kind of information the campaign will need to plan strategy and tactics. They are roughly analogous to the market research that is done in the private sector before new products are introduced or major advertising campaigns are started. *See also: POLLS*

BLAB WORDS abstract, general, or complex words like fairness, government, policy, reform, and so on. These sort of blab words are frequently used in poll questions such as "Do you think the tax laws should be reformed" or "Do you think our foreign policy is working." The difficulty with blab words is they have so many possible meanings that the respondent's understanding of the word may be quite different than the interviewer's.

Public opinion specialists refer to the different meanings that people have for various words as the "frame of reference problem." One way that pollsters deal with the frame of reference problem is to make the meanings they are using as clear as possible in the question itself.

Polls that use a lot of blab words without somehow defining them are suspect. They are likely to contain misleading information because people are answering questions they may not completely understand. *See also: POLLING; POLLS*

BLIP a slight and impermanent factor in public opinion. The term blip has been borrowed from the operation of radar scopes in which it is a small spot of light on the screen of the radar receiver.

In politics a blip is a matter of small importance and little stability—something that is likely to have no long-term influence. *The Philadelphia Inquirer* used the word in late 1983 to describe the fading fortunes of a presidential candidate " . . . poll after poll shows that (Senator) Hollings is largely a blip on the political radar screen" (Oct.12,1983).

BRUSHFIRE SURVEY *See POLLING*

CALL BACKS return telephone calls or home visits to people randomly selected to be poll respondents—who were "not at home" during an earlier call. Call backs are very important in polling. The reliability of a poll might be compromised if those initially listed for interviews are not actually contacted.

Completing interviews with every randomly chosen individual almost always requires returning to some households several times. From 25% to 50% of all initial calls are not completed for one reason or another.

Call backs produce decreasing returns after several calls. Pollsters find that 80-85% of all respondents who can be reached are on the first call. About 95% of those who can be reached are reached by the third call. Additional calls after three raise the overall completion rate by only two or three percent.

Call backs are also expensive and time consuming. Moreover they often present interviewers with reluctant or otherwise difficult respondents. But they are essential if a trustworthy poll is to be produced. Polls which do not complete call backs are suspect and almost certainly defective. *See also: POLLING; POLLS; RANDOM SAMPLING; RESPONDENTS*

CELL a technical term used in the analysis of polls. A cell is part of a larger set of data known as a table. Cells are arranged within tables to show the distribution of responses to questions.

An example illustrates the relationship between cells and tables. Say all respondents in a poll have been asked the horse race question—and the responses revealed that 52% of the sample supported candidate A while 48% supported candidate B. The results from these questions could be presented in a table that shows how respondents are distributed by age—i.e. how did the 18-24 year olds answer, the 25-30 year olds, the 30-45 year olds, and so on. Each of these age groupings makes up a cell; and all of them together make up a table.

The size of cells—i.e. the number of respondents included in them—is of considerable practical importance in polling. This is because pollsters often want to draw conclusions not only about overall samples but also about the cells in that sample. Unfortunately the sampling error for these cells is often quite large.

A common situation illustrates the problem. Blacks make up about 12% of the national population. A sample size of 1200 voters would produce 120 or so blacks. This would be enough to make some findings about overall black political attitudes. But it would not be nearly enough to make confident predictions about the cells within that 120 sample—such as 18-24 year old blacks, college educated blacks, unemployed blacks, and so forth.

The best general solution to this polling problem is over sampling in order to produce enough interviews to allow reliable analysis. Time and money constraints however often preclude this. The result is that a good deal of polling analysis is based on cells that contain relatively few respondents. Consequently the real sampling error in a poll may be several times higher than is reported. *See also: CONTROLLING FOR; CROSS TABULATION; OVER SAMPLING; SAMPLING ERROR; VARIABLE; WEIGHTING*

CHEATER QUESTIONS one monitoring technique used by pollsters to detect so called "curbstone" or "armchair" interviews. These are interviews that are made up by interviewers who fill out the questionnaire themselves instead of talking to the proper respondent.

Pollsters use a variety of techniques to check and establish the authenticity of interviews. Incorporating cheater questions in the poll is one standard practice. Cheater questions have answers which can be checked for internal consistency, inappropriate responses, or other evidence of fabrication.

Another commonly used monitoring device is "respondent verification" in which persons reported as respondents are contacted to determine if they were actually interviewed.

Made up interviews are rare in polling—probably less than 5% of all interviewers ever fudge results. But pollsters take seriously even the possibility of cheating since a few dishonest interviews can easily skew the interpretation given to a poll. *See also: NON-SAMPLING ERROR*

CHI SQUARE *See STATISTICAL SIGNIFICANCE*

CLOSED QUESTION *See OPEN QUESTIONS*

CLUSTER SAMPLING a type of probability sample used in polling. Cluster sampling is employed when very large areas such as entire countries are being surveyed—or when reliable listings of voters cannot be obtained.

The process begins when the population to be polled is divided into geographic units such as states, counties, municipalities, and so on. Cluster samples are then drawn in hierarchical stages until a listing of individuals is produced. Most national polls and many state polls use some version of cluster sampling.

Six stages are common. Stage one might yield a sample of all the counties in a state; stage two then might randomly select several census tracts within each of these counties; stage three picks block groups (several connected blocks) within the designated census tracts; stage four then draws individual blocks within each of the block groups; stage five chooses households within the blocks and stage six selects the appropriate respondents living in these households.

Cluster sampling has some important advantages. It allows probability sampling even when all of the members of an electorate cannot be listed. It also can reduce interviewing costs because it concentrates respondents in clusters. This method does however require somewhat larger samples than some other kinds of probability sampling. It also can result in a higher sampling error than some other types of sampling. *See also: SAMPLING*

COHORT STUDIES *See LONGITUDINAL DATA*

CONFIDENCE LEVEL *See SAMPLING ERROR*

CONTROLLING FOR a technical expression used in the analysis of polls. Controlling for age, sex, race, income, and any other variable removes the influence they may be having on other variables. When pollsters control for some variable, they are really speculating that it is the "cause" of some observed attitude or opinion uncovered by the poll.

Here's a common example. Say the poll reveals that 60% of all Protestants favor a certain policy but only 40% of all Catholics support the same policy. The pollster suspects it is income rather than religion that is really making the difference; so he controls for income and tests the relationship again. If the difference between Catholics and Protestants disappears when income is controlled for, the pollster might infer that it is in fact income rather than religion that explains the apparent differences between Catholics and Protestants.

Much more elaborate controls are possible, holding two, three or more variables constant, but the principle is the same. The technique is essentially a systematic way of looking at the same relationship over and over again—until the real causes can be sorted out and understood. *See also: CELLS; CROSSTABULATION; VARIABLE*

COOKING THE DATA *See WEIGHTING*

CROSS TABULATION a standard technique used in polling that facilitates analyses of the responses given to the pollster's questions. Cross tabulation starts with the overall numbers or "marginals" in a poll—that is 52% for candidate A and 48% for candidate B, or 60% favor Policy X while 40% oppose it. It then examines how important groups in the electorate might differ from these totals—men, women, blacks, whites, Catholics, Protestants, affluent, poor, educated, less educated, etc.

A common situation illustrates cross tabulation. A pollster discovers that 60% of a sample favor some public policy while 40% oppose it. The pollster might then want to know if men and women were similar in their responses (or blacks and whites, or affluent and poor, or Catholics and Protestants, etc.). To find out he would simply classify each respondent as male or female and then compare the responses of the two sexes. It might turn out for example that whereas the overall responses showed 60% for and 40% against, the cross tabulation reveals that men are only 45% for, while women are 75% in favor.

Many other variations of cross tabs can be used to analyze a poll. The purpose of all of them is to allow the pollster to go beyond merely describing what the electorate thinks and believes—to begin to explain the causes of these voter attitudes. *See also: CELL; CONTROLLING FOR; FACE SHEET VARIABLES; POLLS*

CROSS SECTIONAL *See LONGITUDINAL DATA*

CURB STONE INTERVIEWS *See CHEATER QUESTIONS*

DEMOGRAPHICS *See FACE SHEET VARIABLES*

DEPENDENT VARIABLES *See VARIABLES*

EXIT POLLS election day surveys of voters as they leave the polling place. Exit polls are interviews of a sample of voters from key precincts.

In each of these precincts every 2nd, 3rd, or 5th voter is given a ballot and asked to answer 20 to 25 questions. People are asked which candidates they voted for and how they feel about several major issues. Interviewers are trained to observe and record respondent's race, gender, and approximate age.

The major networks are heavy users of exit polling. CBS started their operation in 1967, NBC followed in 1973 and ABC in 1980. The election day operations of all three networks is similar. The New York Times described CBS's procedures in 1984:

> In each of about 2000 precincts around the country workers hired for CBS stopped 75 or more voters as they came out and asked them 25 questions about how they had voted and why. Those 5000 field workers called in their findings to a telephone staff of 100 or more in New York who transmitted the data to a computerized staff of more hundreds for analysis.

Exit polls in politics are similar to so called "intercept surveys" in marketing research. The purpose of the intercept survey is to interview people just after they have visited the store, used a product or made a purchase—while impressions and recollection are still fresh and clear. Exit polls carry this basic idea over to politics by interviewing voters just after they have voted.

The most ballyhooed and controversial use of exit polls is the making of election forecasts or characterizations. Actually the networks never predict a winner solely on the basis of exit polling. Instead the data from these interviews is combined with actual voting returns from key precincts and other data before an election is called.

In any case the most valuable use of exit polling is not the making of election night forecasts. Much more useful is the detailed information they provide about what kind of people voted, for whom and why. This information is used for months and years after election night by social scientists studying the voting behavior of the American electorate. *See also: KEY PRECINCTS; NATIONAL ELECTION SERVICE*

FACE SHEET VARIABLES those characteristics used by pollsters to describe and classify the people they interview. Face sheet variables—also loosely referred to as "demographics"—include age, sex, education, occupation, income, race, residence, religion, and political party affiliation. These are designated face sheet because they commonly are listed on the front or cover sheet of the interview schedule used by interviewers.

Face sheet variables are included in virtually all polls. The theory is that they reveal the real causes of public opinion. In the parlance of the social scientist, they "predict" and "explain" the differences among voters. In practice face sheet variables provide the raw material pollsters need to analyze and make sense of the large amount of data that comes from a poll. *See also: CROSS TABULATION; INTERVIEW SCHEDULE; POLLS*

FILTER QUESTIONS questions asked during a poll in order to sort out voters who have some information about a topic from voters who have little or none. Filter questions challenge respondents to prove they have some knowledge of a subject before their opinion of that subject is considered.

The standard filter question format asks respondents if they have heard or read of such and such topic; if so what did they read or hear?

Here's an example of the filter question as it might appear on an interview schedule:

Q1. Have you happened to hear or read about the governor's plan to reorganize state government?
if—no (interviewer: skip this series of questions)
if—yes (interviewer: go to question 2)

Q2. Can you tell me what you have read or heard about the proposal?
if—don't know or gives inaccurate information, (interviewer: skip this series of questions)
if—respondent offers some knowledge or information about the Governor's proposal (interviewer: go on to question 3)

Q3. Are you in favor of the Governor's proposal to reorganize state government or do you oppose it?

Filter questions are designed to detect lack of knowledge and misinformation. Both problems are related to what is known as the non-opinion—the tendency of some people to express opinions or attitudes when they really don't have any on a particular topic.

Studies have shown that poll respondents will sometimes manufacture an opinion or invent an attitude when they really haven't thought much about the matter being asked about it. The answers given by these respondents are random. The next time they answer the same question they are likely to answer it differently because they really have no well developed opinion. Apparently people do this to avoid feeling foolish or appearing to be uninformed. For the same reasons people often agree with or express approval of a policy when they actually have no idea what it entails. This is one reason that many proposals lose their apparent public support when the public learns more about them. *See also: MISREPORTERS; SCREEN QUESTIONS; SLEEPER QUESTIONS*

FOCUS GROUPS a research technique used by pollsters and other political consultants. Focus groups are sets of 8 or 12 people convened by a moderator who encourages them to talk about a particular issue, candidate or campaign. Pollsters use focus groups to supplement their polling data, while media consultants use them to test political advertising.

Usually focus groups begin with the moderator asking very general questions—for example—"a lot of people are talking about the upcoming election here in River City, does anyone have any thoughts on that?" As people begin to talk the moderator follows up with increasingly focused questions, relying on the dynamics of the group to carry the discussion along.

Interviews are held in specially designed rooms or conference settings. They last for about two hours and are usually taped. Sometimes respondents are observed from behind a two way mirror or via closed circuit television.

Unlike polling respondents, focus group participants are not chosen randomly. Instead they are a "purposive sample"—people especially recruited to represent an important voter group or demographic cleavage. A typical focus group might be made up of people past 65, or upper income professionals, or members of labor organizations, or a particular racial or ethnic group.

Recently newspapers and news magazines have begun to use focus group research as part of their election coverage. These media base some of their stories and features on the research produced by the focus groups. *See also: POLLS.*

FRAME OF REFERENCE *See BLAB WORKS*

HIGH NEGATIVE a low rating given to public figures by respondents in a poll. High negatives are measured on the basis of job ratings, approval ratings, and other indicators of performance. In the typical polling question, a respondent might be asked to rate a public figure on a scale which runs from +5 to −5. Another standard question asks respondents to picture a large thermometer scale and to indicate how warm or cold they feel towards a public figure.

A politician who was rated low or cold on either of these questions is said to have a high negative—although in principle several similar questions should be assessed before any final rating is determined. High negatives are almost always an indicator of substantial problems ahead for any candidate or elected official. *See also: JOB RATING*

IN THE FIELD the interval in which polling interviews are actually carried out. In the field time for political polling can range from several hours to two or three days. Normally polls should not be in the field for longer periods. The passage of time allows important intervening events to occur that can influence the results and produce misleading information. Long drawn out polling is usually not reliable.

Time affects polls in several other ways. The part of the day interviewers call is important because different types of respondents tend to be home at different times. Good procedure is to vary the time of calls during the day and evening hours. Time is also a factor in the durability of a poll. The "shelf life" of a poll—that is the time for which results remain valid—ranges from a few days to several months.

Shelf life depends on the volatility of the electorate, the stage of the campaign and the nature of ongoing events. It is longer for polls taken during general election periods than for polls done during primary elections. And it is longer for polls completed early in the campaign than for polls finished during the last few weeks. *See also: INTERVIEW SCHEDULE; POLLS*

INCH DEEP AND MILE WIDE a popular figure of speech used to describe the political strength of a politician who may be widely known, but whose public support is shallow and superficial. Some politicians score highly on name recognition polls and approval ratings, but voters can provide little un-aided information about them. Often voters have no strong feelings about them either. Such politicians are said to have support that is an inch deep and a mile wide.

The figure of speech is also applied to candidates who do well in trial heats until "heavy weight" competition emerges. The designation was used to describe Walter Mondale in the 1984 presidential campaign. Late in 1983 an Iowa pollster found that Mondale had 41% of the vote against 12% for his nearest rival. Despite this impressive margin, the pollster concluded that Mondale's real support in Iowa was "an inch deep and a mile wide." *See also: SOFT SUPPORT*

INDEPENDENT VARIABLE *See VARIABLES*

INSTRUMENT *See INTERVIEW SCHEDULE*

INTERCEPT SURVEYS *See EXIT POLLS*

INTERVIEW SCHEDULE the questionnaire or "instrument" followed by interviewers taking a poll. Interview schedules guide the conduct of interviews. They include the written questions, the order in which they are to be asked, and detailed instructions about how to proceed through the questionnaire.

Pollsters employ a more or less standardized sequence of questions in their interview schedules. After a brief introduction to the poll comes a series of screen questions designed to sort out likely voters from unlikely voters. Next is often a set of questions about the voter's partisan leanings—are they Republicans, Democrats or what.

These questions might be followed by questions that deal with specific issues and then by questions that ask about feelings toward candidates. About the middle of the interview schedule comes the horse race question—which candidate will you vote for on election day? Toward the end of the schedule questions about media usage are asked: What television or radio stations do you listen to?; what time of day?; how often?; etc.

Finally the demographic questions are asked: age, sex, race, education, religion, occupation, and income. These are the most sensitive questions asked during most polls—and those that respondents are most likely to misreport or refuse to answer. They are placed at the end of the interview schedule to improve the chances respondents will answer. *See also: FACE SHEET VARIABLES; MISREPORTERS; OPEN QUESTIONS; POLL; RESPONDENTS; SCREEN QUESTIONS*

JOB RATING a standard question used in polls to measure how well the voters think an incumbent president is performing his job. Job ratings or approval ratings are a widely watched index to a president's overall popularity.

The major pollsters all phrase the job rating question a little differently. Gallup for example asks respondents: "Do you approve or disapprove of the way (the incumbent) is handling his job as president?" Gallup then reports his data in terms of the proportion of people who approve of presidential performance. Harris poses the question this way: "How would you rate the job (the incumbent) has been doing as president—excellent, pretty good, only fair, or poor?"

Job ratings fluctuate a good deal. Harry Truman's approval scores for example ranged from a high of 87% to a low of 23%. The normal pattern is for ratings to gradually decline during an incumbency. But shifts in approval ratings also correspond to short term events. Popularity is affected by economic conditions, international crises, and war.

Each one percent rise in unemployment causes a 3% decline in job rating. Rising prices have a similar negative effect, but domestic or international crises faced decisively by the president usually result in a sharp rise in popularity. War also influences ratings. Initially voters may rally to the call to arms, however protracted war erodes presidential popularity.

Job ratings then follow a predictable pattern. Long term they tend to decline, bolstered up from time to time by the flux of events. Short term, approval ratings are a barometer to the extent to which voters perceive a president is taking decisive action with respect to some current crises. *See also: HIGH NEGATIVE*

KEY PRECINCTS representative local electoral units used by ABC, CBS, and NBC to forecast trends and predict election results. Key precincts are selected to portray the voting patterns of a larger electoral area such as a county, a state or the entire nation.

In earlier times election analysts relied on so called bellwether precincts to forecast elections. These were election districts with long histories of voting in the same proportion as the state or nation as a whole. But bellwethers eventually prove unreliable even though they may be accurate for long periods.

The key precincts used today are carefully selected to comprise a microcosm of the electorate. Information from past years is collected and compared with incoming election returns—often available within 15 minutes after the polls have closed. When this combination of data suggests a pattern, forecasts can be made.

Key precincts are combined with exit polling before an election can be called. Unless an election is very close the use of exit polling with key precinct analysis can accurately predict the outcome with only about 5% of the vote actually counted. *See also: BELLWETHER; EXIT POLLS*

LADDER SCALE *See SELF-ANCHORING SCALE*

LATE DECIDERS *See EARLY DECIDERS*

LEANERS Likely voters interviewed during a poll who initially tell pollsters that they are uncertain for whom to vote—but later indicate that they lean toward one candidate or another. Leaners are undecideds who have been able to specify a candidate preference only after a followup question from the pollster.

The followup question, which is standard in political polling, asks undecideds which candidate they are "leaning toward as of now." Those who reveal they are leaning to a candidate are then counted as supporters of that candidate. Identifying leaners in this way can reduce the proportion of undecideds by more than half. *See also: UNDECIDEDS; INDEPENDENTS*

LIKELY VOTERS eligible voters who are believed very likely to vote in an upcoming election. People are classified as likely or unlikely to vote on the basis of one or more screening questions asked during a poll.

Pollsters classify as likely voters those respondents: who are registered to vote; who know where to vote; who voted in recent elections; who express considerable interest in the election; and who say they definitely will vote.

Unlikely voters are those: who are not registered or are not sure if they are registered; who don't know where to vote; who haven't voted in recent elections; who are not interested in the election; and who say they probably won't vote.

Sorting out likely voters from non voters is particularly important in primary elections and in many state and local elections where turnouts of less than 40% are common. The accuracy and utility of a poll depends upon a successful screening process because the inclusion of non voters can skew the results by several percentage points. *See also: SCREENING QUESTIONS*

LIKERT SCALE *See SELF ANCHORING SCALE*

LITERARY DIGEST a defunct magazine best known for its 1936 prediction that Roosevelt would lose decisively to Landon. Instead, Roosevelt won in a landslide, and the LITERARY DIGEST never recovered its credibility. Today the magazine remains a symbol for those hostile or skeptical toward polls.

But the Digest's poll really had little in common with contemporary polling. It used an extremely large (over ten million) non-probability sample and it relied primarily on respondents to return their own questionnaire.

The modern poll uses relatively small probability samples of a few hundred respondents, and interviews are completed in person or over the telephone. Straw polls like the one conducted by the LITERARY DIGEST are still occasionally done, but they are rarely treated seriously as valid measurements of public opinion. *See also: SAMPLING; STRAW POLLS*

LOADED QUESTIONS questions in a poll that are worded in such a way as to suggest or imply the desired answer. Loading is the bias that results from the different ways that questions may be asked.

"Do you think the government should end its wasteful and expensive farm price support program?" is an obviously loaded question. However, the loading of poll questions is often subtle and hard to detect. It is, in fact, surprisingly difficult to produce a question that is not loaded to some degree. Pollsters are well aware of the bias that the wording of questions can produce. Even slight variations in wording can produce wide differences in the answers given. Pollsters attempt to minimize the problem by using standardized questions and by rigorous field testing of questions before they are incorporated into a poll. *See also: OPEN QUESTION*

LONGITUDINAL DATA survey research that is gathered at several different times instead of all at the same time. The latter type of data—information collected at only one time—is referred to as "cross sectional". Longitudinal data is to cross sectional as a moving picture is to a snapshot. Its most important quality is that it allows a pollster to observe and analyze changes in public opinion.

There are three basic kinds of longitudinal designs: "trend studies", "cohort studies", and "panel studies." Trend studies sample and then poll a population of voters several times in the course of a campaign. Developing trends can be detected and analyzed as new polls are taken.

Cohort studies poll the same population as it ages. For example, 18 year old voters might be studied in 1984, 20 year olds in 1986, 22 year olds in 1988, and so on. Cohort studies permit pollsters to analyze the influence of life cycle effects on public opinion.

Panel surveys poll the same individuals on several successive occasions. A pollster might interview a sample at the beginning of the campaign, and then reinterview that same panel every three weeks during the campaign. When changes in public opinion occur, the pollster can see who is changing—and perhaps explain why. *See also: LIFE CYCLE EFFECTS; PANEL SURVEYS; POLLS*

MARGINALS *See CROSS TABULATION*

MISREPORTERS polling respondents who provide inaccurate or misleading information to pollsters. Misreporters are people who exaggerate their education, stretch their incomes, say they are registered when they aren't, claim they voted when they didn't, or express support for one candidate when they actually prefer another.

Political analysts disagree about the causes of misreporting. Some believe that outright lying is rare and that most misreporting is the result of honest mistakes brought on by fatigue, boredom, or a desire to be cooperative. Others dispute this explanation however, arguing that too much reporting inaccuracy has been documented to dismiss it all as honest error. According to these critics many people consciously lie if they perceive questions to be ego threatening.

While experts differ about the causes of misreporting, no one questions that a lot of it occurs. Careful studies have shown that several kinds of information are routinely misreported. As many as one third of respondents will overstate educational attainment. Up to one quarter will inflate their income and about 15% will misrepresent their age. Even some apparently neutral questions produce misreporting. One study discovered for example, that 10% of the respondents falsely claimed drivers licenses; in the same study 5% invented ownership of a car and 3% lied about home ownership.

Misreporting of political facts is a particular problem in polls. Political scientists estimate that about 1 in 7 respondents say they are registered to vote when they aren't; approximately 1 in 6 will claim to have voted in a past election when they didn't; and 1 in 20 will mislead about their future voting intentions.

Pollsters themselves disagree about the importance of misreporting. Some believe it produces serious distortions in reported data and compromises the findings based on these polls. Other pollsters argue however that misreporting is not a serious problem because so much of it "washes out" as non-sampling error. *See also: FILTER QUESTIONS; NON-SAMPLING ERROR; RESPONDENT; SLEEPER QUESTIONS*

NAME RECOGNITION awareness of a politican measured by a voter's ability to recognize the name. Name recognition scores are the proportion of the electorate who say they know who a candidate is. These scores can range from virtually zero for unfamiliar figures to ninty-five or higher for widely known public officials.

This typical name recognition question came from a statewide poll taken in Pennsylvania:

> Next I'll read some names of public figures, and would you please tell me if you have read or heard of that person. The first public person is . . . . .

Politicians often rely on name recognition to gauge a candidate's chances. In the early trial heats however these scores can be misleading. Before all the candidates are well known, that candidate with higher recognition levels will almost always be the favorite. Later this apparent lead can vanish as other candidates become better known.

Nevertheless, name recognition is an important asset in electoral politics. In "low stimulus" races the widely recognized candidate is particularly advantaged. Opponents will probably not become well known during the campaign and many voters will vote for a candidate because its the only name they recognize.

Low name recognition scores can usually be improved with political advertising. Steady media time buying, reinforced with regular news coverage will raise name recognition sharply. This is in fact often what happens after a campaign gets underway. *See also HIGH STIMULUS ELECTIONS; TRIAL HEATS*

NON-OPINIONS *See FILTER QUESTIONS*

NON-SAMPLING inaccuracy in a poll caused by the practical problems of carrying out surveys. Non-sampling error includes all of the clerical and mechanical mistakes that can occur when collecting and processing data. It also includes poorly worded questions, badly conducted interviews and all forms of cheating.

Non-sampling error can be a more serious cause of polling inaccuracy than is sampling error. Unlike the latter it is impossible to estimate and difficult to detect. On the other hand non-sampling error can be relatively benign, if it is not systematic—that is all in the same direction.

Pollsters usually make strenuous efforts to minimize non-sampling error. Polls are reported however as if non-sampling error had been eliminated or else had simply cancelled itself out. This is not always the case. *See also: SAMPLING ERROR*

NOT AT HOMES *See CALL BACKS*

OPEN QUESTIONS one of the two basic types of questions used in polling. Open questions present some problem or issue and ask respondents to talk about it. One version of a common open question asks about the important concerns people have:

"A lot of people today tell us that they are most concerned or worried about some particular public problem. What particular problem or issue most concerns you?"

Open questions are designed to evoke a spontaneous response without the interviewer suggesting specific possible answers. This type of question differs from so called "closed questions" in which the interviewer does provide a fixed number of possible answers.

A closed end version of the open question above might be worded like this:

"I'm going to read to you a list of problems that people have told us they are most concerned or worried about. Please listen carefully as I go through this list and then tell me which of these problems most concern or worry you:

unemployment
pollution
arms control
taxes
crime
inflation

Both open and closed questions are found in most polls. Open questions are appropriate when not much is known about public opinion and the objective is to explore. Closed questions on the other hand are most valuable when the range of opinion is well understood and the objective is to measure differences among key electoral groups.

Open questions are used much less frequently than are closed questions. They are much more expensive to administer; they require substantially more time to complete because individual responses must be recorded; and they are more difficult to analyze because they produce larger amounts of data. *See also: INTERVIEW SCHEDULE; POLL*

OVERSAMPLING a technical procedure used by pollsters. Oversampling systematically samples a disproportionate number of persons from some key demographic group. This is done to insure that there will be enough interviews completed with the oversampled group to allow useful analysis.

There are two basic circumstances in which oversampling is appropriate. In the first a demographic group might be relatively small in the overall population—say 1 or 2 percent. If the sample size was based on their actual proportion in the population, it would yield such a small number of actual interviews that analysis would be doubtful.

The other circumstance in which oversampling is used occurs when a demographic group is especially important to campaign planning—only a small margin of sampling error can be tolerated. Here the group must be oversampled to insure that this level of sampling error is not exceeded.

Oversampling need not result in a disproportionate number from the oversampled group being included in the overall poll. Weighting can be applied when the complete sample is analyzed. Each oversampled group can be "weighted down"—either by randomly deleting some respondents that were interviewed, or by assigning each respondent interviewed a decimal value less than one.

Occasionally polls do oversample one or more demographic groups—but then fail to weight the results in their overall analysis. These polls of course are defective. *See also: WEIGHTING*

PANEL BACK POLL a unique type of polling which involves setting up a "panel" of likely voters, then interviewing and re-interviewing them throughout the campaign. Panel back polls differ from other polls in which a different group of people are drawn for each successive survey. Panel backs use the same respondents for repeated polls.

Panel back polls have some distinct advantages as well as disadvantages. Their major strength is that they allow pollsters to study individual shifts in attitude or opinion. With panels, pollsters can see who is changing and ask why because the same people are interviewed in each poll.

Panels also allow pollsters to isolate and monitor key voter groups like late and early deciders, switchers and swing voters. Panel backs however have some drawbacks. One is the "mortality" problem. Panels lose members who drop out over time for various reasons. When mortality is extensive it can threaten the representativeness of the sample.

Panel backs can also become very biased samples—due to a problem termed "reactivity" by social scientists. Reactivity occurs when respondents change as a result of being interviewed. They may become more aware of political news, may be following the campaign more closely, or may have been stimulated by questioning to think more about political matters. All of these behaviors—brought on by being polled—might make these respondents seriously unrepresentative of the population of voters from which they were chosen. *See also: POLLS*

POLLING the process of interviewing relatively small samples of people selected from relatively larger populations in order to discover public opinion. Polling procedures entail five basic steps.

1. Writing of questions that will provide answers that pollsters can use to analyze voters' attitudes and opinions.
2. Drawing a scientific (probability) sample that will accurately represent the entire population of voters.
3. Interviewing respondents selected for the sample without biasing their answers.
4. Analyzing the answers given using statistical principles to guarantee the validity and reliability of conclusions.
5. Interpreting the results by assessing their meaning in the context of campaign goals and objectives.

In modern polling each of these five steps is fairly complex and requires considerable skill and training to complete. Most pollsters today in fact have strong backgrounds in social science methods and statistics. *See also:*

CALL BACKS; CROSS TABULATIONS; FACE SHEET VARIABLES; IN THE FIELD; INTERVIEW SCHEDULE; QUESTIONNAIRE; RESPONDENTS; SAMPLING

POLLS surveys of likely voters taken to assess public opinion regarding specific issues and particular candidates. Four kinds of polls are widely used in political campaigns.

One is the benchmark poll. These are baseline surveys which serve as a basic reference point and planning tool for the campaign. They use long series of questions and large samples and are completed six to twelve months before the campaign formally begins. A second type of poll is the "brushfire surveys". These are taken after the campaign is underway. They are short focused polls which follow up on the benchmark poll, evaluate campaign progress, and identify problems and opportunities.

The third type of poll is the panel back survey. Panel backs differ from other polls which use a different sample of voters for each survey. Panel backs use the same respondents for repeated polls so that pollsters can study individual shifts in attitudes and opinions. A fourth type of poll is the tracking poll. These are very short polls taken continuously during the last several days or weeks of a campaign. They monitor voter trends so the campaign can react to last minute changes in the electorate.

Campaigns employ polls to test campaign themes, rate opposing candidates, discover issues, gauge the electorate's mood, and predict voting intentions. There are also some important non-information uses for polls. Fund raising is one of these. Favorable or encouraging polls are regularly circulated among large contributors and PAC's to persuade them to support a particular candidate. Campaigns also use polls to increase media coverage. Positive poll results can improve a candidate's credibility among reporters and convince them to give more attention to that campaign. *See also: BANDWAGON EFFECT; BENCHMARK POLLS; EXIT POLLS; PANEL BACK SURVEYS; TRACKING POLLS*

PROBABILITY SAMPLING *See SAMPLING*

PSEUDO OPINION *See FILTER QUESTION*

PUBLIC OPINION QUARTERLY the most prestigious and influential journal in the field of polling and public opinion research. The Public Opinion Quarterly is published by the American Association For Public Opinion Research (AAPOR) based in Princeton, New Jersey.

Public Opinion Quarterly is a rich authoritative source of articles on polling principles and practices. Pieces range from the theoretical and estoric to the practical and applied. Most are well written and all are scholarly. The contributor list includes some of the most eminent people in the field. George Gallup, Lou Harris, Herman Hyman, Burns Roper and Seymour Sudman have all published in Public Opinion Quarterly.

There are some other journals and periodicals which feature material on polling and public opinion. One of these is the magazine format Public Opinion published by the conservative thinktank American Enterprise Institute in Washington, D.C. It delivers a steady stream of articles on public opinion and public policy issues. Other publications which regularly feature polling related material include the CONGRESSIONAL QUARTERLY WEEKLY, GALLUP'S REPORTS, THE JOURNAL OF POLITICS, and THE NATIONAL JOURNAL. *See also: AMERICAN ASSOCIATION FOR PUBLIC OPINION RESEARCH (AAPOR); POLLS*

QUBE SYSTEM a widely publicized prototype for interactive cable television. The Qube system has been promoted as a new approach to polling. First installed in Columbus, Ohio, it allows subscribers to watch speeches, view debates, or listen to discussion on issues or proposals. Then they can "vote" their opinions or reactions by pushing the appropriate buttons on the computer terminal attached to their sets.

Qube type systems hold out exciting promise to some but they are criticized by others. Enthusiasts dub them "electronic polls" and argue that interactive polling techniques can bring about true plebiscitary democracy—through mass participation in the formation of public opinion. According to this view public opinion will be known instantly, and it will have greater influence on the policies actually carried out by public officials.

Others however claim that Qube type systems are essentially straw polls—available only to paid subscribers and only to those subscribers who choose to participate. According to these critics the non random nature of Qube system sampling compromises the validity of these surveys.

Qube systems and other interactive polling modes will doubtless continue to be used and experimented with. Their serious methodological problems however suggest that this kind of instant poll is not likely to replace traditional public opinion research. *See also: STRAW POLL*

Q SORTS a research technique used to identify voter types or to study attitudes and opinions within the electorate. Q sorts use small samples. Generally 40 to 50 voters are given a set of attitude statements on 3 × 5 cards, then asked to arrange them into several categories according to how much they agree or disagree with the statements. Those items with which they most agree might go into pile one; those items with which they next most agree go in pile two; and so on until after all of the items are assigned to a particular pile.

Q sorts are analyzed with a statistical procedure known as "factor analysis" which compares and contrasts each voter's Q sort with the Q sort of every other voter. When four or five Q sorts show a substantial match, these four or five are said to make up a "Q type".

Q sorts are based on what social scientists refer to as Q Methodology (or Q Method). Q contrasts with R Methodology which is dominant in most of social science. The essential distinction between the two is that R relies on studying the relationships among so called "trait" variables: age, sex, income, education, etc.; Q emphasized the whole relationship among individuals, what does A, B, and C have in common, and how do they differ from X, Y, and Z.

The main application of Q sorts in the political arena have been in the development of targeting programs. They have also been used to supplement polling data and in the development of issue strategies. *See also: GEO-DEMOGRAPHICS; TARGETING*

QUESTIONNAIRE *See INTERVIEW SCHEDULE*

QUESTIONS *See OPEN QUESTIONS*

QUINTAMENSIONAL an interview design that employs five seperate questions to get at a single complex public opinion issue. The quintamensional is attributed to George Gallup who first described it in 1947.

According to Gallup's scheme, the first question in the quintamensional series should explore "awareness"—has the respondent read or heard of such and such?; second comes a question on "general opinion"—what does the respondent think should be done about such and such?; third is a question on a specific proposal—does the respondent approve or disapprove of this idea?; fourth is a question about the reason for approval or disapproval; fifth and last is a question about "intensity"—how strong does the respondent feel about these views?; all five questions together measure the major facets of public opinion.

Here's an example of the quintamensional format used in a series of questions about gun control:

Q1. Will you tell me what the phrase gun control means to you? (probes awareness);
Q2. What if anything should our lawmakers do about gun control? (probes general attitude);
Q3. It has been proposed that all hand guns be banned for private use. Do you approve or disapprove of this idea? (probes specific attitudes);
Q4. Why do you feel the way you do about gun control? (probes reasons for attitude);
Q5. How strongly do you feel about this—very strongly, somewhat strongly, or not strongly at all? (probes intensity of feelings)

The quintamensional has not been widely used in polling. The technique is well known but the application is time consuming and expensive. Perhaps more important, pollsters often feel that it is unnecessary to measure public opinion in the depth that this method allows. *See also: INTERVIEW SCHEDULE; OPEN END QUESTION*

QUOTA SAMPLE a form of non random sample widely used in the early days of polling. Quota samples are drawn to be miniature portraits of the electorate according to sex, age, education, political party, race, income and so on. The design and execution of a quota sample is relatively simple. First current census data is examined to determine the distribution of the overall population by demographic categories.

Next interviewers are given quotas of people to interview in each category: so many women, so many Catholics, so many college graduates, so many affluents, so many blacks, etc. The categories are combined so that interviewers actually seek out so many women who are also Catholics and college graduates, so many college graduates who are black and affluent, etc. Finally interviewers are sent in the field where they choose the actual people to be interviewed.

Quota sampling has some advantages: it is easier to design and carry out than is random sampling; it is less costly since interviewers' time and travel can be reduced; and it has a certain pseudo precision because it reproduces the population in exactly the correct demographic proportions.

These pluses however are usually outweighed by the problems associated with quota samples. The most serious of these is the bias that comes from interviewers choosing their own respondents. Many interviewers will select people who are accessible, easy to interview and most like themselves. The result is that the poll becomes biased toward relatively affluent, educated, middle class people.

Quota sampling fell into disrepute in the United States after the 1948 election in which it was used to forecast victory for Tom Dewey. Nevertheless some polling organizations continue to use modified forms of the technique today. Quota sampling is also still somewhat common outside of the United States. *See also: POLLS; SAMPLING*

RANDOM-DIGIT DIALING (RDD) a widely used procedure for drawing a sample of respondents for inclusion in a telephone poll. Random digit dialing (RDD) allows pollsters to produce representative samples even when no good listing of voters or their telephone numbers exists.

The popularity of RDD owes to the complexity of producing a good sample using only telephone directories. More than 90% of American households have telephones—but up to 50% of these will not be accurately listed in any telephone book: because about 30% of all homes have unlisted numbers and about 20% of American families move each year. Compounding things, some homes have multiple phones, each with different numbers—and many homes are listed in more than one directory.

Random digit dialing solves many of these problems. Basically the process involves four steps. Like all other random sampling procedures, these steps give every voter a known and equal chance of being selected:

1. The pollster determines the geographic area to be surveyed, then ascertains which phone exchanges are in use.
2. A random number table or computerized "random number generator" is employed to list random numbers which will be called.
3. The sample is drawn. Actually many sub-samples or "replicated samples" are produced to assure a balanced and accurate overall representation.
4. Each telephone exchange is "stratified" by determining the proportion of the total voter population that lives in the exchange. If 20% of the electorate live in exchange 516, then 20% of the sample will be drawn from that exchange.

Not every pollster is enthusiastic about RDD. Critics of this sampling approach complain that it produces too many calls to commercial or nonworking numbers, leaves too much discretion to the interviewer and doesn't produce well balanced samples. *See also: PROBABILITY SAMPLE; POLLS*

RANDOM SAMPLE *See SAMPLING*

REACTIVITY *See PANEL BACK POLL*

REFUSALS people included in a poll sample who decline to be interviewed. Refusals occur during virtually every poll. Lately however pollsters report that they have been increasing. Once only 5 to 10% of all prospective respondents were classified as refusals. Today about 10 to 20% will not answer the pollster's questions.

Experts ascribe several motivations to refusals: many people simply distrust the survey process or are intimidated by it; some can't or won't spend the time; and others are just not inclined to be cooperative. Undoubtedly interviewer skill is also an important factor in eliciting respondent participation.

Pollsters generally don't consider refusals to be a problem unless the refusal rate gets above 20%. Their premise is that the people who do answer questions don't differ importantly from those who don't. This assumption is important because it allows survey data to be analyzed without weighting it or otherwise adjusting for possible bias.

Refusals are not the only kind of response problem that occurs in polls. Pollsters are also confronted with another type of respondent resistance—unwillingness or reluctance to answer specific questions. From 20% to 30% of those polled will balk at one or more of the questions put to them.

Most frequently this problem is encountered with the personal questions asked of all respondents—their age, education, income, etc. Of these the income question by far evokes the most hesitancy. For this reason it is usually the last question asked in a poll. *See also: MISREPORTERS; POLLS; RESPONDENTS; WEIGHTING*

RESPONDENT any person interviewed during a poll. Respondents answer questions providing the data that pollsters use to report findings, reach conclusions and make recommendations.

The number of respondents included in a poll varies. About 250 is the bare minimum while some national surveys will interview 3000 or more. Gallup polls use samples of just over 1500. Regional, state and local polls range from 450 or so to about 1200.

The decision on how many respondents to actually survey depends on the accuracy needed and the financial resources of the organization that sponsors the poll. In general the more interviews, the more accurate is the poll—but costs also rise as respondents increase.

Pollsters classify their respondents according to some more or less standard demographic categories—age, income, education, ethnic group, political party, etc. Using cross tabulation analysis, comparisons can then be made of how these various groups differ in their attitudes and opinions.

The selection of respondents is carefully planned in order to ensure the process is random. Samples are drawn so that individual households all have an equal chance of being selected. Interviewers are not given any discretion even after a particular home has been called or visited. Instead they are trained to use "respondent selection tables" which automatically choose who is to be interviewed, based on the characteristics of the people who live there. *See also: FACE SHEET VARIABLES; POLLS; PROBABILITY SAMPLE*

SAMPLING any procedure which involves selecting people from some larger population, then making inferences about that population from studying the sample that has been drawn. Sampling underlies all polling.

Social scientists distinguish between two broad types of sampling: Probability (random sampling) and non-probability (non-random sampling). Probability sampling is used in all so called scientific polls. It has several versions including such variations as simple random sampling, systematic random sampling, stratified sampling and cluster sampling. All of these are employed in modern polling.

Non-probability sampling differs from probability in one key respect. Non-probability samples are drawn without regard to the established laws of probability theory—the most important of which requires that every person in the population be given a known and equal chance of ending up in the sample.

Before 1936, few polls used probability sampling. The techniques were not well known and they were more laborious than non-probability. The Literary Digest embarrassment and the early successes of George Gallup changed this by bringing non-probability straw polls into disrepute. After 1948 when polling failed to predict a Truman victory all the major pollsters turned to probability sampling.

Non-probability sampling still survives in newspaper straw polls and other informal surveys. No reputable American pollster still uses it—although a version known as quota sampling is still found in European and South American polls. *See also: LITERARY DIGEST; POLLS; QUOTA SAMPLE; SAMPLING ERROR; STATISTICAL SIGNIFICANCE*

SAMPLING ERROR inaccuracy in a poll due to differences between the people actually polled—the sample—and the larger population from which the sample was taken. Polls are usually subject to sampling error in the range of 3 to 5%. This means that the reported results might differ from the actual electorate either plus or minus that amount.

Thus if candidate A is found to be leading candidate B in the horse race by 3 points—and the sampling error is 3 points—the actual race may be a tie between the two candidates, or candidate A might have a 6 point lead.

Sampling error is commonly set at the so called 95% "confidence level", which means that 95% of the time the reported results would be within the reported sampling error range. In principle this means a poll would produce a bad sample of voters only 5% of the time; in practice pollsters use various techniques to guard against even the 5% chance of a bad sample. Sampling error occurs in all polls to some extent. It becomes of more practical importance in close elections where the candidates are separated by margins that are less than the sampling error. Polls in fact cannot infallibly predict close elections unless they reduce the sampling error by using very large samples.

Sampling error is not the only type of inaccuracy that can affect polls. They are also subject to non-sampling error which include all the practical problems of carrying out surveys. Some experts believe non sampling error is more serious than sampling error because it is harder to detect. *See also: NON-SAMPLING ERROR*

SCREEN QUESTIONS a series of related questions asked during a poll in order to sort out likely voters from unlikely voters. Pollsters differ in the exact questions they use and the weight they give to them. But a good screen includes questions that 1) determine voter registration, 2) test knowledge of voting procedures, 3) gauge interest in the election, 4) ask about recent voting behavior, and 5) ascertain the intention to vote on election day.

Screen questions are critically important to the accuracy of a poll because they determine who will be counted. Unfortunately they are not consistently reliable. Even the highly respected Gallup Poll estimates its screening procedures produce a sample of which only 87% actually vote. Some other polls do less well. It is common for 80% of respondents to pass screens as likely voters, while actual voter turnout might be 50% or lower.

The increase of Independents in the electorate has complicated the problem of designing effective screen questions. The volatility of these voters makes it very difficult to predict if they will vote. *See also: FILTER QUESTIONS; INTERVIEW SCHEDULES; LIKELY VOTERS*

SECRET BALLOT TECHNIQUE *See UNDECIDEDS*

SELF ANCHORING SCALE a standard technique used in polls to measure respondents' attitudes today, in terms of how they felt sometime in the past and how they expect to feel sometime in the future. Self anchoring scales were developed by polling pioneers Lloyd Free and Hadley Cantril in the 1950's.

They work like this: the respondent is shown a picture of a ladder—or asked to imagine a ladder—with ten rungs numbered from 0 (bottom rung) to 10 (top rung). He or she might be asked to imagine the worst possible state of affairs and assign that to 1 on the ladder; then think of the best possible state of affairs and assign that to 10 on the ladder. After these extremes have been anchored the respondent might be asked to decide what the real state of things are today, then assign that to a rung of the ladder.

Self anchoring scales are popular because almost everyone is familiar with ladders and able to express opinions and attitudes in terms of the ten rungs on the ladder. Pollsters like them because they allow measurement of the electorate's shifting pessimism or optimism. For example, if voters rate the past more highly than the present or the future, they are probably becoming more pessimistic. On the other hand if voters rate the future more highly than the present or the past, they are expressing growing optimism.

Self anchoring scales have one other important quality. The ladder device creates what statisticians call a ratio scale. This allows pollsters to use an accuracy of measurement and precision of analysis not possible for many other types of questions. *See also: HIGH NEGATIVE; JOB RATING*

SLEEPER QUESTIONS a technique employed by pollsters to detect the amount of guessing going on by respondents. Sleeper questions introduce a fictitious name, an imaginary problem, or an invented issue, then ask people to answer a question or provide information about the made-up item.

For example, during a candidate name identification question featuring several prominent public figures, a "dummy name" might be inserted as a control to determine how valid the scores really are. Or a respondent might be asked to comment on such and such policy issue or evaluate such and such government agency—all concocted.

Sleeper questions sometimes produce startling results. Pollsters have found from 5% to 15% of those surveyed will claim to know a "candidate" who is really only a fictitious name. Still others will say they have heard of public issues that have been wholly manufactured.

Sleeper questions are a special form of filter questions. Both are designed to detect and correct for the so called "non-opinion"—the tendency of some people to express opinions or attitudes even though they really have no understanding or knowledge of the topic about which they are commenting. Apparently, people express non-opinions to avoid feeling foolish or appearing to be uninformed. *See also; FILTER QUESTIONS; MISREPORTERS; NON-SAMPLING ERROR*

SOFT SUPPORT intentions to vote for a candidate which are not firm. Soft support is voter approval given with some reservations or qualifications. As many as one-third of those voters who say they will vote for a specific candidate can be soft supporters.

Sometimes the weak commitment is due to the presence of cross pressures. Voters feel pulled in two different directions—away from the candidate for some reasons and toward the candidate for others. Other times soft support occurs because the favored candidate, is not really well known to the electorate—his support is an "inch deep and a mile wide."

Soft support also results when the candidate's strength comes from the opponent's weakness. This kind of soft support generally erodes if the opponent turns their own campaign around and begins to gain more support from the electorate. *See also CROSS PRESSURES; INCH DEEP AND MILE WIDE*

SPLIT BALLOT TECHNIQUE a procedure used by pollsters to test the quality of their questions. Question wording is a major concern in polls. Small differences in the framing of a question can result in substantial variation in the answers given by respondents. In fact the reported discrepancies between polls is often due largely to different question wording. The split ballot technique controls for these differences by dividing the polling sample into two groups. Each group is given a different version of each question. If there is a significant difference in responses to the two sets of questions, the pollster can assume that question wording is responsible.

Split ballots are also employed to test the accuracy of the "secret ballot technique"—which is a tool designed by pollsters to reduce the number of respondents who claim to be undecided. After the secret ballots have been collected and counted, the split ballot procedure is used to evaluate the difference (if any) between those who voted in secret and those who did not. *See also: BLAB WORDS; UNDECIDEDS*

SPLIT HALVES TECHNIQUES *See SPLIT BALLOT*

STATISTICAL SIGNIFICANCE a technical term used by pollsters in connection with the analysis of polling data. Statistical significance has to do with the relationship between the sample of respondents who are actually asked questions and the much larger population from which the sample was drawn.

When pollsters say this or that poll finding is statistically significant they mean that the finding is real and not just a statistical fluke in the sample. For example, if a particular question reveals a difference between men and women on some policy issue, statistical significance tests would show whether these same differences would also be found in the population from which the sample came.

A common measure used to test statistical significance is the chi square. The chi square can determine if there is a real association between (for example) income level and preference for a particular candidate—or if there is a real difference between (for example) younger voters and older voters on some policy position.

Pollsters report the statistical significance of their findings in order to demonstrate the technical validity of their data. Unfortunately the meaning of statistical significance is sometimes misconstrued by both the media and the public—to imply that the reported data is also meaningful beyond the statistical sense.

The fact is that not every statistically significant finding is also a meaningful finding. Percentage differences of a single point or less are often statistically significant when large samples are used. But whether these are also significant in a practical sense is a separate matter. *See also: CELLS; CONTROLLING FOR; CROSS TABULATION; POLLS*

STRAW POLL any election survey done without regard to probability sampling or other principles of scientific polling. Straw polls are taken by newspapers, broadcast outlets, community groups and others.

These polls have a long tradition in American politics. The first was taken by the Harrisburg Pennsylvanian before the 1824 presidential campaign. Newspaper straw polls soon became regular features of campaign coverage and remained so during the 19th and into the 20th Century. The Literary Digest catastrophe in 1936 did bring straw polling into general disrepute. Several newspapers however continue the tradition. Probably the best known of these is the New York Daily News whose presidential straw poll is widely reported.

Recently television and radio stations have invented a new form of straw poll in which the audience calls in their vote on a special telephone line (sometimes for a fee). Even network television has experimented with these "instant" reaction polls—a practice criticized by many. Another variant of the modern straw poll is the Qube system. Qube allows subscribers to vote their opinion on some issue by pressing the appropriate button on the computer terminal attached to their TV sets.

The latest twist on the straw poll is the candidate polls conducted at cattle shows and other early events in presidential primaries. These polls are sponsored by state party organizations who invite the candidate in to meet and mix with them for an evening. They gained prominence during the 1976 presidential primaries when Democrat Jimmy Carter used them to catapault himself into serious contention. Since then both Republicans and Democrats have begun to use them, despite some misgivings about their appropriateness. *See also: CATTLE SHOWS; LITERARY DIGEST; POLLS; QUBE SYSTEM; SAMPLING*

SURVEY RESEARCH *See POLLS*

THERMOMETER SCALE *See HIGH NEGATIVE*

TRACKING POLLS continuous short polls taken during the last several days or weeks of a campaign. Tracking polls use small samples and brief interviews to monitor trends in the electorate during the final critical period of the campaign.

Tracking requires daily samples of 50 to 2000 respondents. A system of moving averages is used to build up a large sample over several days. To keep data fresh only the most recent 4 or 5 days interviews are retained. For example if 150 voters are interviewed each day, the last 5 day surveys—750 interviews in all—become the sample. Each day the most recent 150 interviews are added and the oldest 150 are discarded.

Tracking allows the campaign to gauge the electorate's reactions to late events and react to developing problems and opportunities. It is especially useful in media oriented campaigns where much of the press coverage and political advertising are concentrated in the last days and weeks. *See also: POLLS*

TREND STUDIES *See LONGITUDINAL DATA*

TRIAL HEAT a polling question which pits perspective candidates against each other to determine who might win a future election. Trial heats pose some version of this question: "if the election was being held today, and the candidates were X, Y, and Z, which one would you vote for." Candidates, journalists, and even political professionals often place too much emphasis on the significance of trial heats. These early horse race questions can reveal problems and opportunities that lie ahead, but they are not particularly reliable forcecasters of who will win or lose a future race.

Trial heats are notoriously misleading in predicting the eventual strength of a candidate. Before primary elections trial heats tend to reflect name identification. Before general elections they are influenced by the party identification of the voter being surveyed. Both of these factors usually diminish in importance as the campaign gets under way.

UNDECIDEDS prospective voters who reveal while being polled that they are uncertain about the candidate for which they intend to vote. Undecideds are critically important because this category of voters can make the difference in close races.

The percentage of undecideds reported in a poll will range from 1 to 2% to as high as 50%. Pollsters use two standard techniques to keep the undecideds as low as possible. One of these involves the use of followup or probe questions. When respondents say they are unsure about the candidate they prefer, they are then asked which candidate they are "leaning" to as of now.

A second technique used to reduce the size of the undecideds is the "secret ballot." Toward the end of the interview, respondents are handed a sample ballot, asked to mark a candidate choice on it, fold the ballot and deposit it in a cardboard ballot box carried by the interviewer. Both the probe question and secret ballot techniques can reduce undecideds by half or more.

As a rule the undecided vote is higher in primary elections probably because there are no party cues to assist voters in making choices. In general elections, undecided voters tend to come from among Independents and ticket splitters. Pollsters consider reported undecideds of more than about 20% to be the mark of a flawed poll. *See also: LEANERS*

UNLIKELY VOTERS *See LIKELY VOTERS*

VARIABLE a technical term used in polling. Variables are behaviors or attitudes that can vary from one person to another. They are the things that differentiate people and groups. The common variables measured in polls include these: age; income; education; occupation; sex, race; ethnic group; religion; and political party affiliation.

Pollsters sometimes distinguish "independent variables" from "dependent variables." Independent variables are these which cause things to happen. In the idiom of social science they "explain" and "predict." Dependent variables are those which are caused by the independent variables. They are the things pollsters are interested in explaining and predicting.

Traditionally certain variables are treated as independent while others are usually dependent. For example income, education, occupation, political party affiliation, sex, and race are normally examined as independent variables that explain why people vote as they do.

On the other hand voting intentions and turnout are the traditional dependent variables, those that are caused or explained by the independent variables. Voting intentions and turnout are in fact the most important variables used in polls. In one way or another almost the entire poll is devoted to the study and analysis of these two variables. *See also: CELLS; CONTROLLING FOR; CROSS TABULATION*

WEIGHTING a technical procedure used by pollsters to correct imperfections in their sample. Weighting is done to make the sample more representative of the population from which it was taken. Weights are applied if one or more key demographic groups—blacks, farmers, union members, white collar workers, women, etc.—have been overrepresented or underrepresented in the sample.

The mechanics of weighting is straightforward and is done during the data processing stages of polling analysis. Samples are compared to census data or other demographic information. If a population group is underrepresented in the sample, it is weighted up by multiplying those persons in the sample by a factor that will bring them into balance. For example, if a survey of 1,000 produced 50 blacks or 5% of the sample, but blacks actually constituted 10% of the population, the answers of the 50 black respondents would be weighted by two.

On the other hand if a population group is overrepresented in the sample, it is weighted down by randomly deleting some respondents that were interviewed. For example, if the 1,000 survey cited above included 125 blacks when their actual proportion of the population should produce only 100, then 25 of the 125 would be randomly removed from the sample.

Pollsters who weight samples are sometimes accused of "cooking" their data to insure it comes out right. Probably some unethical pollsters do manipulate their samples this way. Most don't, however. Moreover, weighting is a legitimate and necessary procedure when random chance has produced an unrepresentative sample—as it will do about 5% of the time. In fact, pollsters who do not weight when it is appropriate to do so run the risk of producing a bad sample about one out of every twenty times. *See also: OVERSAMPLING*

4

ELECTORAL STRATEGIES AND TACTICS

ACCESS the political status of those who can ask for and consistently expect to receive the attention and responsiveness of government officials. Having access means that one can arrange an opportunity to see a key official, that one's problems or concerns will be treated seriously, and that one is perceived as a friend and supporter.

The term access is often used to describe the quid pro quo that is believed to exist between political candidates and their financial supporters. It is generally supposed that political money buys government access. Regardless of any specific goal or objective a contributor may have in mind, they reasonably expect future access to the candidate to whom they contribute. This view of the relationship between politicians and their supporters has generated some sharp disagreements among political observers. Some find the notion of access unsettling in that it implies an unequal distribution of power and influence to those who possess the financial resources to contribute to campaigns. But others defend the role of access in public affairs as an appropriate one in the context of the bargaining and compromise that characterizes a pluralist system of government. *See also: HANDICAPPING; PAC'S*

AGGREGATE ELECTION DATA one of two broad classes of data that are used in planning campaign strategies and analyzing election results. Survey research or poll data is the other.

Aggregate data is made up of the election returns from past elections; these are mainly voting totals broken out by party or candidate for each level of electoral organization: precinct, ward, municipality, county, congressional district, and state.

This information allows the analyst to study gross voting patterns over time and to compare one electoral region with another in terms of overall trends and outcomes. A major use of aggregate data in planning campaign strategy is to "target" campaign resources and efforts in areas that have performed well in the past.

Aggregate data is widely available and inexpensive to access. Frequently it is available in libraries or in local government offices. Its major limitation is that it does not allow the user to carry analyses to the individual voter level or to know with confidence what causes to ascribe to overall voting patterns.

The great risk of aggregate data is the so-called aggregative or "ecological fallacy;" this is the logical error of imputing behavior or motivations to individuals because they belong to a group that seems to manifest that behavior or motivation. *See also: POLLS; TARGETING*

ANNOUNCING making the official announcement of candidacy for public office. Announcing involves careful planning and timing. The timing of the formal announcement is in fact one of the major strategic considerations of the political campaign. This is so because announcing triggers both legal and political consequences that impact different candidacies in different ways.

Incumbents and very strong candidates often announce early, exploiting the opportunity to discourage other candidates who might be thinking of making the race. Announcing early also can facilitate fund raising and the job of building a campaign organization. Non-incumbents—especially long shot candidates—also sometimes announce early in the hope that doing so will allow them to build credibility as viable candidates. And where public financing is involved, announcing early may be necessary to qualify for the public funds.

While many candidates do announce early, most do not. Delaying the announcement usually doesn't preclude a candidate from either raising funds or building an organization as an "unannounced candidate." And waiting allows avoidance of the FCC's equal time rule which requires that radio and television stations give equal time to all announced candidates. Late announcing also permits a candidate—especially an incumbent—to appear to be above politics and more statesmanlike. Finally, the act of not announcing can generate valuable media speculation about whether and when an announcement will occur. *See also: EQUAL TIME RULE; FILING; PUBLIC FINANCING*

BALLOT POSITION the order in which a party or candidate's name appears on the printed ballot. The conventional wisdom among politicians is that first listing on the printed ballot will gain them additional votes compared to the votes that they would receive were they listed elsewhere.

There is some evidence that the order in which a candidate's name appears on the ballot can alter the outcome of an election. Apparently, many voters will cast their votes for the first name on the ballot simply because it is the first that they see. This seems to be especially the case in direct primaries, non-partisan elections, and in elections where the candidates for an office are not well known.

Individual states vary in the way that ballot position is determined. Frequently, the party that won the last major statewide election is assigned the first column in party column ballot states. In states using office block ballots, candidates are usually listed alphabetically under each office. In primary elections, candidates often draw lots to determine their ballot position.

Some jurisdictions attempt to neutralize the advantage of first listing by rotating candidates' names so that each is placed on the top of roughly the same number of ballots. *See also: BALLOTS*

BASE OFFICES any political office that traditionally has served as a vehicle for election to higher office. Base offices are the "stepping stones" in political careers. The notion of base office, includes the expectation that politicians who have occupied these offices will share common experiences with others who have also occupied them. And these common experiences will broadly socialize politicians into similar ways of thinking and behaving.

The offices that are considered base offices vary from state to state and even within states. For example, the office of local prosecutor or district attorney is a traditional base office in some areas, while in others it is not. The office of mayor is a base office in some states but not in others. Usually, the office of U.S. Representative is a base for statewide office while governorships are bases for the U.S. Senate. Recently the U.S. Senate has come to be considered a base for the presidency. *See also: POLITICAL BASE*

BASE RACE a prior election that is believed to reflect the hard partisan vote that exists in any political jurisdiction. The base race reveals the percentage of the vote that would be cast for or against a candidate simply because of the party line that candidate occupies on the ballot.

Political strategists sometimes analyze one or more base races. Usually, the base race selected is a low visibility non-controversial office. The assumption is that voting in such elections is largely determined by the partisan leaning of the electorate—rather than on the basis of either issues or candidate preference.

At the local level the less prominent row offices, such as assessor or clerk of courts are good base races. Statewide, the fiscal offices such as state treasurer, are used as base races. But elections in which the candidates are well known, such as congressional and gubernatorial elections, are usually not thought of as base races. This is because the influence of party on voting behavior diminishes as voters get more information about particular candidates. *See also: NORMAL VOTE*

BATTLEGROUND STATES the large two party industrial states that usually figure prominently in the Electoral College strategies of presidential candidates. These battleground states are generally considered to be California, Illinois, Indiana, Michigan, New York, Ohio, Pennsylvania, and Texas.

These states are influential in presidential elections because the operation of the Electoral College system gives more weight to the vote from the large two party states. Under the unit rule a state casts all its electoral votes for the candidate receiving the most popular votes in that state. Candidates receiving lesser numbers of popular votes receive no electoral votes at all from that state. The consequence of this is that the strategic importance of the larger states is amplified.

The battleground states account for a large number of electoral votes. Combined they cast 214 of the 270 required for election to the presidency. Normally, these states are not in the solid electoral base of either major party and are, therefore, states that either candidate could win. And because they are so important to their electoral strategies, presidential candidates tend to spend much more time campaigning in them than they do in the smaller states. *See also: UNIT RULE*

BIG EIGHT STATES *See BATTLEGROUND STATES*

BLACK ADVANCE *See DIRTY TRICKS*

BULLET VOTING a tactic sometimes used when there are several seats to be filled for the same office, such as school board, county commissioner or city council. Bullet voting strategy calls for the supporters of a candidate to vote only for that candidate and no other.

Here's a common example. Say there are three seats up for city council, but six candidates running. Each voter is entitled to three votes for three different candidates, but the bullet voter would use only one, voting only for the favored candidate. The consequence of this is to magnify that single vote threefold since no other candidate receives the other two.

Strategists employ bullet voting in two basic electoral situations. One is the at large election where winners are chosen from among a field of candidates on the basis of order of finish. For example if five school board seats are up and 15 candidates are running, the five seats will be filled by the top five finishers. Bullet voting here calls for supporters to vote for only one (or perhaps two) candidates.

The other electoral situation in which bullet voting occurs is the multimember legislative race where several legislators are elected in the same district. These contests especially encourage the minority party to concentrate their voting strength on a single candidate.

Near synonyms for bullet voting are "sling shooting" (rare) and "single shooting". The latter is loosely used and can also refer to the practice among PAC's of deciding support for a candidate on the basis of a single test issue or critical vote. *See also: CAMPAIGN STRATEGY*

CALL'EM AND-RAISE' EM an expression of the classic maneuver for handling political mud slinging and attacks. Political scientists Nelson W. Polsby and Aaron Wildavsky offer some tongue in cheek advice along these lines in their book PRESIDENTIAL ELECTIONS (1984:189)

> if all else fails, it is always possible to take advice attributed to a Chicago politician who said that in politics, as in poker, the way to meet scandalous charges is to 'call'em and raise em'. If you are denounced as a fool, call your opponent a damned fool; if he says you are a crook, call him a robber; if he intimates that you are careless with the truth, tell your audience that he is a pathological liar.

Strategies for dealing with attacks from opponents are largely based on the belief prevalent among politicians that "negatives" influence voters more strongly than do "positives." The common wisdom is that no politician can afford to allow a charge or criticism to go unanswered. And the best defense is usually a good offense. One consequence of these beliefs has been a steady increase in the use of negative advertising in American politics. *See also: NEGATIVE ADVERTISING*

CAMPAIGN STRATEGY the planning of campaign operations for the purpose of achieving victory or avoiding defeat. A great deal of campaign strategy is improvisation based on a situational assessment of the unique conditions that prevail in each campaign. Campaigns react and adapt to the issues that emerge, the strengths and weaknesses of opponents, the verdict of polls, the facts of incumbency and registration, the availability of money, and so on.

Yet beyond the day to day calculations that shape strategy, there are some widely held beliefs that also influence campaign thinking and planning. Some of these derive from the insights of voting behavior research. The maxim that campaigns should mainly "reinforce" partisans and "activate" latent supporters is an example.

Other traditional campaign strategies come from intellectuals who specialize in politics. The precept that politicans should take a middle of the road position on most issues—because most voters are moderates—was established by political scientists Richard Scammon and Ben Wattenberg (1972). And writer-analyst Kevin Phillips (1969) set forth the now familiar premise that the Republican Party could build a electoral majority by appealing to southern and western conservatives.

Still other strategies used in campaigns are simply blends of conventional political wisdom and practical political experience. The adage that tickets should be balanced to represent important groups in the electorate—or that candidates should never mention the name of a less well known opponent—or that minority party candidates should not refer to their party affiliation—are all examples of those political strategies that get passed from politician to politician and campaign to campaign as long as they seem to work. *See also: ENCLAVE STRATEGY; MOMENTUM; NORMAL VOTE; PEAKING; POSITIONING; REPRESENTATIVE RACE; UNCERTAINTY*

CEMETERY VOTE a fraudulent vote cast in the name of a deceased voter. Cemetery votes were a staple item for the old political machines who reportedly voted entire graveyards when circumstances dictated the need to do so. Modern registration procedures and ballot security measures have reduced, but not eliminated this form of vote stealing.

There are probably more old political stories about cemetery voting than about any other kind of voting fraud. One of the best of them is told by Warren Moscow in POLITICS IN THE EMPIRE STATE. Moscow quotes an early New York state politician who is describing his philosophy about cemetery voting:

> We never vote a man unless he would have voted our way if he were still alive. We respect a man's convictions.

Republican Senator John Heinz of Pennsylvania may have enunciated the definitive strategy for candidates facing the prospects of a heavy and unfavorable cemetery vote. Up against an entrenched Philadelphia Democratic organization in 1976, Heinz was asked how he planned to hold down the opposition's vote. The Senator replied that his campaign planned to pave over the city's cemeteries before election day. *See also: VOTING FRAUD*

CHAIN BALLOT a voting fraud that can be perpetrated when paper ballots are in use. Known also as the "tasmanian dodge," a chain ballot is started by a corrupt party or campaign supporter who first gets an unused ballot, marks it for his candidate or slate, and then passes it to a voter.

That voter then gets his own ballot from election officials and goes into the voting booth. Once inside, the voter exchanges his own unmarked ballot for the already marked ballot and deposits the latter in the ballot box. The voter then returns his own unused ballot to the corrupt supporter to prove that a fraudulent vote was actually cast.

The payoff is usually money, although it can be alcohol, groceries or even future favors. The chain starts again after the corrupt supporter marks the new ballot and gives it to another voter. Vote buyers usually start the day with a large supply of unmarked ballots so that several chains can be operated simultaneously.

In practice, it is difficult to operate a chain ballot without the knowledge and connivance of officials stationed at the polls on election day. Several ballot security measures guard against this type of a voting fraud. Probably the most effective of these is a numbered stub system which permits the ballots cast to be compared to the detached stubs maintained by election officials. The widespread substitution of voting machines for paper ballots has sharply reduced the opportunity for this kind of voting fraud. *See also: BALLOT BOX STUFFING; VOTE BUYING; VOTING FRAUD*

CHLOROFORMING a metaphor for an assortment of political ploys and techniques designed to suppress the turnout of an opponent's likely voters. Chloroforming is intended to confuse and bewilder an opponent's supporters so that they fail to vote.

As a tactic it is distinguished from most others in its emphasis on reducing overall voter participation rather than increasing it. It is based on the belief that committed persons rarely switch allegiance from one candidate to the other—but they will switch from committed to non-voter status if they are heavily cross pressured.

Chloroforming strategies attempt to create the cross pressures that will raise doubts about a favored candidate. For example a direct mail piece impugning the honesty or character of an opponent might be sent to his or her supporters a few days before the election. Often these efforts are highly targeted so that one's own supporters are not exposed to a campaign message that could create a backlash. *See also: NEGATIVE ADVERTISING*

CLUSTER TARGETING *See GEODEMOGRAPHICS*

CONNECTIONS knowing personally or having access to governmental decision makers. Connections are links between political power on the one hand and those who would do business with government on the other—between someone inside government and someone outside government.

Connections have always been important in doing business in the public sector. Those having them can command the attention of government officials and can often expect an inside track for business opportunities. The connected become so in two main ways—by making campaign contributions that open up access, and through personal political activity that increases influence and visibility.

Connections shade the greyer area of public morality. When they are used merely to gain access to an official they are probably both legal and ethical. If they provide honest graft they are still legal but may not be ethical. And when connections lead into clearly dishonest and unlawful schemes they are both illegal and unethical. *See also: ACCESS, HONEST GRAFT*

CROSSFILING an electoral practice under which a candidate may file nominating petitions for both the Democratic and Republican primaries. Crossfiling is defended as a means of increasing the quality and quantity of choices available to voters in party primaries. Critics of crossfiling—and there are many—argue that it confuses voters and weakens the already feeble political parties.

California allowed crossfiling for 45 years until 1959. Candidates there could file in both parties, however, voters could vote only in their own party primary. When candidates won both primaries—which was not unusual—they would normally be unopposed in the fall general election.

Today the New York State Conservative and Liberal Parties permit crossfiling. Usually Democratic candidates crossfile for the Liberal Party primary and Republican candidates crossfile for the Conservative Party primary. In the Fall general election the Democratic nominee will be listed on the Liberal Party line and the Republican nominee will be listed on the Conservative Party line. The practice has given New York's third parties more influence in state politics than is usual.

Several states permit crossfiling for judicial offices as a means to reduce the influence of partisan politics on the courts. The device seems mainly to confuse voters and chagrin politicians. In a recent Pennsylvania appellate court election a Democrat won the Republican nomination while a Republican won the Democratic nomination. In the subsequent general election the Republican judge ran as a Democrat while the Democratic judge ran as a Republican. *See also: FILING; FUSION TICKET*

CUMULATIVE VOTING an electoral system which allots two or more votes to each voter, who may then distribute them among several candidates or cast them all for a single candidate. Cumulative voting is not widely used. There are scattered examples in Europe but in the United States only Illinois has adopted this form of voting.

In that state three members of the lower house are elected from each legislative district and each voter is given three votes. These may be allocated according to that voter's preferences. For example all three could be cast for a single candidate, or one and one half each could be cast for two candidates or one vote each could be cast for three candidates. Other combinations of votes are also possible.

Cumulative voting permits third parties to gain some legislative represention. It allows their members to concentrate all of their votes on one candidate while major party supporters are spreading their votes among many candidates. But this system of voting can only be used in multimember districts from which more than one legislator is chosen. Since most elections in the United States are from single member districts, cumulative voting is unlikely to ever be an important feature of the American electoral system. *See also: BULLET VOTING; PROPORTIONAL REPRESENTATION*

CUTTING the practice of surreptitiously working against a candidate of one's own party—especially on election day. Cutting is usually carried out by local ward and precinct leaders who publicly support candidates while privately opposing them.

Candidates are cut for a number of reasons: intra-party rivalry; personal animosities; conflicting political alliances; and in return for the payment of street money.

Party leaders cut candidates by both omission and commision. The former category includes failure to pass out a candidate's slate card at the polls or refusal to allow a candidate's literature to be prominently displayed. Commission includes active discouragement of voting for the candidate and overt solicitation for a rival candidate.

Cutting is more common and more consequential in low level, low visibility races where voters tend to look to local political leaders for guidance before voting. The practice is easy to discover if there are only a few pockets within a jurisdiction that fail to support party or endorsed candidates. It is more difficult to detect when it is widespread. *See also: ELECTION DAY ACTIVITIES; STREET MONEY*

DIRTY TRICKS illegal, unethical or unfair tactics used to win a political campaign. Dirty tricks include a long list of sabotage and intrigue. Traditionally some dirty tricks have been viewed as less serious than others.

Among the minor dirty tricks are such ruses as sending hecklers to opponent's speeches, tearing down opponent's signs, and dumping opponent's literature. More serious dirty tricks involve running whispering campaigns against opponents, making last minute smears or undocumented charges, and disrupting press conferences or other media events.

The most serious dirty tricks include trading in documents stolen from an opponent, campaign espionage such as electronic bugging and eavesdropping, and actually placing a campaign spy in the other side's camp. Voting fraud is also properly classified as a dirty trick.

In years past there was an almost cavalier attitude about dirty tricks and their performers. Both were looked upon as not very important. The legendary purveyor of dirty tricks was one Dick Tuck, an amusing figure who haunted the Goldwater and Nixon campaigns in the 1960's. Most of Tuck's tricks were pixyish—as were the antics of many others in that era.

Watergate, with its revelations of systematic spying, sabotage, and blatant lawlessness altered public perceptions of the gravity of dirty tricks. Today the press takes them seriously and so do most politicians. *See also: BOOTLEG; CAMPAIGN SPY; FAIR CAMPAIGN PRACTICES; ROORBACK*

DOUBLE RIDING making contributions to both candidates in the same race. Double riding or double giving is a common practice among PAC's and some wealthy individual donors.

According to the public interest group Common Cause, some 91 PAC's were double riders in 1984 just in U.S. Senate races. At least 35 of these PAC's contributed to both sides in an Illinois race, another 26 gave to both in an Iowa race and 21 supported both candidates in a Kentucky race. No comparable figures are available for individual contributors, however the incidence of double giving from private citizens is probably substantial.

Double riding does not necessarily mean that competing campaigns receive the same amount. Wide differences are not unusual. For example in the U.S. Senate races mentioned above, one PAC gave $7500 to the Republican candidate, but only $250 to the Democrat. In the same contest another PAC gave only $1500 to the Republican, but $5000 to the Democrat.

Double riding is a form of handicapping—a process in which large contributors systematically determine where to allocate their campaign contributions. Handicapping is calculating the odds before the horse race is over. Double riding on the other hand is a hedge bet that covers all the possibilities. Regardless of who wins the election the double rider is assured of some future access. *See also: HANDICAPPING; HELP THE HEALTHY AND SHOOT THE SICK; PAC'S*

ELECTABILITY the real prospects that a candidate will be successful. Electable candidates are those who have the qualities needed to actually win the election. Unelectable candidates are those who have one or more deficiencies that mar their electoral chances.

Without the perception that a candidate is electable there is almost no way a campaign can attract any substantial amount of early support, contributions or press coverage. Fund raising is especially sensitive to expectations about a candidate's ability to win. Serious givers are very influenced by the likelihood of victory.

Sometimes major party candidates try to promote their electability as a tactic to undermine their primary election opponents. Gary Hart did this in 1984 when he claimed that he had more support than Walter Mondale with those voter groups needed to defeat Ronald Reagan. The strategy didn't work for Hart as it hadn't worked for earlier presidential candidates who tried it like Nelson Rockefeller (1968), Edmund Muskie (1972), Henry Jackson (1980) and George Bush (1980).

Voters are apparently less swayed by a candidate's chances than are large contributors or professional politicians. Most voters do not make their decisions on the basis of which candidate seems most likely to win in November. Electability arguments may stir professional politicians and other political insiders but it probably doesn't influence the rank and file voter.

See also: BANDWAGON EFFECT; EARLY MONEY

ELECTORAL COLLEGE STRATEGY *See BATTLEGROUND STATES*

ELEVENTH COMMANDMENT the political maxim that Republicans ought to eschew public criticism of other Republicans. According to the eleventh commandment Republicans running against each other in primaries should confine their campaigning to issues while avoiding personal attacks on their fellow party members.

While the eleventh commandment is often associated with Republicans it actually embodies an attitude that is prevalent among both Democrats and Republicans. Professional politicians in both parties work to keep intraparty strife low. The theory is that fractious primary contests lead to general election defeats. These conflicts weaken the party and leave a residue of bitterness that makes it difficult to bring about unity for the fall campaign. Whether this conventional wisdom bears out seems to depend on the particular circumstances of a given nomination fight. In presidential politics, protracted intense primary battles did not prevent John Kennedy (1960) or Jimmy Carter (1976) from winning the general election. On the other hand many observers believe that primary struggles doomed Hubert Humphrey (1968) and George McGovern (1972)—while contributing to the losses of Gerald Ford (1976) and Walter Mondale (1984).

Contested primaries also have a mixed legacy in state and local elections. Established, well known candidates forced to put on expensive hard fought campaigns are usually much the worse for the experience—even when they win. Money is spent that will not be available for the general election, issues are raised that the Fall opponent might later exploit, and potential support is lost because of hurt feelings among followers of defeated candidate(s).

But for candidates not so established or well known, the consequences of a tough primary can be quite different. Candidates with low name recognition, little political experience, or weak support, can actually increase their general election chances as a result of a hard primary. If they win they almost certainly will have become better known and more skilled as campaigners. Their ability to raise money, attract volunteers, and command credibility can all be enhanced by the primary exposure.

ENCLAVE STRATEGY campaigning only in safe and controlled surroundings. Enclave strategies are adopted by campaigns which want to avoid serious gaffes while insuring that news coverage is restricted to media events that present the candidate in a positive light. Enclave strategies used by sitting presidents are referred to as "rose garden strategies"—after the practices of several presidents of combining official White House duties with unofficial campaigning.

President Gerald Ford was probably the first to adopt a rose garden strategy so elaborate that it became itself an issue. Ford's approach involved remaining in the White House for much of the campaign—attracting wide and favorable media coverage for bill signings, routine meetings with foreign leaders, and other White House ceremonies.

Incumbent President Carter followed Ford's example by limiting most of his campaigning to White House functions. Carter's campaign posture was based on repeated statements that he was too busy managing the Iranian crisis to leave the White House. Incumbent President Reagan adopted similar tactics—campaigning mostly in friendly territory before enthusiastic supporters.

All modern presidents since John Kennedy have used some kind of enclave strategy—and for some good reasons. Americans may or may not like any given president, but they love the presidency. Voters respond positively to the symbolism and traditions associated with the office, and they prefer to see their presidents acting presidential rather than partisan.

The White House or similar enclave offers an ideal backdrop for doing this. White House ceremonies and news coverage of official presidential actions dramatize the fact of incumbency and project the image of a strong competent leader. All of this is achieved without much chance of a major mistake that might be exploited by an opponent. Incumbent presidents are understandably loath to give up these advantages for the risk and uncertainty of campaigning is less favorable environments. *See also: CAMPAIGN STRATEGY*

FREE RIDE an opportunity to run for higher office without giving up the office one now holds. Free rides allow politicians to take their next career step without risking their present office.

The American electoral system is stacked against free rides. Some jurisdictions actually prohibit them by requiring an incumbent to resign before running for another office. Even where they are allowed they are unusual because an incumbent must have a term that overlaps the term of the higher office.

Free rides do occur however under certain circumstances. U.S. Senators can get free rides in running for national office if their term doesn't end in the same year as the presidential term. Governors sometimes get free rides in running for the U.S. Senate when a senate seat comes up during their gubernatorial term. And state legislators and local officials can get free rides when the office they seek has a different term than the office they hold.

There are some other relatively rare, but nonetheless important sources of free rides. The best known of these are special elections in which vacancies are filled between regular terms. Incumbents of other offices can usually compete in these without giving up their own office. Free rides are also available in those states where election law allows a candidate to run for two offices in the same election. This practice is known as "simultaneous elections."

Some states which sanction simultaneous elections also allow what is known as "simultaneous offices"—or holding more than one office at a time. In New Jersey for example it is possible for an office holder to be both an elected local official and a state legislator. *See also: SPECIAL ELECTION*

FUSION TICKET a joint election slate produced by two seperate political parties, both of whom nominate the same candidates. Each party holds its own line on the ballot, and the candidates nominated appear on both ballots.

Fusion tickets are unusual but not unheard of in American politics. Occasionally they have been used in municipal elections by out parties trying to oust an entrenched in party. They have also been used by third parties trying to increase their bargaining leverage with majority parties.

The best current example of a fusion ticket is the practice of New York state's Liberal Party and Conservative Party. Both of these third parties regularly run fusion tickets with Democratic and Republican parties respectively.

New York state election law permits third parties to nominate candidates who are also nominated by one of the major parties. Most other states however have regulations which prohibit fusion tickets. These "anti-fusion laws" forbid a candidate's name to appear on more than one line of the ballot.

Some states also have "anti-raiding laws" which compel candidates to belong to the party that nominates them. Anti- fusion and anti-raiding statutes are part of a pervasive system of obstacles and restrictions faced by American third parties. *See also: CROSSFILING; FILING; RAIDING; THIRD PARTIES*

GENERATED MAIL postcards, letters, and telegraphs sent to elected officials as part of an organized campaign to influence legislation or policy. Generated mail is usually orchestrated by a PAC or other organized interest group.

The availability of high speed printers and other sophisticated direct mail technologies has substantially increased the amount of this stuff that is delivered—and probably substantially decreased its influence. Politicians as a rule take their mail from constituents seriously, but they tend to discount much of the generated mail they receive. *See also: DIRECT MAIL*

GEODEMOGRAPHICS a sophisticated approach to voter targeting that uses census data, public opinion research and marketing research to locate those voter blocks that are most likely to support a candidate or issue. Geodemographics, or cluster targeting as it is also called, is generally used with polling data. The poll identifies favorable voters by demographic grouping (age, income, education, etc.). The geodemographic analysis indicates where those voters live. The principle of geodemographics is that people who live in a similar cluster tend to vote and behave the same way.

The most widely known geodemographic system is the Claritas system. It allocates voters into one of 40 lifestyle clusters—each made up of neighborhood or "block groups" of people that have similar backgrounds and lifestyles. For example, cluster 27 is made up of upper class mobile managers with older children, and cluster 6 is made up of poor, grade school educated racially mixed rural neighborhoods. Once polling data indicates that cluster 6 or 27 is important, geodemographic analysis helps to locate those clusters in the electorate.

Geodemographics is sometimes distinguished from psychodemographics although in practice the two are used together. Occupation is a geodemographic variable, but hobbies and leisure are psychodemographic. Income is a geodemographic variable, but disposable income patterns are psychodemographic. Geodemographic targeting supports such campaign activities as canvassing, direct mail, and telephone banks. *See also: POLLS; TARGETING*

GOTV an acronym for "get out the vote" activities and other campaign strategies aimed at increasing voter turnout. GOTV is an election day activity which is often planned weeks or months in advance.

Its objective is to get favorable voters to the polls. In the modern campaign, GOTV is likely to be organized around a telephone bank operation or door-to-door canvassing effort—perhaps supplemented with direct mail, a literature drop or even radio and television appeals.

Traditionally, the Democratic party has put more emphasis on GOTV than has the Republican. This is because control of turnout is critical to the Democrats whose partisan supporters tend to vote at a lower rate than do Republicans. *See also: ELECTION DAY ACTIVITIES; VOTER CONTACT*

HELP THE HEALTHY AND SHOOT THE SICK a kind of political euthanasia practiced by many large campaign contributors who habitually favor incumbents over challengers and stronger candidates over weaker ones. PAC's (Political Action Committees) are especially noted for their inclination for giving generously to incumbents and likely winners—regardless of party affiliation or ideological leaning.

The usual explanation for this is that large contributors intend to invest in future access. Incumbents in particular are more likely to be there when that access is needed. Recently, in fact PAC's have begun to handicap political races in order to target their contributions to those campaigns in which they will have the most impact. *See also: HANDICAPPING; INCUMBENTS; PAC'S*

HIT LIST incumbent politicians targeted for defeat and removal from office. Hit lists in some form are probably as old as organized politics. Since about 1980 many PAC's have formalized this old political tradition by targeting their opponents with sophisticated campaigns of direct mail and slick expensive media.

The so-called ideological PAC's like NCPAC have been especially enthusiastic users of hit lists. Who is and who isn't on the major hit lists is usually a popular topic among political insiders. The actual electoral consequences of hit lists is unclear; however, there is evidence that they can create a sympathy backlash for their intended victims. *See also: NCPAC; NON-CONNECTED PAC'S*

INCUMBENTS someone who already holds an elective office. Incumbents who run for reelection have some impressive advantages. They are almost always better known to voters than are their challengers. Their name recognition scores are often twice or more the level of their opponents. Incumbents are also generally more experienced campaigners and they usually find it easier to raise money. PAC's and other large contributors heavily support incumbents regardless of party.

Then too incumbents receive some office perks which can significantly aid their reelection campaigns. These include a paid office staff, office space, travel expenses, printing facilities and (for congressmen) the franking privilege. Finally incumbents command media attention because they are public figures carrying out public business. Their free media exposure is almost always more than any challenger is able to attract.

These substantial advantages produce victory for most incumbents who run for reelection. For example in the 1984 primaries, no incumbent governor or U.S. Senator lost and only three U.S. House members failed to win (and two of these were in their first term). General elections reveal similar patterns. Over 90% of U.S. House incumbents who run are reelected.

In fact some political scientists believe that incumbency has replaced party loyalty as a voting cue. Voters no longer automatically vote for a particular party's candidate, but instead search the ballot for the name of a familiar incumbent.

Incumbency of course can have some drawbacks. Incumbents acquire records they are obliged to defend and popularity can wane over time, particularly if a politician is forced to make difficult decisions or is involved in controversial issues. *See also: INS AND OUTS; MARGINALS; OPEN SEAT*

INSIDE STRATEGY a reference to political tactics that concentrate on securing support from party leaders and gaining control of party machinery, rather than appealing directly to rank and file voters. Before the mass media and the direct primary become such a dominant influence in politics, an inside strategy was used by most aspiring presidential candidates.

A candidate would work to achieve the support and endorsement of major party leaders and elected officials with the expectation that if this were successful the sought for nomination could be delivered by these insiders. Today not all candidates adopt inside strategies. Since the mid 1960's several major presidential candidates have employed a predominately "outside strategy"—a campaign based on direct appeal to rank and file voters, grass roots organizations, running and winning in primary and caucus contests, and climbing steadily in the public opinion polls.

There are several contemporary examples of both types of strategy in presidential nomination politics: Barry Goldwater in 1964, Hubert Humphrey in 1968, Gerald Ford in 1976, and Walter Mondale in 1984 all used inside strategies; Eugene McCarthy in 1968, George McGovern in 1972, Jimmy Carter in 1976, and Gary Hart in 1984 all used outside strategies. *See also: DELIVERING; ENDORSEMENT*

KNIFING *See CUTTING*

LEAST OBJECTIONABLE POLITICIAN (LOP) a phrase coined by media consultant Tony Schwartz (1973) to characterize the strategy of making a candidate into the least objectionable politician (LOP) in the race.

The LOP is really an analogue for the theory in television known as least objectionable programming. According to it, audiences watch the least objectionable program on television rather than seek out a specific preferred program. And they will continue to watch a station as long as they are satisfied with the least objectionable programming on it. But if a program comes on that is controversial or otherwise objectionable, the audience will switch to another station.

The LOP notion in politics is essentially negative. It assumes that as a class politicians are disparaged by the public and associated with other social pariahs like (according to Schwartz) salesmen, landlords, tax collectors, and meter maids. Given this public attitude, a positive campaign won't work so the best strategy is to depict a candidate as the best of the worst—i.e., the least objectionable politician in the race. *See also: NEGATIVE ADVERTISING*

LOCKS registered voters who can be reliably counted on to support a candidate or faction within a political party. Local political organizations sometimes hold down registration and turnout in party primaries to their loyal partisans or locks. They do so in order to maintain control over the nomination process. Tom Bucci, a Bridgeport, Connecticut politician, described the tactic to the WASHINGTON POST (Haynes Johnson, 1984):

> The history was to keep the enrollment down to those individuals you knew, your so-called 'locks' . . . the people you've got a lock on. That was the old traditional . . . politics for a generation or two: keep the rolls limited to individuals you can pick up on the phone and call. It was a closed political system. If you keep control over those on the voting rolls, you don't have to worry about control of the party.

This kind of strategy encourages political parties to restrict access to registration and to promote low turnout in primary elections. It also can create a dilemma for the general election—particularly in competitive two-party systems—when every vote may be needed to win. *See also: LOW TURNOUT STRATEGY; REGISTRATION; TURNOUT*

LOW TURNOUT STRATEGY a political tactic which encourages low voter turnout in order to control the outcome of primary elections. Traditionally, political machines used low turnouts to get those voters to the polls who could be depended upon to vote the party's slate of endorsed candidates. The principle behind this strategy is that a political organization can influence party regulars through the use of patronage and other incentives. But the party may lose control of the election if the turnout increases to include people who are beyond party domination.

Today, primary elections usually record low turnouts. This is, however, due more to voter apathy than to manipulation by party organizations. Nevertheless, low turnouts in primaries do increase the chances that the party endorsed slate of candidates will win nomination. *See also: CHLOROFORMING; LOCKS; SLATING*

MOMENTUM the increasing pace and movement of a political campaign—reflected in added press coverage, rising support in the polls, and growing fund raising success. Momentum—or big mo—is a major objective in many campaigns. Campaigns said to have momentum are catching on and gaining support with the electorate. A candidate may be behind in the polls, but if he appears to be moving up, he has momentum.

Campaigns build momentum through carefully planned and skillfully executed increments in campaign activities. In the physical world momentum is the product of mass and velocity. In politics that mass is the growing presence of the campaign reflected in campaign events, fund raising, press coverage, candidate scheduling and political advertising. Velocity is the increasing tempo of these campaign functions—more events, more advertising, more candidate appearances, and so on.

Many political professionals believe momentum is the key to a successful campaign. A good deal of strategy is based on the notion that a campaign should build and sustain momentum which peaks on election day. Losing campaigns in fact are often described as never having generated momentum or having peaked too soon because of poorly timed momentum. *See also: CAMPAIGN STRATEGY; DECOMPRESSION; PEAKING*

OCTOBER SURPRISE any last minute strategy, issue or event that can change the basic direction of a campaign and alter its outcome. October surprises were originally dramatic and unexpected actions by an incumbent president. The phrase now is loosely applied to any late action that might increase support or build momentum for a candidate.

Incumbents generally have more opportunity to control events than do challengers. And candidates who are behind are usually more interested in surprises than are candidates who are ahead. Naturally enough then it is usually incumbents who are behind who hint mysteriously about October surprises to come—while challengers who are ahead become most anxious about them actually occurring.

Expectation of an October surprise is prevalent in campaigns. Nevertheless, most end without ever seeing one. In fact a standard rejoinder that comes out of many losing campaigns is this one liner:

> The October surprise in this campaign was that there was no October Surprise.

Despite the scarcity of the real thing, the anticipation grows as election day nears. In 1976, Democrats were convinced that incumbent President Ford would undertake some bold foreign policy initiative to capture public attention. And in 1980 Republicans were just as sure that incumbent President Jimmy Carter would use the Iranian situation to improve his election prospects. Neither did and both lost. *See also: MOMENTUM*

OUTSIDE STRATEGY *See INSIDE STRATEGY*

PEAKING finishing a political campaign strongly—in a climaxing crescendo of support and energy. Peaking is a strategy that emphasizes the importance of generating a steady momentum which gradually increases until election day.

Peaking is based on two related ideas. The first is the notion that campaigns should start slowly, gradually building momentum as they go on. The second idea is that elections are ephemeral events in the lives of most voters. Since the electorate's attention is temporary, campaigns should focus their impact in that brief period toward the end of the campaign when most voters are paying attention.

Sometimes campaigns are said to have peaked too soon. These are campaigns in which voter support reached its maximum, but then declined before election day.

Other campaigns are described as never peaking or late peaking. These are campaigns for which voter support never achieved its maximum before election day.

Early peaking is a particular danger in campaigns which overexpose the candidate or which receive too much media attention long before election day. Late peaking is a hazard in campaigns which begin too slowly or have trouble attracting media attention. *See also: ELECTION DAY ACTIVITIES; MOMENTUM*

PIPS the acronym for what is more formally known as the "precinct information priority system." PIPS is a relatively sophisticated approach to targeting. It combines hard numbers and other data with political judgement—in order to establish priorities among precincts for use in scheduling, fund raising and other campaign planning.

Four steps are necessary to construct a PIPS. First those voter characteristics that will influence the voting outcome should be listed. These vary but might include party registration, turnout history, incidence of ticket splitters, income levels, and ethnic patterns.

After these characteristics have been identified the second step is to assign a weight to each characteristic (say 1–5) depending on how relatively important that factor is expected to be to the voting outcome. For example if turnout was considered very important, a history of high turnouts could be given a five weight.

The third step is to go through every precinct in the voting jurisdiction and calculate a PIPS score for each by adding all the weights together (computers can do this very efficiently).

The final step is ranking of each precinct according to the combined score it accumulates on all the weights. This done, strategists can easily ascertain the relative importance of any precinct when called upon to make decisions about the allocation of campaign resources. *See also: TARGETING*

POLITICAL BASE the hard core support in votes and resources that a politician has built up and may count upon. Political base is usually the home turf election district or other geographic area.

Sometimes though a politician's base is perceived to be ideologic or even ethnic. Among contemporary politicians Ronald Reagan's base is said to be in the conservative wing of the Republican Party. Jesse Jackson's base is in the black electorate; Walter Mondale had his base in the traditional labor liberal coalition of the Democratic Party.

Local and state candidates might have their bases in particular geographic areas such as Northern New Jersey, Southern California, Eastern Washington or Western Pennsylvania. Ethnic groups—Poles, Irish, Italians, Hispanics, are also political bases for some candidates.

Politicians employ their bases in two ways. One use is shoring up for reelection. A healthy base might provide an incumbent with one-third or more of the votes needed on election day.

The other major use of the political base is running for higher office. Here the base becomes a launching pad—solid and reliable and something that can be counted on in the new political wars. Strong political bases also give ambitious politicians some additional credibility and legitimacy. Since they already represent one important political group, they are entitled to be heard and taken seriously in a quest for higher office. *See also: CONSTITUENCY; SLACK*

POLITICAL JUDGEMENT shrewd, sound and balanced understanding of the political world based on knowledge and experience. Political judgement is the capacity to evaluate situations critically and respond appropriately.

Political judgement is a mark of stature and achievement among professional politicians. Someone who has it should be taken seriously, listened to, sought out for advice and always included in planning strategy. Anyone without it is an amateur, non-political, a technician and maybe a lightweight.

Politicians themselves can't always describe exactly what political judgement is but they will claim always to recognize it. Political consultant Beatrice Kay put it this way:

> Political judgement comes from understanding politics, in trusting hunches, and in developing an intuitiveness based on correct interpretation of words, actions, deeds, and events in politics. (Kay, 1981:47)

The test of political judgement is the ability to coolly appraise unfolding events, correctly interpret what they mean and then act effectively under pressure. Politicians who can do this rise quickly and have long careers. Those who cannot remain low level hangers-on or even drop out of politics altogether.

POSITIONING a now classic electoral strategy. Positioning is based on work first done in commercial advertising and in marketing. The essential idea as applied in politics is that candidates should be marketed by first finding out in a poll what voters already think and believe. Then a candidate can be advantageously positioned among his opponents by tapping into the feelings and attitudes voters already hold.

In short, positioning discovers through polling what voters already believe about a candidate. It then develops a political advertising campaign built around those existing beliefs. Most important, positioning doesn't attempt to create an image. Instead it trys to evoke feelings by working with the existing images.

Gerald Rafshoon, media advisor to former President Jimmy Carter was one of the early proponents of positioning. However, many other media specialists have been influenced by it.

Recently pollsters have developed a research tool known as the "Kelly Grid." With the Kelly, pollsters can determine what qualities voters use to evaluate politicians. After these have been determined, individual candidates can be measured on each of them and then compared with opponents. Once a candidate's position has been carefully located in relation to all opponents a positioning strategy can be developed. *See also: CAMPAIGN STRATEGY; CANDIDATE IMAGE*

POWER BASE *See POLITICAL BASE*

PROXY CANDIDATE a stand in for another candidate who will later run for office in his own right. Proxy candidates provide the rare but interesting situation in which a would be candidate allows or requests someone to occupy their position on the ballot.

Usually this happens when the would be candidate fails to qualify for the official ballot for one reason or another—perhaps they are out of the jurisdiction, hesitant about running, or simply late to file. A proxy candidate then files in their place with the intention of resigning from the ballot before the general election.

Election laws in many places give tacit approval to proxy candidates by authorizing party officials to replace candidates who leave the ballot between primary and general elections. Nevertheless the practice is apparently not widespread. *See also: BALLOT ACCESS; CANDIDATE; FILING*

PSYCHO DEMOGRAPHICS *See GEODEMOGRAPHICS*

RAIDING the tactic of voting in another party's primary election in order to nominate a weak opponent for the general election. Raiding is a form of crossover voting in which voters of one party will participate in the primary of another party and then cross back over to their own party for the general election. The practice is very difficult to document and so there is some considerable differences of opinion about how common it is.

The possibility of raiding is frequently raised as an argument against the open primary. Critics charge that the open primary makes a party vulnerable to crossover voting and raids. The whole issue is largely theoretical because there is very little empirical research on the behavior of voters in open primary states. It seems likely however that voters who do crossover to vote in opposition party primaries are more motivated by the lack of a contest in their own primary—or by an attraction to a candidate of the other party—than they are by a desire to raid the other party. *See also: CROSSOVERS; OPEN PRIMARY*

REPRESENTATIVE RACE a previous election which is believed to be similar in important respects to a current or upcoming campaign. Representative races match the races with which they are compared on as many strategic factors as possible. The theory is that the earlier electoral experience provides the current campaign with the opportunity to assess their strengths and weaknesses.

The representative race might simply be the previous election if the candidate was either an incumbent or challenger in that contest. On the other hand the representativeness criterion might suggest a totally different office in another jurisdiction. For example a white Jewish female non-incumbent running for a state legislative slot might have to look well outside her district for a similar race.

Representative races are never exactly the same as the current race. No two elections are perfectly comparable—not even when both candidates are the same. Conditions change, voters enter and leave the electorate, issues ebb and flow. Still a carefully chosen representative race can provide solid insight into the opportunities and pitfalls that lie ahead. *See also: BASE RACE; NORMAL VOTE*

RIFLE SHOOTING *See DIRECT MAIL*

ROORBACK any false charge, slander, slur, or smear made during a political campaign. Roorbacks are vicious and untrue attacks on the integrity or reputation of a candidate—especially those made so late in a campaign they cannot be refuted.

Roorbacks are named after one "Baron Roorback" who appropriately enough never himself existed. The fictional Baron was invented by the enemies of presidenial candidate James Polk in 1844. Roorback's name was signed to published excerpts from a bogus manuscript titled, ROORBACK'S TOUR THROUGH THE WESTERN AND SOUTHERN STATES IN 1836. The counterfeit material viciously maligned Polk who nevertheless went on to win the presidency.

The term roorback is still used although it has become archaic. It may survive because it doesn't have many good synonyms. For some obscure reason the American political lexicon does not include a lot of terms for campaign lies or smears.

Perhaps this is because modern political mudslinging is mild compared to what it used to be. Past candidates including presidential nominees have been regularly referred to as buffoons, liars, cheats and crooks—and regularly accused of being drunkards, adulterers, swindlers, and tyrants.

Today such abuse is not unknown, but it tends to be relatively tame. Television more than any other influence is probably responsible for elevating the level of contemporary invective. TV makes personal attacks seem harsh or petty and politicians tend to avoid them for fear of backlash. Then too the speed of modern communications technology makes it difficult as well as dangerous to spread lies about an opponent. *See also: DIRTY TRICKS; FAIR CAMPAIGN PRACTICES*

SHORT COUNTING a voting fraud in which election judges or vote tellers purposely miscount the vote. Short counting happens after the polls close. The scam has two basic variations.

In one version crooked election judges call the votes inaccurately as they read them to vote tellers whose job it is to tally the votes. The other version of the fraud features the vote tellers themselves recording phoney votes even though election judges have read them off correctly.

Election districts with histories of voting irregularities may employ poll watchers to detect short counting as well as other types of voting fraud. Before actual counting begins one poll watcher positions himself behind the election judge who opens the voting machine or ballot box. Another poll watcher sits with the vote teller. The first poll watcher then makes certain the votes are called out honestly, while the second sees that they are recorded accurately.

Short counting is a serious problem in some places. When it occurs it can be more of a threat to the integrity of the election process than other dishonest practices like ballot box stuffing or vote buying. Unlike these frauds which require votes to be stolen one by one, short counting allows gross cheating that may involve hundreds or even thousands of votes. *See also: ELECTION JUDGES; POLL WATCHERS; VOTING FRAUD*

SIMULTANEOUS ELECTIONS *See FREE RIDE*

SIMULTANEOUS OFFICE *See FREE RIDE*

SLING SHOOTING *See BULLET VOTING*

SMEAR *See ROORBACK*

SWIMMING UPSTREAM starting behind in a political contest because of some built in disadvantage. Swimming upstream often describes candidates who run against heavy registration odds.

For example in Pennsylvania, Republican statewide candidates always swim upstream because Democrats have a voter registration edge of about one million. But in Indiana it is the Democrats who swim upstream because Republicans outnumber them by about a half million voters.

Swimming upstream is also a popular sport for challengers who run against incumbents and for Independents or third party candidates who have major party opponents. Today in fact the prevalent campaign ethic among many large contributers is help the healthy and shoot the sick. These contributers habitually favor incumbents over challengers and stronger candidates over weaker ones. *See also: HANDICAPPING; HELP THE HEALTHY AND SHOOT THE SICK*

TARGETING establishing priorities for the allocation of campaign resources. Targeting is based on the principle that campaigns have limited time and money. Therefore candidate scheduling, media expenditures, voter contact projects and other campaign efforts should be concentrated in those areas likely to yield the largest number of favorable voters.

Two kinds of targeting are used in modern campaigns. One type—the oldest and most traditional—relies on voter history, registration, and turnout data to locate and mobilize supporters. This election data targeting can be used to identify those precincts or wards with the most Republican or Democratic registrants, the most ticket splitters, the most swing voters, and so on.

The other type of targeting used today, is known as geodemographics or cluster targeting. It combines census data, polling and marketing research to identify and locate those voters most likely to support a candidate. The survey data identifies favorable voters by demographic grouping (age, income, education, etc.) Then the census data indicates where these voters live.

Geodemographics differs from election data targeting in that it stresses the importance of demographic characteristics—while election data targeting is based on accumulated voting statistics. Both types of targeting are usually closely linked to a program of voter contact effort such as direct mail, canvassing, and telephone banks. *See also: GEODEMOGRAPHICS; PIPS; SCHEDULING*

TASMANIAN DODGE *See CHAIN BALLOT*

THEME a guiding idea, basic issue or main topic that ties the political campaign together. Themes are the central motifs or story lines that run through all campaign messages.

Campaigners often put a good deal of effort into developing the campaign theme. Strategists believe the theme should be established early and then worked into all political advertising speeches, press conferences and other campaign activities.

Themes are often translated into campaign "slogans." These are catchy phrases that are repeated over and over again during a campaign—in brochures on television and radio spots, and in other forms of political advertising.

Themes and slogans differ. Some examples make the distinction clear: "Jobs" or "Unemployment" is a theme: "He'll put us back to work again" is a slogan. "Integrity" is a theme; "A politician you can trust" is a slogan. "Experience and competence" is a theme; "The second toughest job in America" is a slogan.

The function of a slogan is to sum up the theme in an appealing phrase that voters will recognize and remember. Through repetition the slogan reinforces the theme and reminds voters what the candidate stands for and the campaign is about. *See also: POLITICAL ADVERTISING*

UNCERTAINTY the one certainty in almost every political campaign. Uncertainty is also a formal approach to problem solving and decision making that emphasizes the importance of knowing the real value of choices that can be made—and the probability that these values can actually be achieved.

A political campaign is faced with uncertainty, for example, if it must decide whether to spend its last $10,000. on a final "media blitz" or put it into election day activities. The problem is that no one really knows which choice will yield more votes.

Political scientist Gary Jacobson describes the nature of campaign uncertainty in his book, THE POLITICS OF CONGRESSIONAL ELECTIONS (1983: 61–62):

> . . . the central motif of almost every discussion of campaign strategy is uncertainty . . . . The effects of uncertainty about what works and what does not pervade campaign decision making . . . . Successful candidates are inclined to do what they did in the past; they must have done something right even if they cannot be sure what; a degree of superstition is understandable. Other candidates also follow tradition . . . (some things are used like) yard signs, bumper stickers, and campaign balloons . . . not so much because they have been shown to be effective but because everyone expects them and their absence would be noticed. . . .

Uncertainty prevails in campaigns not because campaigners lack knowledge or expertise. The tactics and strategies of campaigning are well known and widely used. But there is no certainty among political professionals that one thing will work better than another. Understandably, a favorite cliche among campaigners is that half the money spent in campaigns is wasted—the trouble is nobody knows which half. *See also: LAW OF MINIMAL CONSEQUENCES*

VOTE BUYING one of the most direct and least complicated forms of voting fraud. Vote buying along with ballot box stuffing, short counting, and chain ballots has always been a popular way to try to steal an election. Dick Simpson, a political scientist and political activist in Chicago, reviews some of the basics in WINNING ELECTIONS:

> Finally, there is the old tried and true method of vote stealing developed by such legendary politicians as Bathhouse John Coughlin and Hinky Dink Kenna. Simply buy the votes you need to win. Now buying votes is not as easy as it might appear—there is an art to it. In unguarded precincts a captain can just stand outside the door of the polling place and give money to voters on their way in or out. But a wiser captain will put the money in a matchbook and hand those to voters or slip the money to voters with a handshake which is harder to detect. A really good precinct captain disdains even these methods. Instead, he sets up an account at the pub, a cafe, or grocery. Then voters do not get cash but are given so much in groceries, drinks, or food. The only giveaway of this fraud is a steady stream of voters leaving the polling place and going directly to the pay-off place.

Despite the appeal of simplicity and long tradition, the practice of vote buying is probably in decline. It was always a high cost, labor intensive, and risky way of accumulating votes—a technique more suited to the "retail politics" of an earlier era than to the media centered, wholesale politics of today. As voting fraud evolves and adapts to modern politics, there will probably be fewer and fewer cases of traditional vote buying. *See also: CHAIN BALLOT; VOTING FRAUD*

WEATHER thought to be a factor in the outcome of some elections because of its influence on voter turnout. In earlier times, rainy weather was believed to favor Democratic candidates because it discouraged the Republican farm vote. Fair skies, on the other hand, were considered to be Republican weather because the rural vote would be more likely to come out.

Today weather is a factor of a different sort. In primary elections bad weather may mean a low turnout dominated by party activists. Party organization and well organized campaigns can dominate a low turnout primary because they are able to get out their own vote on election day. Good weather primary elections, however, often means that turnout will increase. This makes it more difficult for party leaders to control the outcome.

In general elections bad weather usually means that overall turnout will be lower than normal for both parties. And those who do vote are more likely to be strong supporters of a candidate or party. Good weather in general elections means higher overall turnout in both parties and a greater number of voters who are Independents or weak partisans. *See also: LOW TURNOUT STRATEGY; ELECTION DAY*

WHATSISNAME an expression popular with politicians ahead in the polls who do not want to directly mention their opponent's name. Candidates are often counseled to avoid publicizing their opponents. They are told to refrain from naming them in speeches, referring to them while answering questions or alluding to them in commericals. This advice is particularly emphasized when the opponent is far behind in the polls or not well known. The logic of whatsisname is that name identification in politics is a major factor in voter approval and electoral success. In many elections the candidate with the highest name identification will win the election simply because he or she is better known.

Beyond this, leading or incumbent candidates often won't mention their opponent's name because they believe doing so gives the opponent equal stature and credibility. Refusal to debate is sometimes based on this line of thought.

When candidates adopt a whatsisname strategy they might use it throughout the campaign—even in circumstances where refusal to mention the opponent is more amusing than effective. It's a sure sign that this type of race is tightening up when the taciturn frontrunner suddenly begins to drop his opponent's name at every opportunity.

5

PARTIES AND PAC'S

ACCEPTANCE SPEECH a major address to the convention by presidential and vice-presidential nominees. Acceptance speeches are designed to promote party unity and to create enthusiasm for the fall campaign.

Political parties now manage their conventions carefully to assure acceptance speeches are delivered before large television and radio audiences in prime time. Before the media era, however, presidential nominees did not even appear at conventions. They usually accepted their nomination in a separate ceremony weeks after the convention.

Franklin D. Roosevelt broke this tradition for the Democrats in 1932 and Thomas Dewey broke it for the Republicans in 1944. Since then acceptance speeches by the presidential and vice- presidential nominee have been the final scheduled events of both the Democratic and Republican conventions.
See also: CONVENTIONS

AGENCY AGREEMENT an arrangement whereby a state political party formally agrees to allow a federal level committee of its national party to act as its agent. Agency agreements between state parties and their national counterparts allow the often wealthier national party committees to support federal candidates within particular states much more generously than would otherwise be possible.

Under the Federal Election Campaign Act (FECA), various kinds of expenditure limitations are imposed with respect to the amount of money that the national parties and their committees may spend on behalf of their candidates for federal office. The Federal Elections Commission (FEC) has ruled however that state political parties may spend as much on behalf of federal candidates in their states as does the national party.

When state parties lack the resources to match their federal level counterparts, they may enter into agency agreements with a federal level party committee. These agreements permit the national committee to pick up both their share and the state's share of allowable expenditures.

The United States Supreme Court has ruled that agency agreements are legal and that they are in fact legitimate ways to promote party accountability. *See also: FEDERAL ELECTION CAMPAIGN ACT (FECA); SOFT MONEY*

AMATEURS AND REGULARS terms coined by political scientists to contrast the two major types involved in American politics. Both are usually discussed in the context of their political party activity.

Amateurs are issue oriented and often reform minded. They are likely to be associated with a cause or public policy which motivates them to enter politics. Regulars are organization loyalists and seldom reform minded. They are more likely to be motivated by material rewards such as patronage and power.

Amateurs and regulars also differ in their attitudes toward election strategy and the pursuit of electoral victory. Amateurs place the highest priority on the accomplishment of their policy goals; they are much less inclined than regulars to compromise on issues or candidates in order to win an election. Regulars on the other hand place their highest priority on winning elections; they are much more inclined than amateurs to employ bargaining and compromise to build coalitions and win elections.

The distinction between amateurs and regulars was probably more useful in the heyday of political party organization and influence. The difference drawn by political scientist Xandra Kayden (1978: 41--46) between vocationalists and avocationalists may be more valid in today's campaign centered electoral politics. *See also: VOCATIONALISTS*

ANTI-PARTISAN an attitude characterized by hostility and disdain toward political parties and their activities. Anti-partisan voters are not merely non-partisan; they are overtly opposed to partisan politics in any form.

Anti-partisan sentiments are not uncommon in the United States. The founding fathers themselves seem to have been infected with some anti-partisan feelings. Certainly, the political system they constructed could hardly have been less hospitable to the development of political parties. And the American electorate as a whole has never held parties or politics in high esteem.

Today there is evidence—in the decline in turnout, the increase in Independents, and the trend toward ticket splitting—that voters are becoming even more anti-partisan. If so, American politics may drift further away from any kind of responsible party government toward a system much less party oriented and much more candidate centered. *See also: NON-PARTISAN: REALIGNING ELECTION*

ANTI-SOREHEAD LAWS in politics soreheads are candidates who run in general elections as Independents after losing in their own respective primary. Anti-sorehead laws are provisions in the election codes of several states which prohibit a candidate who has run in a primary and been defeated for nomination, to become an Independent candidate in the subsequent general election.

These laws are intended to protect the integrity of the party primary process. They also tend to reduce the number of candidates who run in general elections while increasing the probability that the winning candidate in general elections will receive a majority of the votes cast. In 1984 about a dozen states had an anti-sorehead law. *See also: ELECTORAL SYSTEM*

ASSESSMENT *See MACING*

AUXILIARY POLITICAL GROUPS organized groups which have developed outside the formal structures of the two major political parties. Auxiliary political groups are in principle usually designed to supplement the work of the Republican or Democratic parties. In practice they appeal to and represent distinct factions within the major parties.

Examples of auxiliary groups are the National Federation of Republican Women, the Young Democrats, the College Republicans, and the College Democrats. The ideology oriented groups which operate mainly within the context of one of the two parties are also properly classified as auxiliary groups. These include such organizations as the Young Americans for Freedom, the Americans for Democratic Action, and the various local Republican and Democratic clubs where they exist.

Auxiliary groups should be distinguished from special groups which are voter groupings made up of people with similar ethnic or religious backgrounds, or who share other sociological traits. Special groups are generally organized ad hoc for the duration of a campaign or candidacy. But auxiliary political groups often become permanent fixtures on the political scene. *See also: SPECIAL GROUPS*

BEAUTY CONTESTS *See ADVISORY BALLOT*

BIG LABOR a term generally applied to the AFL-CIO and its 98 affiliated unions. Big Labor has big resources that can be converted to the political campaigns of those it supports.

Nationally, Big Labor counts over 15 million union members who with their families comprise a potentially vast array of campaign resources and voters. Equally impressive is the demonstrated ability of labor to raise money. In 1984 the AFL-CIO is estimated to have contributed about 2 million dollars to candidates for federal office alone. Millions more is raised and spent in registration drives and GOTV efforts, such as telephone banks and canvassing.

But in spite of these very substantial political resources, an endorsement from big labor does not always result in electoral success. For one thing, labor itself is often divided between or among the candidates, reducing the impact of any labor vote.

For another, labor's endorsement does not always influence the rank and file vote. Workers who are union members often ignore the preachments of their unions and vote for other candidates. Finally, the endorsement or support of big labor can be a two edged sword that galvanizes opposition to a labor backed candidate with some voters, just as it attracts support from other voters. *See also: DEMOCRATIC COALITION; UNION BUG; UNION HOUSEHOLDS*

BINDING PRIMARY *See ADVISORY BALLOT*

BLANKET PRIMARY *See OPEN PRIMARY*

BLIND PRIMARIES presidential primaries in which delegates are listed on the ballot without any information about the presidential candidate they support. Blind primaries make it difficult for voters to know how to vote for the delegate(s) of their preferred candidate—and they have been generally criticized for this.

Blind primaries encourage competing presidential campaigns to recruit delegates who are well known, and therefore likely to attract votes. The Democratic party no longer allows blind primaries for the selection of presidential delegates. The Republicans still use them in a few of the larger states. *See also: ADVISORY BALLOT; DIRECT PRIMARY*

BOLT *See TAKING A WALK*

BONUS RULE a longstanding policy of both the Democratic and Republican parties that awards extra convention delegates to state parties that achieve certain electoral performance standards. Bonus rule delegates are given for such things as carrying the state for the presidential nominee, electing a governor or United States Senator, or winning a majority of congressional seats.

Republicans have been using some kind of bonus system since 1916. Democrats did not adopt their's until 1940. Both parties had similar systems until 1972 when the Democrats changed their bonus formula to one based on a state's population and its popular vote for the last Democratic presidential candidate.

The Republicans have continued the practice of awarding a flat number of bonus delegates—regardless of a state's population—to those states that have carried the Republican presidential nominee in the last election or which have elected a governor or United States Senator, or a majority of congressional candidates.

Bonus systems tend to favor small states and states where one or the other party dominates. They have been criticized because they create unequal representation at the convention unless they are based on state population. They also accelerate the trend to ever larger delegations. The Democrats now certify over 4,000 convention delegates, the Republicans almost 3,000. *See also: CONVENTIONS; RULES COMMITTEE*

BOSS a political party leader who controls the sources and the use of political power in a city, country, or state. Bosses gain and exercise their power through control of party nominations and access to the fruits of patronage. The great bosses of American political legend—figures like Tweed, Crump, Kelly, Hague, De Sapio, and Long—wielded iron control over entire cities and states. Bosses of this type are now gone from American politics. Their demise was caused by the same factors that contributed to the general weakening of political parties: rising income and education; widespread adoption of civil service systems; growth in public welfare systems; population shifts from city to suburbs; the introduction of the direct primary; and the technologies of the new politics.

It is an exaggeration to say that all bossism has disappeared from American politics. There are still dozens of local and state party leaders who exercise great power and influence through their control of party organizations. But unlike their legendary predecessors, they tend to share power rather than monopolize it. And the party organizations they control are much weaker and less effective than the earlier party machines. *See also: PATRONAGE*

BROKERED CONVENTION a convention in which the early ballots fail to produce a nominee. Brokered conventions feature bargaining and negotiation among party leaders until a nominee is selected. The term is usually applied to the national political conventions, but a brokered convention can also occur in state level conventions or caucuses.

Traditionally, brokered conventions were controlled by party leaders and favorite son candidates who had come to the convention in command of large numbers of delegates. These power brokers could commit their delegate strength to a favored candidacy in return for the promise of future political favors.

Today, the growing influence of the presidential primaries and caucuses, and the elimination of the old Unit Rule, all make this sort of brokerage unlikely in national conventions. In fact not since 1952 has either of the major political parties gone beyond one ballot in selecting a nominee. *See also: OPEN CONVENTION*

CAUCUS one of the three main mechanisms used by political parties to nominate candidates. The other two are direct primaries and conventions. Caucuses involve a succession of multi-level meetings that span several months in the election year—typically February to June.

The first round of meetings is the precinct level caucus which are local mass gatherings open to all members of the political party. The precinct caucuses select delegates to county meetings which in turn select delegates to go to congressional districts and state level meetings. Eventually congressional and state level caucuses select the delegates who will represent the state at the national conventions.

Precinct meetings are the most important level in the caucus system. People elected there determine who will go on to congressional and state level where the national delegates are finally chosen. Turnout at precinct caucuses however is low—generally not above 10%. And those who do participate tend to be party leaders and political activists. Because of this, campaigning in caucus states usually emphasizes grass roots organization and personal campaigning, rather than political advertising and mass media exposure.

The caucus has gone full cycle in American politics. It was used heavily during the early 19th Century to select presidential candidates as well as other party nominees. But it was replaced in the mid-nineteenth century by conventions which in turn gave way to direct primaries in the 20th Century.

There is now however some movement back to the caucus as a nominating device in presidential elections. Although 27 states are still using presidential primaries, 15 have adopted the caucus and 8 more use mixed systems that combine primary and caucus. *See also: CONVENTIONS; DIRECT PRIMARY*

CHALLENGE PRIMARY a nominating mechanism which combines features of a convention with those of a direct primary. Four states—Colorado, Connecticut, New York and Utah provide for a challenge primary.

Connecticut is representative. There each party nominates its candidates at a convention. These nominees are placed on the Fall general election ballot unless challenged to a primary by another candidate. To challenge, a candidate must have received 20% or more of the votes cast by convention delegates. In effect then, candidates must demonstrate some support in the party convention in order to gain access to the party primary.

Even when candidates have achieved the minimum threshold of support at the convention, they do not always challenge. In fact, more often they don't. Connecticut for example went 15 years before a convention winner was forced to run in a challenge primary.

Prospective challenges face the prospect of creating intra-party strife that might reduce the party's strength in the general election. The problems of attracting supporters and raising money also discourages potential challenges. *See also: CONVENTION; DIRECT PRIMARY*

CLOSED PRIMARY a nominating election authorized by a particular political party and open only to voters who are members of that party. Closed primaries require a perspective voter to be registered with the party or willing to make some affirmation of affiliation and support.

About 75% of the states use the closed primary. The theory behind them is that they strengthen political parties because they allow each party to nominate its own candidates without outside interference.

Political party leaders usually favor closed primaries because they prevent raiding by crossover voters from other parties. Voters however often resent closed primaries because they limit their choices. Independents in particular are affected by them. These voters are disenfranchised during closed primaries because they can't vote in the primary of either party.

Closed primaries are often contrasted with open primaries in which voters may choose the party primary in which they vote. In practice however the differences between closed primary states and open primary states is often not that significant. It is more accurate to think of the states in terms of a wide continuum—which ranges from the few states which have completely closed primaries to the few states that have completely open primaries. Most states use a combination of the two types. *See also: DIRECT PRIMARY; OPEN PRIMARY*

COALITION shifting alliances of political interests that come together to win elections—often staying together only until that purpose has failed or succeeded.

The major coalitions in American politics overlap with the traditional constituencies of the national Democratic and Republican parties. Republicans for example are said to be made up of upper income earners, whites, small town dwellers, professional and white collar workers, Protestants, and Westerners. Democrats on the other hand include lower income earners, blacks, inhabitants of large cities, ethnic groups, blue collar and technical workers, union members, Catholics, Jews and residents of the large industrial states.

Historically these customary alliances have been loose and volatile—inherently unstable arrangements that guarantee no constancy from one election to the next. Nevertheless most American politicians think in terms of putting coalitions together, or taking them apart. And American political scientists and professional journalists regularly study and analyze politics in coalitional terms. *See also: BLOC VOTING; DEMOCRATIC COALITION*

CONVENTION CALLS official announcements establishing the date, site and procedures for the next national convention. Convention calls are issued by both the Democratic and Republican National Committees to their respective state parties.

Calls include a great deal of information on the rules and regulations that will govern the convention. They establish the size of a state's delegation, and its membership on the key Rules, Credentials and Platform committees. Convention calls are issued about 12–14 months before the scheduled start of the next convention. They have been coming earlier in recent years as the pre-convention presidential primary and caucus period lengthens. *See also: CONVENTIONS*

CONVENTIONS a regularly scheduled gathering of political party members or their delegates. Traditionally American political conventions nominate candidates, write party platforms, select party officers, and kick off the election campaign.

National conventions have been held continuously by both major political parties since 1852. Since 1960 however, they have been declining in importance in terms of their influence on nominations. Primaries and Caucuses now choose most delegates and have determined the outcome of presidential contests since 1968.

Modern national conventions have become tightly scheduled media events. The order of business doesn't change much from one convention to another. On Monday the delegates are welcomed by a succession of speeches before hearing the Keynote Address—traditionally delivered by a rising political star. On Tuesday the major convention committees make their reports and the platform is adopted. If there is to be a fight for the nomination it often surfaces here— in skirmishing around platform planks.

On Wednesday the presidential nominating speeches are given, followed by balloting and by eventual selection of a presidential candidate. Both parties now require a simple majority to nominate. No major party convention has gone beyond the first ballot since 1956. On Thursday Vice Presidential nominating speeches are given, followed by balloting. Almost always the eventual nominee has been handpicked by the presidential candidate. After the Vice Presidential selection, both nominees make formal acceptance speeches. These are followed by massive campaign rallies complete with balloons, horns, and marching bands.

Conventions have also survived in several of the states where one or both parties use them instead of holding direct primaries. In these states conventions may select delegates for national conventions, nominate candidates for statewide office, and adopt party platforms. Even in these states, however, the exclusive use of conventions to make nominations is rare. Usually political parties may choose between conventions and direct primaries, and candidates defeated in a convention can request a challenge primary. *See also: CREDENTIALS COMMITTEE; PLATFORM COMMITTEE; RULES COMMITTEE*

CONVERTING ELECTION *See MAINTAINING ELECTION*

COUNTY CHAIRMAN *See COUNTY COMMITTEE*

COUNTY COMMITTEE the political party organizational level that fits between precincts or wards and state committee. County committees are usually made up of precinct leaders and are headed by a county chairman. These committees are traditionally the most important unit of party organization. Patronage is more commonly found at the county level than at the local or state levels of government. And many of the more important offices, like judges, district attorney, and sheriff are elected countywide— or like state legislators and U.S. Congressmen, are based on county constituencies.

The vigor and influence of county committees varies considerably across the nation's odd 3200 counties. In some counties they perform all of the classical functions of political parties. They recruit candidates, administer campaigns, raise money and participate in government. But, in other counties these committees do few or none of these things and even have trouble filling their party offices.

When strong active political parties are found in the United States, it is usually at the county level. In fact state political parties are built upon these local organizations and are never stronger than the local precincts and county committees that make them up. *See also: NATIONAL COMMITTEE; STATE COMMITTEE*

COUSINS v. WIGODA a 1975 United States Supreme Court decision which clarified existing laws with regard to how conflicts between state laws and rules of the national political parties should be resolved.

Cousins v. Wigoda grew out of a struggle between rival Illinois delegations to the 1972 Democratic national convention. One faction—a pro mayor Richard Daley group—went to a state court for injunctory relief after the convention's Credentials Committee had refused to seat them. The Credentials Committee had determined that the pro Daley group was chosen in violation of Democratic national party rules. But the Illinois state court ruled that state law had been properly followed and it injuncted the rival anti Daley group from taking seats or participating in the convention.

The dissidents ignored the order, which was then upheld in an Illinois Appellate Court. The U.S. Supreme Court, however, in Cousins v. Wigoda, took the case on appeal and overturned the earlier state court orders. In their decision the Supreme Court laid down the rule that the national political parties are the final arbiter of credential disputes between rival delegates. And, the court established the clear principle that the rules of the national political parties usually prevail over state statutes when the two conflict. *See also: CONVENTIONS*

CREDENTIALS COMMITTEE one of the three major committees employed by the Democratic and Republican Parties to carry out the business of their national conventions. The other two are the Platform Committee and the Rules Committee. The Credentials Committee is charged with reviewing any challenges made to the roll of delegates compiled by the party's national committee. Hearings are held on these challenges and committee recommendations are prepared and sent to the convention floor for final approval.

Most of the time the work of the Credentials Committee is routine, but not always. Some of the most pitched battles in convention history have occurred over credentials disputes. In the Republican Party, credentials fights have usually centered on the legitimacy of southern delegations chosen from so-called rotten boroughs. In the Democratic Party most credential contests have been linked to civil rights issues and questions about party loyalty.

The most intense credentials fights occur when one or more of the presidential candidates become identified with a credentials challenge. Then the issue may become a test of strength between opposing candidates. And when this happens, the convention's decision on the seating of the disputed delegates usually accurately forecasts the eventual presidential nominee.

Recently both the Democratic and Republican Parties instituted formal pre-convention procedures to review credentials challenges well before the convention opens. These procedures have substantially reduced both the number and the significance of credentials challenges. In the future, serious convention clashes are more likely to occur over the platform or the rules than over delegate credentials. *See also: CONVENTIONS; PLATFORM COMMITTEE; RULES COMMITTEE*

DARK HORSE a political candidate who is generally regarded as having little chance to win his party's nomination. Dark horses are usually presidential candidates, although the term is also used to describe weak candidates in state and local primary elections.

The expression dark horse is one of a long list of race track metaphors that grace the prose of journalists and authors who write about American politics. Some other common ones are horse race; front runner; running; also ran; stretch run, and trial heat. The regular use of this sort of imagery reflects some tendency to look at politics and campaigns as sporting events with set rules, established standards of competition, a clear winner and—most important of all—another scheduled race to follow.

In their book PRESIDENTIAL ELECTION (1984:113) political scientists Nelson W. Polsby and Aaron Wildavsky describe the strategy of dark horse candidates:

> the dark horse is a possible candidate who picks and chooses among primaries and avoids much open campaigning . . . is content to be everyone's friend and no one's enemy . . . the strategy of the dark horse is to combine with others to oppose every front runner. His hope is that when no front runner is left he will appear as the man who can unify the party by being acceptable to all and obnoxious to none . . . .

During this century there have been three dark horse candidates who eventually won their party's nomination: Warren Harding did it in 1920; Wendell Willkie in 1940; and Jimmy Carter in 1976. Many others of course have tried but failed. Dark horse candidates, by any measure, are long shots. *See also: HORSE RACE*

DEALIGNMENT *See REALIGNING ELECTION*

DELIVERING coming through with the support needed to win an election or carry a political fight. Delivering usually refers to producing votes. The old political machines were said to be able to deliver—which meant that precinct captains and ward leaders could produce wide vote margins for organization candidates.

Delivering once also played an important role in presidential politics. Before presidential primaries became widespread, local and state political leaders controlled the delegate selection process. At the national convention these party leaders often had enough influence to deliver all or most of their state's delegation to a favored presidential candidate.

Today both kinds of delivering is rare. The disciplined reliable political machines no longer control turnout or voting. And national conventions are governed by delegate selection processes—primaries and caucuses—that greatly reduce the influence of party leaders in presidential politics. Even the legislative caucuses of the political parties are more and more made up of members who resist being delivered by party leadership.

All of these changes are linked to larger political forces—in particular the decline of the political parties and the steady substitution of wholesale politics for retail politics. Should these trends continue it seems doubtful that delivering will ever again be an important part of American politics.

See also: WHOLESALE POLITICS

DEMOCRATIC COALITION the agglomeration of social, economic, regional, religious, and ethnic groups that make up the electoral strength of the national Democratic Party. The Democratic coalition is traditionally thought of as comprising the following major constituencies: union families; Catholics; Jews; blacks; southerners; poor; large city dwellers; and youth.

These groups vary substantially in the strength of the support they provide Democratic candidates. At one extreme are blacks who give up to 90% of their votes to Democrats; at the other extreme are Catholics, union families, and southerners who give barely half or even less of their support to Democrats.

Opposing the Democratic coalition is the traditional Republican coalition. The mirror image of the Democratic constituency, it is usually described as including the following groups: non union families; Protestants; whites; northerners; affluents; small town and farm dwellers; and the middle aged.

As is the case with the Democrats these groups vary in the support they provide to Republican candidates. For example affluent voters give up to 80% of their votes to Republicans; on the other hand Protestants and whites provide 50% or less of their votes to Republicans.

Recent political history suggests to some observers that a permanent shift or realignment is occuring among the groups of the Democratic and Republican coalitions. Those who interpret recent Republican victories as evidence of realignment forecast a continuing abandonment of the Democratic Party by its traditional supporters—and a continuing increase in the support these groups give to the Republican Party.

Not everyone believes that the traditional constituencies are breaking down. Some analysts argue that the present flux among Democratic supporters is only a brief flirtation after which these traditional Democrats will "come home."

At least a few observers expect neither realignment nor continued Democratic dominance. Instead they forecast dealignment—a steady and gradual breakdown in the electoral coalitions of both major political parties.

See also: BLACK VOTERS; BLOC VOTING; COALITION; ETHNIC GROUPS; JEWISH VOTERS; REALIGNING ELECTION; UNION HOUSEHOLDS; UPSTATE AND DOWNSTATE

DEMOCRATIC NATIONAL COMMITTEE (DNC) *See NATIONAL COMMITTEE*

DEVIATING ELECTION *See REALIGNING ELECTION*

DIRECT PRIMARY a nominating election sponsored or authorized by a political party. There are two basic types of direct primary used in American politics: closed primaries and open primaries.

Closed primaries are elections closed to anyone not a member of the sponsoring political party. The main argument for them is that each political party should be able to maintain the integrity of its own nominating process without interference from raiding or crossover voters.

The other basic type of direct primary is the open primary. These are nominating elections open to any eligible voter regardless of party affiliation. Voters in open primaries can choose the party election they will participate in after entering the voting booth. The rationale for these is that they provide a wider choice of candidates while allowing voters to maintain secrecy about the party ballot they select.

Some version of the direct primary is used in every state except Delaware. The closed form is dominant—about 3/4 of the states use it—although in practice the difference between a closed primary state and an open primary state is often not great.

A distinction is sometimes drawn between direct primaries and so called indirect primaries. In the direct primary, voters directly choose candidates who will run for office in a subsequent general election, but in the indirect primary, voters only select delegates to a subsequent nominating convention. These delegates in turn finally choose (or nominate) candidates. Indirect primaries are still used in some states in connection with the selection of delegates to nominating conventions. Most presidential primaries are also properly classified as indirect primaries. *See also: ADVISORY BALLOT; BLIND PRIMARY; CHALLENGE PRIMARY; CLOSED PRIMARY; CROSSOVER; OPEN PRIMARY; RUNOFF PRIMARY*

ENDORSEMENT a formal public expression of approval and support for a political candidate. Endorsements are made by newspapers, PAC's, political parties, other politicians, and even celebrities from the entertainment and sports industries. The value of endorsements is disputed. The issue is how much difference does an endorsement make and do some kinds of endorsement make more difference than others?

Newspaper endorsements apparently can have a significant affect on voting. Some studies have reported that five to ten percent of voters are influenced by them. These endorsements probably weigh more in low visibility races where the candidates are not well known.

Endorsements by PAC's or other interest groups such as labor, business, farmers, etc. can be important if they produce campaign workers or contributions. Few large organizations today can deliver their membership to a candidate or political party. But some—labor is an example—can produce large amounts of money or volunteers.

Political party endorsements have mixed results. Formal party support in a primary election can be very effective when a strong political organization backs it up on election day. On the other hand party endorsements more often today carry no substantial resources with them. In fact some party mavericks have successfully flouted party endorsements and won their primary contests by advertising that they were not the endorsed candidate.

Personal endorsements by celebrities or other politicians probably have only slight value. Like party endorsements these usually bring no tangible campaign resources with them. And few public figures have the kind of influence with their followers that allows them to transfer their won popularity to a political candidate. The major importance of personal endorsements is the publicity they provide—and the credibility they can create with the media and among the politically active. *See also: COATTAILS; DELIVERING*

EVERYONE PARTY a waggish reference to the Democratic Party and to the broad base of diverse constituency groups it comprises. The Democratic party is the everyone party in the sense that almost every important demographic group in the country includes more Democrats than Republicans. Democrats outpull Republicans among: whites, blacks, blue collar workers, white collar workers, college educated, ethnics, Catholics, Protestants, Jews, rural residents, and city dwellers. With the exception of those with incomes above $35,000, the Democratic party has the two party majority of virtually every significant crossection of the population.

The designation of the Democratic party as the everyone party is however somewhat misleading. A more important characteristic to emphasize is probably the basic heterogeneity of the two major parties. Both the Democratic and Republican parties contain substantial numbers of all the principal constituencies, and they draw significant proportions of their vote from all of them.

With few exceptions neither party can afford to ignore any large social group. This political reality encourages the parties to take moderate and largely similar positions on many domestic issues. In a very real way both major parties are the everyone party. *See also: COALITION; DEMOCRATIC COALITION*

FAITHFUL DELEGATE RULE *See ROBOT RULE*

FAVORITE SONS state party leaders, often a governor or U.S. Senator, who are the choice of their state's delegation to the national convention. Favorite son candidates are not usually serious contenders for the presidential nomination. They generally are popular and powerful local leaders who offer themselves as candidates in order to hold the delegation together and to improve its negotiating strength in the convention.

Favorite sons were common before primaries and caucuses became so influential in the nominating process. Just the nominations of favorite son candidates often required a full day or more of convention time. The established practice for many state parties was to promote a favorite son as a bargaining chip or as a strategy to block the front runner.

Such candidacies have now become rare in both parties. The Democrats all but abolished the practice in 1972 when they required that any nomination have the written support of at least 50 delegates spread over three delegations. The custom has also virtually ended in the Republican party. *See also: UNCOMMITTED DELEGATES*

FIREHOUSE PRIMARY a delegate selection and presidential nominating process which incorporates features of both the direct primary and the caucus systems. Firehouse primaries utilize a primary type mass meeting in the first stage followed by a congressional district level convention in the second and final stage.

Firehouse primaries are used in some of the smaller states. they differ from the multi-tiered caucuses used in larger states in that they involve only two stages. Rank and file voters also have a much more direct impact on selection of the national convention delegates in firehouse primary states. *See also: CAUCUS; CONVENTION*

FRIENDLY PRIMARY a primary election in which two incumbents of the same party vie against each other for a congressional or legislative seat. These primaries are races between two incumbent Republicans or two incumbent Democrats—candidates who face each other as a result of the reapportionment of their respective districts.

Friendly primaries usually occur in states that must relinquish legislative seats because their population growth has fallen behind other areas of the country.

For example the 1980 census and subsequent reapportionment reduced Pennsylvania's congressional delegation by two seats. (Other states also lost congressional seats as a result of this reapportionment.) Pennsylvania Democrats held both of these lost seats. The former constituents of both congressmen were merged into the districts of two other congressmen who also happened to be Democrats. The result—four Democratic congressmen and only two congressional seats—set the stage for friendly primaries in both reapportioned districts.

Friendly primaries are not always all that friendly. An air of civility and even amicability is often maintained, however no marquise of queensbury rules are enforced or expected. In fact some nasty bitter battles occur in friendly primaries, but this is not surprising. Colleagues and friends are pitted against each other for survival. Both understand that the winner will continue a career, while the loser will have ended one. *See also: APPORTIONMENT; DIRECT PRIMARY*

FRONT LOADING establishing an election calender that schedules many of the caucuses and presidential primaries early in the political season. Front loading squeezes the early nomination contests into a critical few weeks.

Pressures to shorten presidential campaigns have led particularly the Democratic party to search for ways to condense the pre-convention period. In 1984 the Democrats front loaded their presidential nomination process by selecting almost 50% of their pledged delegates by the end of the first month of the schedule.

Front loading places a heavy strain on campaigns and on campaigners who must run in several states at the same time. It favors well known candidates and well organized campaigns. Front loading especially makes it difficult for challengers to overtake a front runner or any candidate who has established momentum. *See also: WINDOW*

GAIN-DEFICIT RULE one of several rules of thumb that have evolved to predict the outcome of presidential nomination contests. The Gain-Deficit Rule—known also as the Rule of 36—was formulated by political scientists Donald S. Collat, Stanley Kelly, Jr., and Donald Rogowski. It holds that the candidate will eventually win, who first gains on any one ballot 36% of the net votes needed for nomination.

For example, if a candidate is 100 votes short of nomination, and then gains 36 or more votes on the next ballot, that candidate will ultimately be nominated according to the Gain-Deficit Rule. The Rule works whether it is applied to the multi-ballot conventions common before 1952, or to the more recent single ballot conventions that now occur in both major political parties. For the latter, the rule simply substitutes wire service delegate counts for the convention ballots of the earlier era.

The Gain-Deficit Rule is the most accurate of any of the various systems that have been devised to forecast the outcome of nomination contests. Since 1952 the rule has correctly predicted the eventual victor in every convention struggle. The success rate of the other leading rules of thumb has been much less consistent.

One of these, the "polling majority rule," predicts that the candidate will be nominated who first wins a majority of delegates in press polls. But this rule has forecast the winner in only four of nine contested races. Another leading rule of thumb, the "front runner rule," predicts that the candidate will be nominated who has the most early support. But this rule has forecast the winner in only seven of nine contested races.

A third leading approach, the "threshold rule," predicts that the candidate will be nominated who first receives the support of 41% of the convention delegates. But even this rule has forecast the winner in only seven of eight contested races. Unless the Gain-Deficit rule fails in one of the next several conventions, it is likely to become the generally accepted approach to forecasting the outcome of contested presidential nominations. *See also: CONVENTION*

GERRYMANDERING drawing electoral areas, especially state legislative and congressional districts along geographic lines that blatantly favor one party over another. Gerrymandering is a time honored American political tradition.

It dates back at least as far as its namesake Elbridge Gerry who was governor of Massachusetts in 1812 when the first recorded gerrymander took place. The principle of a gerrymandering strategy is to create election areas that either concentrate your opponent's voters in as few districts as possible— or disperse them across as many districts as possible. In either case the objective is the same— to minimize the opposition's ability to affect the outcome of an election. When gerrymandering is skillfully done, a party having only a minority of voters may nevertheless control a majority of the seats in a legislative body.

Since the one man, one vote court decisions of the 1960s, state legislatures must now reapportion voting districts after each decennial census. The party in control of the legislature at the time of reapportionment is usually able to draw those districts to their advantage. However, the federal courts have consistently shown that they are not reluctant to intervene if the reapportionment is glaringly partisan or if it contravenes the principle of one man, one vote. *See also: APPORTIONMENT; ONE MAN, ONE VOTE*

GOING FISHING *See TAKING A WALK*

HANDICAPPING the process of systematically determining where to allocate campaign contributions—usually with respect to where those contributions will have the most impact. Handicapping in politics is calculating the odds on the candidates. It is especially prevalent among Political Action Committees or PAC's.

PAC'S contribute to campaigns for many different reasons, and all of them are criterion that are used in handicapping political races. Access to the eventual winning candidate is important. Beyond that, PAC's look for ideologically compatible candidates who are in close races in which PAC money might make a difference. Other considerations include evidence of a clear philosophical difference between candidates and PAC desire to reward their friends and punish their enemies.

PAC's weigh all these factors differently and sometimes "hedge their bets" by contributing to both candidates in the same race. This later practice— known as double riding—is used by political givers who wish to cover all possibilities and insure future access regardless of who wins the election. *See also: DOUBLE RIDING; EARLY MONEY; HELP THE HEALTHY AND SHOOT THE SICK; HORSE RACE; PAC's*

HARD COUNT a firm and reliable reckoning of the delegate support and opposition that exists for a candidate. Hard counts are usually made for the strategic use of a campaign organization prior to a major vote in a

convention or party caucus. One of its purposes is to identify uncommitted delegates or delegates whose support is "soft."
Recently, the mass media have begun to do hard counts of the delegate accumulations of candidates during presidential primaries. Some political analysts believe that the publication of these and other hard counts may generate momentum for leading candidates that has a bandwagon effect. *See also: CAUCUS; CONVENTION*

IDEOLOGICAL PAC'S *See NON CONNECTED PAC'S*

IN PARTY *See INS AND OUTS*

INS AND OUTS the present holders of power and future holders of power respectively. Ins are in power, but someday will be outs. Outs are out of power but eventually will be ins.
The phrase "ins and outs" reflect a pervasive anticipation found in two party systems; eventually the in party will accumulate problems, incur disfavor with the electorate, overstay their welcome, and become the outs. Meanwhile the out party waits for their next chance to be the ins.
The expression also suggests cynicism about any real differences between the Republican and Democratic parties. As columnist William Safire put it in his POLITICAL DICTIONARY (1978):

> When asked 'What is the basic difference between the Republicans and the Democrats?' A host of political figures have been credited with the remark: 'The only difference is—they're in and we're out.'

How the outs become ins and the ins out is of considerable interest to working politicians. The best evidence is that voters don't vote the outs in so much as they vote the ins out. The goal of the in party in these circumstances is to avoid major mistakes and failures while the function of the out party is to call attention to the shortcomings of the in party while waiting to assume power.
The electorate generally will vote for a change only if the in party has shown itself incompetent to govern and the out party seems to present a reasonable alternative. But there often isn't much the outs can do to become ins until the ins have proven to a majority of the voters that they deserve to become the outs. *See also: TWO PARTY SYSTEM*

INSTRUCTED DELEGATE a delegate to a political party caucus or convention who has been formally bound to support a particular candidacy or platform proposal. Usually primary and caucus delegate selection processes attempt to instruct delegates in some way. Lately, however, both major political parties have been moving away from the so called robot rules which deny discretion to individual delegates.
In 1984 the Democratic Party eliminated any regulation that would have bound national convention delegates to the support of any candidate.

Continued elimination of instructed delegate status might produce a more volatile and lively national nominating convention. But most political experts doubt it will have that consequence because the presidential primaries and caucuses have come to so completely overshadow conventions. *See also: ROBOT RULE; UNIT RULE*

INTEREST GROUP RATING *See REPORT CARDS*

KEYNOTE ADDRESS *See CONVENTION*

LETTERHEAD COMMITTEES *See SPECIAL GROUPS*

LIBERAL PARTY a minor political party in the United States that enjoys some attention because of its prominence in New York politics. The New York Liberal Party differs from most other third parties in the custom it follows in nominating candidates for office. Usually, it nominates the candidates of the Democratic Party instead of separate candidates of its own. The Liberal Party's line on the ballot provides a bargaining chip that can be used to encourage the Democratic Party to nominate candidates or adopt policy positions that are acceptable to Liberal Party members. The implied threat is that the Liberal Party will nominate a separate candidate and draw support away from the Democratic ticket. This tactic has allowed the Liberal Party to have some influence in New York politics while remaining a third party. *See also: THIRD PARTY*

LIBERTARIAN PARTY a minor party in the United States that regularly runs presidential campaigns and fields candidates for federal and local office in many states. Electorally, the Libertarians are strongest in Alaska and parts of the western United States. The party maintains at least some organizational structure in most of the states. The Libertarian political philosophy is a blend of conservatism and liberalism that stresses individual equality, arms control, the value of private property, and individual initiative.

The Libertarian Party attracted some national media attention in 1980 when it ran a serious and well financed campaign for the presidency. Overall, however, the party has not had much electoral success. Their problems are those usually faced by American third parties: low visibility, lack of financial support, and the traditional American apathy toward alternatives to the Democratic and Republican Parties. *See also: THIRD PARTIES*

LITMUS TEST ISSUE *See REPORT CARD*

LONG BALLOT a ballot which lists a large number of offices and candidates. Long ballots are also referred to as "bedsheet ballots." They are contrasted with short ballots which list only a few offices to be filled by election. Electoral jurisdictions which use long ballots elect a large proportion of their public officials, while those which use short ballots elect relatively few public officials—and rely on these to appoint others.

Long ballots became popular during the Jacksonian period in the United States, when it was argued that they increased democracy by enlarging the number of public officials who are elected. Today this notion is challenged by many political scientists who believe that accountability and rational voting is more likely with short ballots for which voters may concentrate their limited time and attention. Despite some movement toward short ballots, the long ballot prevails today in most areas of the country.

Long ballots have two major and conflicting effects on political parties. They probably augment the dominant party's control of the minor offices because voters are unable to distinguish among all the offices and candidates on the ballot. On the other hand, they also diminish party unity by pitting candidates from the same party against each other for the same limited political resources. *See also: AUSTRALIAN BALLOT; BALLOTS; VOTER FALLOFF*

LOOPHOLE PRIMARY presidential primary elections which allow the otherwise outlawed "winner take all" method of selecting delegates to national conventions. Loophole primaries are permitted exceptions to the general rule in the Democratic party that delegates be selected mainly on the basis of the proportional vote received by each candidate within the state.

The exception or loophole is that delegates may be elected directly from districts if the district is not larger than a congressional district. When delegates are elected directly, the plurality winner in each district may get all of the delegates within that district.

This system enables a presidential candidate to win all or most of a state's delegation while receiving substantially less than all of the vote. Critics of the loophole primary charge that it violates the spirit of the Democratic party's efforts to eliminate winner take all systems. *See also: UNIT RULE*

MARGINAL SEAT a legislative district in which the incumbent won the last election by less than 55% of the vote. The spread between winners and losers can be as much as 10% in these races, but marginal seats often feature contests won (or lost) by only two or three percentage points.

Non-marginal seats are those in which the incumbent won the last election with at least 55% of the vote. If the incumbent won with 60% or more of the vote a seat is said to be "safe."

Most legislative seats are won by more than 55% of the vote. In fact about 70% of all congressional seats are now considered safe seats because their incumbents win elections with 60% or more of the vote. Similar patterns exist in most state legislatures.

The high proportion of safe seats means that real political party competition does not exist in most legislative races. Two factors explain this pattern, known to political scientists as the "vanishing marginals." One of these is the virtual one party domination that characterizes many areas of the

country. Even states with vigorous two party competition for state offices still have local elections dominated by one or the other political party.
The other factor responsible for the high incidence of safe seats is the influence of incumbency. Most incumbents run for re-election. And when they do run, over 90% of them are re-elected.
Today it is the so called open seat races which provide the main competition in legislative districts. These are contests between non-incumbents, open because the incumbent is leaving office for some reason. Open seat contests produce most new legislators. Indeed about 75% of all congressmen initially win their office in open seat elections—in spite of the fact that only about 12% of all congressional seats actually fall open in any one election year. *See also: INCUMBENTS; OPEN SEAT*

MINOR PARTIES *See THIRD PARTIES*

NCPAC a prominent example of the so called non-connected or ideological PAC. NCPAC—the National Conservative Political Action Committee—is probably the best known of those PAC's which operate free of any corporate, union, or trade association sponsorship. NCPAC's stock in trade is independent expenditures made with money raised by direct mail solicitation from thousands of committed conservative ideologues.
NCPAC gained some notoriety in the early 1980's when it raised and spent millions of dollars to defeat mostly liberal Democrats. The tone and stridency of their negative advertising probably created some sympathetic backlash for some of those on the NCPAC hit list. Like many other non-connected PAC's, NCPAC also sponsors candidate schools and provides polling and media services to favored candidates. *See also: HIT LIST; INDEPENDENT EXPENDITURES; NON-CONNECTED PAC's; PAC's*

NATIONAL CHAIRMAN *See NATIONAL COMMITTEE*

NATIONAL COMMITTEE the generic name given to the governing body of both major political parties. National committee for the Democrats is known as Democratic National Committee or "DNC"; its Republican counterpart is Republican National Committee or "RNC."
DNC is more than twice the size of RNC. The Democratic National Committee authorizes up to 355 members. These include the state and territorial party chairmen (55); the next highest ranking party official of the opposite sex (55); committeemen and committeewomen apportioned to the states according to national convention representation (200); elected officials and national committee staff (20); and up to 25 more members to provide balance.
RNC is half the size of DNC. It has 162 members. These include the state party chairmen (50); one committeeman and one committeewoman from each state (100); and territorial representatives (12).
The two major political parties differ in the way they apportion national committee members to the individual states. The Republican system is

simplest. It assigns each state and territory three members regardless of population. California gets three, so does Vermont. Democrats however allocate their delegates to give the larger states more members than the smaller states. The Democrats also stress greater representation for women and minorities.

Originally national committees were intended to be the principal campaign committees for the party's presidential nominee—their activity limited mostly to the election year. Today however both parties now maintain year round organizations with full time staffs headquartered in Washington, D.C. Modern national committees are particularly active in convention planning: selecting the convention site; allocating delegates; establishing convention committees; and making convention arrangements.

Recently both national committees have also begun to provide research, consulting, fund raising and other technical services to candidates and campaign organizations. Most observers believe that RNC does a better job of providing support for its candidates, although the DNC is steadily improving its services. Ironically neither national committee is usually heavily involved in the presidential campaign itself—the main purpose for which both were created. *See also: COUNTY COMMITTEE; STATE COMMITTEE*

NEPOTISM favoring of relatives in employment, awarding of government contracts or appointment to public office. Nepotism—literally nephew-ism—is one form of patronage. It is a particularly obnoxious one to those voters who believe all relatives are incompetent or corrupt.

Some notorious examples of nepotism have occurred in the past several years—involving governors, congressmen and big city mayors. But blatant partiality is less prevalent than it once was. Public scrutiny, ethics laws and civil service regulations have all reduced the opportunities for it.

Employment favoritism in high visibility offices is especially rare. Instead, patronage of other sorts, such as lucrative contracts and awards, sometime favor relatives. Today these government business connections are more prized than many government jobs.

But old fashioned relatives on-the-payroll nepotism has not disappeared. In local governments and state legislatures, family employment ties are still common. Wives (or husbands) are hired to oversee offices, children are brought in for summer work, and assorted uncles, aunts, and cousins fill other staff positions.

Certainly not all nepotism is improper or unsavory. A reasonable standard to apply to the practice is whether the advantaged relative would have been qualified in the absence of any family ties. *See also: PATRONAGE*

NON-PARTISAN ELECTION an election in which candidates are listed on the ballot without any party designation. Non-partisan elections are widely used in the United States to fill local offices. Almost 70% of American cities over 25,000 population use them to elect mayors, councils, school boards and other municipal officials.

Advocates of non-partisan elections argue that they reduce corruption and eliminate wrangling among party supporters. Evidence suggests however that removing political parties from the ballot does not always prevent them from participating in elections.

Often in fact the non-partisan ballot is only a formality. Parties still actively endorse and support candidates and voters are aware of partisan distinctions. Even where parties are inactive, non party factions such as civic groups, business interests, labor unions, and even local newspapers often perform many of the same functions as do parties.

Non-partisan elections probably favor certain groups and types of voters. In fact, turnout in these elections is about 30% less than in partisan elections. Much of this decline is attributed to reduced participation by low income, ethnic, black, and less motivated voters.

Non-partisan ballots are rarely used in state elections and never used for federal elections. Every state includes party labels on ballots for governor, U.S. Senator and U.S. Representative. A few states do hold non-partisan elections for statewide offices like superintendent of schools and treasurer, but the vast number of state offices are filled in partisan elections. Only Nebraska of the 50 states uses a non-partisan ballot to elect its state legislature. *See also: BALLOTS; ELECTORAL SYSTEM; PARTY SYSTEM; POLITICAL PARTY*

OFF THE RESERVATION *See TAKING A WALK*

OPEN CONVENTION a convention in which none of the candidates has a clear majority of the delegates needed for nomination. The convention is therefore open to the deliberations of the delegates as to who the nominee should be. An open convention should be distinguished from a brokered convention. In the latter the nominee is chosen by party leaders and other power brokers, while in the former the delegates themselves choose the nominee.

In recent years the call for an open convention has usually been made by factions opposing the front runner, who hope to prevent a stampede to him. Truly open conventions have been rare in American politics, however presidential nominees have sometimes thrown conventions open for the selection of their vice-presidential running mates. *See also: BROKERED CONVENTION*

OPEN PRIMARY a nominating election open to any eligible voter regardless of party affiliation. Open primaries allow voters to choose the party election they will vote in after they enter the voting booth. Republicans may vote in the Democratic primary and Democrats may vote in the Republican primary. Usually Independents may vote in either.

Open primaries are often compared to closed primaries which require a prospective voter to be registered with a political party or willing to make some affirmation of affiliation and support. Usually Independents are banned completely from closed primaries.

About 25% of the states use some form of the open primary. Supporters of the concept argue that these elections provide a wider choice while allowing voters to maintain secrecy about the party ballot they choose. Critics however charge that open primaries encourage raiding by crossover voters, while they discourage strong responsible political parties.

A rare version of the open primary is the so called "blanket primary." In the blanket primary not only may voters vote in any party primary they wish—but they may switch back and forth between the parties-voting for this party's candidate for governor, that party's candidate for mayor, and so on.

Political party leaders and most political scientists think even less of blanket primaries than they do of other open primaries. But rank and file voters—especially Independents—seem to favor them. Currently the blanket primary is used in only two states: Washington and Alaska. *See also: CLOSED PRIMARY; CROSSOVERS; DIRECT PRIMARY; RAIDING*

OUT PARTY *See INS and OUTS*

PAC'S political action committees authorized under the Federal Elections Campaign Act (FECA). PAC's are basically voluntary organizations of like minded people who hope to influence elections by contributing money to political campaigns.

The Federal Elections Commission (FEC) classifies PAC's into six distinct categories. Four of these—Corporate PAC's, Labor PAC's, Trade/membership/Health Organization PAC's, and Non-Connected PAC's make up more than 95% of all political action committees. Altogether about 4,000 PAC's are now registered with the FEC and are active in federal elections. Thousands more operate at local and state levels.

Modern PAC's were authorized by an obscure provision in the Federal Elections Campaign Act which gave corporations permission to use corporate funds to start and operate political action committees. Until then PAC's were used only by labor organizations. But now corporations, trade associations, ideological groups, and others can establish them.

Under federal law PAC's can make direct contributions to candidates of up to $10,000—$5,000 in the primary and another $5,000 in the general election. Overall Democrats receive about 55% of this, Republicans 45%. But it is those already in office who receive the bulk of this money. Incumbents of both parties get about 65% of all PAC contributions. By contrast challengers receive only about 20%—while about 15% goes to open seat races.

PAC's are criticized by some who accuse them of weakening the political parties and exercising undue, even corrupting influence on elected officials. Others defend PAC's however arguing that they allow interest groups to operate in the clear light of public scrutiny, and provide balance to the power of big government, big business, and big labor. *See also: FEDERAL ELECTION CAMPAIGN ACT (FECA); HANDICAPPING; HIT LISTS;*

INDEPENDENT EXPENDITURES; NCPAC; NON-CONNECTED PAC'S

PARTY SYSTEMS a term employed by political scientists to designate the type of political party competition that exists at a particular time or in a particular place. Party systems include three main kinds of competition: one party systems; two party systems; and multi-party systems.

One party systems are those in which a single party dominates election after election. These occur regularly in the individual states. Political scientist Austin Ranney lists 8 states in which the opposition party is never a factor—and another 20 states in which the opposition party is only rarely a factor. Most of these states are in the South and West.

Two party systems are those in which the Democratic and Republican parties seriously vie against each other for electoral offices. U.S. national politics is a two party system because both parties regularly compete for the presidency. Some states also have two party systems. Currently there are 22 states, mostly in the Midwest and Northeast, which feature two party competition. (Keefe, 1984: 37–41)

Multi-party systems are those in which three or more parties are relatively strong and competitive. These are found in Europe but not in the United States. Now and then an American third party does gain enough support to act as spoiler or even win an occasional election, but this is unusual. Overall third parties receive little support from the electorate, rarely win elections, and almost never share power.

The term party systems has one other use. Political historians use it to delineate five eras of political party history. These differ from each other in the particular parties that existed at that time and the relationships between those parties. the shift from one historical party system to another is usually preceded by a realigning election. *See also: POLITICAL PARTY; RANNEY INDEX OF COMPETITION; TWO PARTY SYSTEM*

PATRONAGE the exchange of government jobs, contracts, licenses, or other favors for political support. Patronage systems flourished in the United States during the 19th and early 20th Centuries. Patronage then meant using jobs and appointments to reward loyal party workers, build effective political organizations, and ensure a steady flow of campaign contributions. Today however government jobs are no longer the cornerstone of most patronage systems.

Civil service merit systems have reduced the supply of available jobs—and public unionization has limited officials' ability to fill even non-civil service positions. Even more important, rising standards of living and expanding economic opportunities have made government employment less attractive than it once was. Instead of jobs the most sought after patronage are franchises, legal fees, bond work and other discretionary government business.

Some of this "new patronage" involves questionable behavior. Both legal and ethical issues are raised by such common practices as awarding large legal fees to politically connected law firms, hiring only architects and engineers who support the incumbent party, giving insurance business to generous contributors, and favoring party loyalists for lucrative "non-bid" contracts.

Politicians usually like patronage because it provides them resources that can be traded for political support. Even many political scientists are ambivalent about the value of patronage. They condemn the abuses and corruption often associated with it, but they also point out that patronage strengthens and nourishes political parties.

PAYING YOUR DUES giving support, labor, and loyalty to a political party or organization. Paying your dues is to work in the political vineyards to prove that you deserve and merit advancement.

At one time politicians paid their dues before they ran for major office or became eligible for important patronage positions. The traditional way to do this was to get involved in local politics, perhaps serve as a committeeman or committeewoman, work at the polls on election day, campaign for party candidates, and even run for minor office.

Paying your dues still matters today in some places at some times. But it is less important than it was when political parties were stronger. The new politics—with its emphasis on technology, media, and candidate centered organization—makes it possible for aspirant politicians to by-pass the political party. Today the lateral entry candidate can enter politics without ever serving in lower level offices or working for a party. *See also: LATERAL ENTRY; NEW POLITICS*

PLANKS *See PLATFORM COMMITTEE*

PLATFORM COMMITTEE one of three major committees used by the Democratic and Republican Parties to carry out the business of their national conventions. The other two are the Credentials Committee and the Rules Committee.

The Platform Committee drafts the policy proposals the party intends to run on in the Fall. These planks as they are called are crafted after platform committee hearings have provided an opportunity for party factions to press their case that this or that issue be addressed in the party platform.

Historically the platform committee—as well as the Credentials and Rules Committees—has been the site of early tests of strength between opposing presidential candidates. When these battles are taken to the convention floor, they are usually accurate barometers of the competing candidates' first ballot strength among delegates.

The conventional wisdom has been that party platforms are vague and ambiguous documents that don't differ greatly between the two parties and that don't provide a reliable guide to a party's future action. But political scientists Gerald Pomper and Susan Lederman (1980:161–165) have recently presented some findings that seem to contradict this view of party platforms.

According to these scholars, 2/3 of platform pledges are made only by one of the two parties. Moreover platform promises have been a good guide to a party's future performance. Depending on the time interval cited, platform promises have been acted upon in some way from 2/3 to 3/4 of the time. *See also: CONVENTION; CREDENTIALS COMMITTEE; RULES COMMITTEE*

PLATFORMS *See PLATFORM COMMITTEE*

POL *See POLITICO*

POLITICAL CLEARANCE *See SPONSOR*

POLITICAL PARTY ENDORSEMENTS *See ENDORSEMENTS*

POLITICAL SPONSOR *See SPONSOR*

POLITICO a pragmatist who accumulates and uses political power according to the principle of what works. Politicos are incrementalists who rely on bargaining and compromise to reach consensus and get things done.

Usually the term is fairly neutral, however it can be used as a mild epithet by speakers who view politics as cynical and calculating. When real disparagement is intended the word often used is "pol." This is a politician who functions mainly to put deals together and exercise power—but who lacks any larger sense of purpose.

PRECINCTS the neighborhood unit of political organization. Precincts have a dual function in the United States. They are in most states the basic administrative units for operating the electoral machinery. The about 175,000 local polling places are located in precincts. Votes are counted and reported from precincts and election officials like pollwatchers and election judges work in precincts on election day.

Precincts also have another function. They are the bottom rung organizational level for the political parties. Precincts make up wards which in turn make up municipal and county party structures. Within the political parties precincts are headed by a committeeman and committeewoman (in some places these leaders are called precinct captains.) Every two years (usually) precinct officials are elected either in local caucuses or during primary elections.

Theoretically precinct leaders are expected to be the tireless footsoldier for the political party—the person voters can go to during the year to get help with government officials, have a street paved, a tax bill changed or even get a job for themselves or a relative. In return precinct leaders are expected to deliver the vote on election day.

Outside of a few political machine areas few precincts actually operate like this today. Most committeemen and women are hard pressed just to keep their street lists up to date and mount some semblance of an election day organization. In fact the political parties are themselves pressed to even fill the precinct leader positions. Studies have revealed more than half of them to be vacant in some states. *See also: COUNTY COMMITTEE; NATIONAL COMMITTEE; STATE COMMITTEE; STRATARCHY; WARDS*

PRIMARY ELECTION *See DIRECT PRIMARY*

R'S AND D'S insider shorthand for Republicans and Democrats respectively. R's and D's connotes a partisan flavor tinged with respect and even admiration. Politicians themselves use the term the way that members of some exclusive club might refer to a rival club: a mixture of privileged familiarity and open regard.

Popular opinion often holds that there isn't much real difference between R's and D's—"not a dime's worth of difference" as former presidential candidate George Wallace was fond of repeatedly telling his audiences. Political scientists, historians, journalists, and even humorists however generally disagree—pointing out with various evidence that R's and D's generally come from different backgrounds, have different philosophies, belong to different social groups and favor different policies.

Most research bears out the experts' opinions. For example polling data from the 1984 election reveals that there are substantial differences between R's and D's on the basis of income, political philosophy, sex, race, and religion: Republicans tend to be richer, more conservative, younger and whiter. They also tend to live in the West or Midwest. Democrats tend to be low and middle income, more liberal, older and more likely to be black. Democrats also tend to live in the East or South and to be Jewish or Catholic.

Moreover the available evidence is that the professional politicians in both parties differ sharply on ideology. In fact Republican activists are much more conservative than Democrats or even rank and file Republicans. And Democrat activists are much more liberal than Republicans or even rank and file Democrats. *See also: DEMOCRATIC COALITION; UPSTATE AND DOWNSTATE*

RABBI *See SPONSOR*

RANNEY INDEX OF COMPETITION a rating system developed by political scientist Austin Ranney (1971) which gauges the degree to which the Democratic and Republican parties actually compete with each other in a given state. The Ranney Index of Competition is a rough guide of the extent to which American elections feature serious contests between the two major parties.

According to Ranney, competitive elections are those that include candidates from both the Democratic and Republican parties, in circumstances in which either party has a reasonable expectation of winning. By this measure actual party competition varies considerably among the 50 states.

Virtually every state is now competitive in presidential elections, however this is not the case for other offices such as U.S. House, U.S. Senate and Governor.

In fact, the current Ranney Index indicates that over 50% of the states—28 states mostly in the South and West—do not feature genuine two party competition for offices below the presidency. Eight of these 28 are "one party states" in which the opposition party is never a factor; the other 20 non-competitive states are "modified one party states" in which the opposition party is only rarely a factor.

Only 22 states then—mostly in the North and Midwest—have competitive two party systems in which both the Democratic and Republican parties regularly vie against each other for state offices. Interestingly, competition between the two parties also varies by specific offices within a particular state. Some offices are consistently held by the same party in election after election—while other offices in the same state are usually competitive. *See also: PARTY SYSTEMS; TWO PARTY SYSTEMS*

REALIGNING ELECTION an election which results in a fundamental restructuring of the existing pattern of political power. Realigning elections are those in which the electorate permanently shifts its support and loyalty from the prevailing majority party. The minority party wins and in the process becomes the new majority party.

Political scientist Angus Campbell (1960) has developed a widely used classification system which labels American national elections as either "maintaining elections," "deviating elections" or "realigning elections." Maintaining elections are the most common. In them the majority party wins and the electorate's underlying loyalties and voting patterns are unchanged. Political analysts consider 1960, 1964 and 1976 to have been maintaining elections.

Deviating elections are next most common. In them the majority party loses because of some short term forces peculiar to that election, but the basic partisan attachments of the electorate remain unchanged. The presidential elections of 1952, 1956, 1968, and 1972 were all deviating elections. Realigning elections are the least common. In them the majority party loses because of permanent changes in the loyalties and voting patterns of the electorate.

Scholars disagree whether there have been three, four, or five realigning elections in American history. Most however list the elections of 1860, 1896, and 1932 as realigning. All of these featured great political and economic turbulence amid fierce debate over the future direction of the nation.

Recently some political analysts have speculated that changes in the electorate may be signaling a new realignment era. Specifically they point to the increase of Independents, the rise in ticket splitting and the steady erosion in the strength of the majority Democratic Party. In fact some analysts believe that the 1980 election was a realignment.

Others however doubt that any realignment has occurred or is imminent. They argue that instead a "dealignment" is occurring in which the old partisan loyalties and voting patterns are disappearing, without being immediately replaced by new ones. Dealignment brings a period of flux and instability—during which the electorate gropes for new political continuity and the political parties compete to become the next majority party.

REPORT CARDS ratings produced by organized interest groups which measure the voting record of legislators. Report cards, also known as score cards, are usually based on a few "litmus test" issues considered vital by the rating organization.

Some 70 lobbying organizations issue report cards for Congress. Among these are such interest groups as the AFL-CIO, U.S. Chamber of Commerce, Americans for Democratic Action, National Taxpayers Union, and the National Federation of Independent Businesses.

The evaluation systems used are not complicated. Legislators are rated on the percentage of "right votes" cast on a scale of 0 to 100. Individual members can receive very different ratings depending on the interest group involved. In 1984 for example the AFL-CIO rated Senator William Armstrong (R-Colo.) as 0%; but the U.S. Chamber of Commerce rated him 84%, and the National Taxpayers Union rated him 73%. For the same year, Senator William Bradley (D-N.J.) was rated 82% by the AFL-CIO, but only 32% by the U.S. Chamber, and 29% by the Taxpayers Union.

Scoring well on the report card of a major interest group can be important to a political career. Ratings are circulated among members who may use them to assess an incumbent's performance. Often more important, the scores are used by interest groups to make decisions about campaign contributions and other forms of support.

Political analysts often charge that report card rating systems are misleading and unfair. They point out that the scoring measures only the easiest to count aspect of legislative service—voting. Committee work, constituency service and even legislative leadership are ignored. Critics also complain that the report cards include only a sample of the votes actually taken and don't therefore accurately reflect overall voting records. *See also: HANDICAPPING; OPPOSITION RESEARCH; PAC's*

REPUBLICAN COALITION *See DEMOCRATIC COALITION*

REPUBLICAN NATIONAL COMMITTEE (RNC) *See NATIONAL COMMITTEE*

ROBOT RULE a controversial party rule adopted by the Democrats during their 1980 convention. It required delegates elected in primaries or caucuses to vote on at least the first ballot for those candidates to whom they were pledged. Known also as the "faithful delegate rule" and more formally as Rule 11 (h), the issues raised by the Robot Rule are very old ones in representative democracy. James W. Davis in his definitive book on national conventions put it in this perspective:

> (The robot rule) defined in essence the role of delegates at a national convention. Should they be able to cast their votes only for the candidates they were instructed, often months earlier, to represent, or should they be free as "Trustees" to change their minds and vote their consciences? . . . this dispute symbolized the classic conflict between the Progressive instructed delegate versus the Burkean—party regular concept of representation . . . .
> (Davis, 1983:90)

The debate and convention vote on the Robot Rule was the focus of a key test of delegate strength between Carter and Kennedy in 1980. The Carter forces favored rule 11 (h) and the Kennedy forces opposed it. Kennedy lost and shortly thereafter withdrew from the race.

The Robot Rule however was short lived. In 1981 the Democratic National Committee appointed the Hunt Commission to review delegate selection processes. The Commission recommended repeal of the Robot Rule and the Democratic National Committee did so in 1982. Now even though delegates may be pledged to a candidate they are essentially free to support any candidate they wish on any ballot. *See also: CONVENTIONS; RULES COMMITTEE*

ROCK RIBBED REPUBLICANS *See YELLOW DOG DEMOCRAT*

RULE OF 36 *See GAIN-DEFICIT RULE*

RULES COMMITTEE one of the three major committees used by the Democratic and Republican Parties to carry out the business of their national conventions. The other two are the credentials committee and the platform committee.

The Rules Committee establishes the basic regulations and procedures under which each convention operates. Normally the rules adopted in each convention are similar to those used in earlier conventions, and they are not controversial. The Rules Committee however has been the scene of some monumental clashes between supporters of rival presidential candidates. When these conflicts are taken to the convention floor, their outcome almost always predicts accurately the convention's eventual presidential nominee.

Serious rules disputes have occurred in at least one of the two major party conventions since 1968. These battles have usually overshadowed any that might be going on in either the Credentials or Platform Committees. In each instance the victor in the rules fight was also able to control the convention itself and win the presidential nomination. This pattern has become so regular that some political analysts believe that struggles over convention rules—rather than those over credentials or even platforms—have become the most reliable indicator of who will win in close nomination contests. *See also: CONVENTION; CREDENTIALS COMMITTEE; PLATFORM COMMITTEE*

RUNOFF PRIMARY a primary election following a previous primary election in which none of the candidates received at least 50% of the vote. Runoff primaries are contests between the top two vote getters in the first primary. Nine southern states, plus Oklahoma and Washington, D.C. require runoff primaries if no candidate wins a majority of the votes cast in the first primary. Runoffs date to the late 19th Century and are historically linked to the collapse of the Republican Party in the South. The traditional argument for runoffs was that the primary in the (one party Democratic) South was equivalent to the general election in other parts of the country. Since the Democratic nominee would rarely face real Republican opposition it was important that candidate did have the support of a majority of Democratic primary voters.

Recently runoff primaries have become politically controversial. Black leadership has opposed them, equating runoffs with literacy tests, poll taxes, white primaries and other vestiges of past voting discrimination.

The fundamental black argument is that runoffs foster racial bloc voting— whites vote for whites and blacks vote for blacks. Whites usually win these contests and blacks usually lose even when black candidates have finished first in the earlier primary. Allegedly the ultimate result of all this is de facto disenfranchisement of black voters and continued white majority rule.

Wrangling about runoffs emerged in the Democratic party during the 1984 presidential campaign when many black leaders demanded national party support for their abolishment. The issue looms as a serious dilemma for the Democratic party. Many analysts believe that elimination of runoffs would bring about large scale southern white defection to the Republican party. *See also: DIRECT PRIMARY; WHITE PRIMARY*

SAFE SEATS *See MARGINAL SEATS*

SAMPLE BALLOT *See SLATE CARD*

SCORE CARD *See REPORT CARD*

SITTING ON THEIR HANDS *See TAKING A WALK*

SLATE a list of candidates for office compiled by political party officials and presented to voters in a primary election. Slates are the party ticket— the candidates selected to represent the party or political organization in the future general election. Candidates endorsed by party officials in advance of the primary are said to have been slated.

Two kinds of slatemaking processes are found in the United States. One type, informal slatemaking, is practiced in those areas which still have strong party organizations. Cities like New York, Chicago and Philadelphia are prominent examples.

Their slating committees screen the credentials of prospective candidates. Often an interview is held and candidates are given the opportunity to present their qualifications. Subsequently a team of candidates are chosen who are promoted and supported by the party organization during the primary campaign.

With informal slatemaking there is no legal basis for endorsing candidates and slated candidates are not designated on the official ballot. But the second kind of slatemaking used in the United States is quite different. This type, formal slatemaking, is based on state law and slated candidates are identified on the ballot.

In those states which use formal slatemaking, candidates are usually endorsed only after a pre-primary convention open to other candidates. Whether done informally or formally, slating is one of the tools still available to political parties who want to control the nominating process in their own direct primaries. *See also: DELIVERING; ENDORSEMENTS*

SLATE CARDS postcard size facsimilies of the official ballot which usually emphasize the name and ballot position of one or more candidates. Slate cards—also known as "palm cards" and "sample ballots"—are prepared and distributed on election day by a political party or candidate organization.

The emphasis on them varies among local political jurisdictions. They are more heavily used in urban areas and in jurisdictions where excessively long ballots confront the voter with dozens of offices to fill and hundreds of names from which to choose.

In primary elections, precinct and ward officials sometimes sponsor competing slates and then charge candidates street money in return for a listing on the sample ballot. In some locales there are even AM and PM slate cards. Candidates pay the going rate to be listed on the sample ballot for the morning, a different rate to be listed on the afternoon-evening ballot, and perhaps a special combined rate to be listed on both.

Slate cards probably do influence the outcome of some elections. Their impact is certainly slight if any in highly visible top of the ticket general elections. At the other extreme they can be decisive in obscure low interest multi-candidate primaries. *See also: BALLOTS; ELECTION DAY; POLLING PLACE; STREET MONEY*

SORE LOSER LAW *See ANTI SOREHEAD LAW*

SPECIAL GROUPS campaign nomenclature for any voter groups both large enough and important enough that competing candidates vie for their support. Special groups become special when a campaign puts together an organization designed to appeal to group members on behalf of a candidate or party.

Ethnic groups are traditional special groups—Polish, Irish, Jewish, etc. Almost as common are groups based on professional associations like lawyers, doctors, accountants, teachers, etc. Becoming more frequent are special groups organized by age or sex—women, youth, retired etc. Special groups are also organized to represent issue concerns like abortion, gun control, and nuclear power.

Sometimes special groups amount to no more than "letterhead committees"—paper organizations which are set up with an impressive list of officials and titles, but with no real functions or activities.

When special groups are bonafide, campaigns use them to appeal to voters who are members of the group. Tactics vary but special groups usually formally endorse their candidate in a news release or even at a press conference. They also recruit volunteers and undertake fund raising. Ethnic special groups particularly often carry on registration programs and operate GOTV efforts on election day.

No one knows for certain what influence all of this has on voting. Research does indicate however that some bloc voting does go on and some voter groups are influenced by special appeals to them. *See also: BLOC VOTING; COALITIONS; ETHNIC GROUPS*

SPONSOR an influential patron who uses power and influence to advance the political career of someone less well connected. Sponsors are mentors who promote, protect and guide their political charges. They are people who by dint of hard work, personal prestige, or large campaign contributions have become influential within a particular political party of organization.

Sponsorship comes into play in two kinds of circumstances. The first and most common involves employment. Where patronage is used, sponsors are often required to attest to the qualifications of a job applicant. Usually political reliability is the main qualification of interest.

Sponsors also might be expected to help a job seeker gain "political clearance" by championing them among other power centers in the party. Not infrequently sponsors even compete with other sponsors for available jobs.

Sponsorship can also be important when lucrative government contracts are awarded. Sponsors might write a letter or make a call to facilitate the business transaction—or in other ways use the access their connections provide.

"Rabbi" is a near synonym. "Rabbi's" are sponsors who themselves are usually involved in high level active politics. Their political proteges are likely to be senior government officials or even aspiring young politicians. *See also: PATRONAGE*

STATE CHAIRMAN *See STATE COMMITTEE*

STATE COMMITTEE the general name given to the governing body of state political parties. State committee for the Democrats in a given state is referred to as Democratic State Committee, while Republicans are referred to as Republican State Committee. In a few states the appellation is State Central Committee.

State committees are the level of political party organization that fits between county committee and national committee. Their memberships usually include state committeemen and committeewomen chosen at the county or congressional district level of the party.

State committees are headed by an elected state chairman who today is usually assisted by a permanent full time staff. Normally the state chair is an important figure. When his party holds the state house the chair is probably a senior adviser to the governor on political matters and often plays a major role in the dispensing of patronage. When the state chair's party is out of power, he is usually an influential leader and may be the dominant force in the party.

The political role of state committees varies from state to state. In some states they are powerful bodies that can dictate party policy, determine who is slated, and decide how party funds will be raised and spent. But in other states they are not much more than weak advisory committees with no real functions and little influence.

Most state committees provide a program of support activities for their state candidates and local parties. These generally include voter registration drives, GOTV projects, and other voter contact activities. Many state committees also offer research services to their candidates and almost all now conduct campaign management seminars. *See also: COUNTY COMMITTEE; NATIONAL COMMITTEE*

STRATARCHY a form of organization peculiar to political parties and political campaigns. A stratarchy is an organization in which the different "levels" are loosely linked together. Stratarchies resemble confederations more than they do hierarchies.

The term was suggested by political scientist Samuel J. Eldersveld who defines them this way:

> By stratarchy is meant an organization with layers or strata of control rather than one of centralized leadership from the top down . . . each stratum of organization is relatively autonomous in its own sphere . . . there is, thus, (shared) power and decision making and a recognition that lower layers are not subordinant to the commands or sanctions of higher strata.
> (Eldersveld, 1982:99)

The two major political parties are stratarchies. So are most campaign organizations. Thus the parties have a national committee, state committees, county committees and wards and precincts. Campaigns often parallel the party strata. But there is rarely any amount of centralized control or authority between levels. Coordination and cooperation is loose and informal. Power is shared and influence is exerted mainly through bargaining and compromise. *See also: COUNTY COMMITTEE; NATIONAL COMMITTEE; STATE COMMITTEE*

SUPER DELEGATES *See UNCOMMITTED DELEGATES*

TAKING A WALK refusing to support the candidates of one's own party in a particular election. Taking a walk is to amble around the political countryside, but to eventually return home. The phrase was popularized by Al Smith who took a walk in 1936 after Franklin Roosevelt was renominated. Politicians who take a walk plan to get back the day after the election. Those who don't care for walking might be "going fishing." Even more sedentary politicians might be found "sitting on their hands." All of them in any case could be said to be "off the reservation."

Taking a walk is only one of several actions a candidate or faction might take after losing a party fight. Much more serious would be to campaign for the other party, to switch to the other party, or even to set up a rival third party.

Political parties of course try to avoid any of these. The national conventions of both parties end with massive love feasts to reduce the chances of defection. Losing candidates and their dismayed supporters are appealed to come together, close ranks and present a united front for the upcoming general election.

Practicing politicians, no matter how deep their disappointment are usually loath to take a walk. The prospects of the opposition party winning is to be considered as is the possibility that the renegade politician might be blamed for the loss. Political futures can be compromised by animosity over any desertion. Even politicians who do take a walk usually proclaim publicly that they are supporting the ticket.

THIRD PARTIES any political party other than the Democratic or Republican. Third parties in America emphasize issues and ideologies. Most are small and many are temporary.

Political scientist Walter Burnham has suggested that there are two types of third parties: 1) Third parties with long life, but low penetration. These include parties like the Prohibition Party and the Marxist Party. This type of party might become permanent but it never receives wide support. 2) Third parties with short life, but high penetration. These include parties like the Bull Moose Party and the American Independent Party. This type might last only one or two elections, but it has wide appeal during that brief period.

Overall third parties receive little support form the American electorate. They rarely win elections and almost never share power. Only about one percent of all Americans identify with them. And just eleven times in the nation's history have minor parties received five percent or more of the vote.

Nevertheless, third parties have been important in American politics. There have been almost 1100 of them since the early 19th Century. Their traditional function has been to propose new ideas and advocate political reforms. Several third party planks have been adopted over the years. These include the progressive income tax, prohibition, women's suffrage, and several social welfare programs.

In a few states third parties adapt themselves to the two party system by nominating the same candidates nominated by the major parties. In New York State the Liberal Party usually nominates the candidates of the Democratic Party while the Conservative Party sometimes nominates the candidates of the Republican Party. This practice, known as a fusion ticket gives the major parties an extra line on the ballot, while it gives the third party some leverage with the major parties. *See also: FUSION TICKETS; LIBERAL PARTY; PARTY SYSTEMS; SINGLE MEMBER DISTRICT; TWO PARTY SYSTEM*

THRESHOLD RULE a standard used by the Democratic party to govern the selection of convention delegates. In primary elections and caucuses the Threshold Rule stipulates that a presidential candidate must receive a minimum proportion of the popular vote before receiving any convention delegates. This minimum proportion or threshold is set at 15% to 20%.

The Threshold Rule works to the advantage of well known candidates who have broad based support, but it handicaps candidates whose appeal is concentrated among a particular ethnic group or region of the country. In 1984 for example Walter Mondale achieved the threshold in every state primary and was able to win over 50% of the convention delegates with about 40% of the popular vote. Jesse Jackson on the other hand failed to meet the threshold in many states and received only 7% of the delegates despite winning 22% of the vote. *See also: CONVENTION*

TWO PARTY SYSTEM the prevailing system of political competition in the United States and several other western democracies. In two party systems most of the elections are won by one or the other of the two major political parties—in the United States the Democratic or Republican parties. The two parties alternate control of government although there may be long periods in which one holds sway.

Third parties may exist in two party systems, but they win few elections and are never strong enough to prevent one of the major parties from governing. The United States now has a vigorous two party system for presidential elections, however, the situation is less consistent at local and state levels. Many congressional districts are dominated by one party, and are not really competitive. In fact over 80% of all House elections are won by 55% or more of the vote.

Moreover many of the individual states do not have competitive two party systems. Political scientist Austin Ranney (1971) has classified all 50 states according to the degree of two party competition that actually exists. Eight states are classified as one party states, another 20 states are modified one party states; and only 22 states are genuinely two party competitive states.

Today some observers believe the two party system may be breaking down. The rising proportion of Independents in the electorate, the steady decline in influence of the major parties and the burgeoning of special interest groups—may all lead to the development of a multi-party system.

This is possible but similar expectations have risen before when one or the other of the two major parties was in a period of decline. Each time the durable two party system was reestablished as the dominant form of political competition. *See also: PARTY SYSTEM; RANNEY INDEX OF COMPETITION; SINGLE MEMBER DISTRICT; THIRD PARTIES*

TWO-THIRDS RULE a celebrated bylaw that was used in Democratic national conventions for 101 years. The Two-Thirds Rule required that a two-thirds majority of delegates voting were necessary to nominate candidates for president or vice-president. The often controversial rule was first adopted in 1835 at the convention that nominated Martin Van Buren. It was abolished in 1936 at the convention that nominated Franklin Roosevelt for a second term.

Democratic conventions were often protracted affairs while the Two-Thirds Rule prevailed. The rule had the effect of giving every major wing of the party a veto over the presidential nominee. The South in particular, was advantaged by the Two-Thirds Rule which frequently gave it the balance of power in contested conventions.

Repeal of the Two-Thirds Rule brought important changes to Democratic conventions. The number of favorite son nominations dropped drastically. No longer could a few key delegates block a nomination—or stall for the chance to late put together a successful coalition. The number of nominating ballots was also reduced because now only a majority of delegates were required to nominate. Since 1936 in fact there has been only one convention (1952) to go beyond the first ballot.

Repeal of the Two-Thirds rule brought one other important change to Democratic conventions. It made eventual dropping of the Unit Rule (in 1968) acceptable to delegates. These two party bylaws had respectively required extraordinary majorities (the 2/3 rule) and provided the mechanism for achieving them (the Unit Rule). With the former gone, the later became unnecessary. *See also: UNIT RULE*

UNCOMMITTED DELEGATES national convention delegates who are elected in primaries or caucuses as unpledged or who are chosen by state parties as "super delegates." Uncommitted delegates are a smaller proportion of each succeeding Democratic and Republican convention. The trend in the selection of delegates has been toward choosing them in binding primaries or caucuses. About 75% of convention delegates are now chosen this way pledged to specific candidates—whereas in earlier times 60 to 70% of the delegates might arrive at the convention uncommitted.

Many political scientists are troubled by the increasing absence of uncommitted delegates at national conventions. They argue that a convention made up largely of committed delegates is rigid and unable to compromise. Such a convention loses its capacity to function as a deliberative assembly since it can only ratify the results of the primaries and caucuses.

There is some countertrend toward increasing the proportion of uncommitted delegates to national conventions. The Democratic party eliminated the so-called Robot Rule for its 1984 convention and allocated 14% of its seats to super delegates. These delegates are chosen on the basis of their public office or party status and without being formally pledged to a candidate. *See also: ROBOT RULE*

UNION BUG the seal or imprint on an item of campaign paraphernalia that identifies it as union made. The union bug is an important symbol to trade unions who regard its use to be emblematic of solidarity with union aims and values. Candidates who have or hope to have union support are careful to insure that the bug is properly affixed before material is used or disseminated.

Campaign items that are expected to have a union bug include signs, brochures, most other printed matter, and some equipment. A great deal of material has been pulled from campaign inventories after discovering that the union bug had not been properly impressed upon it. *See also: BIG LABOR; UNION HOUSEHOLDS*

UNION HOUSEHOLDS an important category used by pollsters to label poll respondents who are union members or belong to households that include union members. Union households is a socio-economic classification like income, education, and occupation that groups people together who are likely to behave similarly.

Voters who are members of union households are a major part of the so-called blue collar vote in the United States. They generally support candidates of the Democratic Party and traditionally make up a substantial proportion of the Democratic coalition. Union households constitute about 25% of the adult population and contribute an average of about 30% of the total Democratic vote. Their loyalty to the Democratic Party is as high as 80% in some elections.

Lack of solid support from union households for Democratic candidates is a reliable sign that a candidacy is in trouble. Recently, the national Republican Party has attracted substantial support from union members and their families. If this key group of voters began to shift between the two major parties, it could signal the beginning of a new volatility in national politics. *See also: BIG LABOR; DEMOCRATIC COALITION*

UNIT RULE a winner take all system which requires a delegation or slate of electors to cast all of its votes as a bloc for that candidate who has received at least a plurality of those votes in earlier balloting. Until 1968 the Democratic Party allowed states to use the Unit Rule in its national conventions. While in effect, each member of a state delegation bound by the rule was required to vote for that candidate supported by a majority within the delegation. When the Democrats abolished the Unit Rule, they also forbid its use in state and local party caucuses and conventions.

The Unit Rule is still used in Electoral College balloting for president and vice-president. Under election procedures in all the states, those candidates for president and vice-president whose electors receive a plurality of the popular vote are entitled to all of the electoral votes allocated to that state. This is accomplished by grouping together on the same statewide ticket all of a candidate's electors. A vote for any one elector is a vote for the entire bloc of them—and the bloc with the most votes determines the Electoral College delegates who will cast that state's votes for a president.

Neither the constitution nor federal law require the states to follow a unit rule in choosing Electoral College slates. The practice is a result of custom and law in each individual state. *See also: PLURALITY*

VOLUNTEERS unpaid workers found at all levels of political campaigns. Volunteers traditionally do the grunt work in politics: canvassing, working telephone banks, stuffing envelopes, answering mail, and running errands. There are, however, many campaigns in which volunteers fill high administrative and strategic roles. Key positions in small and medium sized campaigns are often filled with volunteers.

There are differences of opinion about the importance of volunteers in modern campaigning. Some political professionals believe volunteers are vital. They point out especially that volunteers provide the manpower for the canvassing and election day activities which seem to make the difference in many campaigns. Other political observers discount the value of volunteers. They argue that today's heavy campaign reliance on electronic media and the computer has made volunteers obsolete.

The actual presence of volunteers in campaigns has declined in recent years. Federal campaign finance laws have limited the money spent for storefront and other activities that attract and sustain volunteer commitment. The new technologies of modern politics has also diminished the demand for volunteers. *See also: AMATEURS AND REGULARS; VOCATIONALISTS*

WALL STREET, MAIN STREET, EASY STREET a metaphorical reference to the three major factions within the Republican party. Wall Street anchors the eastern and liberal wing of the party and symbolizes the ancient east-west conflicts that have historically created deep rifts among Republicans. Main Street is the midwestern and moderate wing of the party which holds the centrist values of traditional Republicanism. Easy Street is the southern and western wing of the party—the newest and the most conservative of the major Republican factions.

Political scientists Don Nimmo and William Rivers have described these traditional cleavages:

> Wall Street is the eastern wing of the party. It is the Republican Party of Thomas E. Dewey and Wendell Willkie, of Dwight Eisenhower and Henry Cabot Lodge, and . . . Nelson Rockefeller. the Wall Street Republicans are usually considered to be the left wing of the party . . . .
>
> Main Street is the midwestern wing of the party, the center of the Republican party both geographically and ideologically. Main Street Republicans are rural and smalltown dwellers, small businessmen and professionals, the party of decent, honest, God-fearing and tight-fisted men . . . .
>
> Easy Street, the Republican party of the nouveau riche, is an altogether new phenomenon. It appeared quite suddenly in the suburbs and boomtowns of the

Sunbelt . . . . Historically, the South and the Southwest were areas of conservative Democratic strength. Therefore, it is not surprising that this new Republican right held a special appeal for former Democrats. (Nimmo and Rivers. 1981).

The Wall Street, Main Street, and Easy Street Republican factions illustrate the great talent of American politics to accommodate right, left, and middle of the road within the same party. The diverse coalitions that make up the Republican and Democratic parties would be, in many other political systems, themselves independent political parties. *See also: COALITION; DEMOCRATIC COALITION*

WARD HEELER a low level political party functionary—a drone. The term is distinctly unsavory. Ward heelers are party workers who perform perfunctory chores usually in the service of a political machine.

In the heyday of the large city political organization, they were expected to canvass their precincts, solve the day to day problems of their constituents, and get out the vote on election day. Today most of their functions have been taken over by the modern precinct captain or eclipsed by the new politics. *See also: NEW POLITICS*

WARDS the level of political party organization between precincts and counties. Generally, wards are composed of election districts or precincts. They, in turn, make up the county level of political organization.

The size of wards differs widely. In some rural areas and small towns, a ward might comprise fewer than a hundred people; in large cities they can include thousands of people. Nationally, there are an estimated 7,000 wards and about 175,000 precincts. The State of Pennsylvania has about 400 wards and 10,000 precincts. The City of Philadelphia in Pennsylvania has 66 wards and 1700 precincts.

The term ward and the phrase "ward politics" often carries an unfavorable connotation which suggest raw patronage, grimy deals, corrupt practices, and cynical politics. Wards themselves, however, are simply intermediate organizational units in the structure of the political parties.

Wards and ward leaders tend to be active and important where local political parties are healthy and vigorous. In cities like Boston, Chicago, and Philadelphia, the ward organizations still exercise considerable influence on the course of political affairs. But in those areas where the political parties have declined, wards are much less important. *See also: COUNTY COMMITTEE; NATIONAL COMMITTEE; STATE COMMITTEE*

WHITE PRIMARY a primary election in which participation is limited to white registered voters. White primaries were used mainly by some southern states. They excluded black citizens from meaningful involvement in the electoral process by restricting membership in the Democratic Party to whites. Since the Democratic Party was then virtually the one party of consequence—winning the Democratic primary was tantamount to being elected—blacks could be effectively frozen out of the elective process.

White primaries were only one of the various ploys once used to prevent blacks from participating in politics. Other tactics included poll taxes, literacy tests, and grandfather clauses. All of these have been declared illegal and unconstitutional. The Voting Rights Act of 1965 and its amendments provided the tools to monitor and enforce federal laws designed to prevent voting discrimination.

Recently, some black organizations have charged that run off primaries are also discriminating to black voters because they encourage whites to vote in a bloc against black candidates. Run off primaries are now widely used throughout the South. *See also: RUN OFF PRIMARIES; VOTING RIGHTS ACT*

WINDOW the time interval between the beginning and the end of a process or series of events. In the political context, the term window is used to delineate the three month period in a presidential election year from early March to early June in which the Democratic party requires its state parties to hold their presidential primaries or first round caucuses.

The NATIONAL JOURNAL used the term in reviewing the Democrat's 1984 primary and caucuses calendar:

> . . . the Democrats retain the window that requires primaries and first tier caucuses to be held no earlier than the 2nd Tuesday in March and no later than the 2nd Tuesday in June . . . by narrowing the window the reformers reduced the period that voters normally spend looking at the candidates and sizing them up . . . .

The national Democrats adopted windows and front loaded their primaries and caucuses in order to shorten the political season and concentrate on the nomination process. The national Republicans do not restrict their state parties as to when they hold their primaries or caucuses. Among Republicans, however, there is also a trend toward tighter schedules and briefer nomination periods. *See also: FRONT LOADING*

YELLOW DOG DEMOCRAT voters who are hard core committed Democrats. The political counterparts of yellow dog Democrats are rock ribbed Republicans. Both are fierce partisans who support their respective party's candidates in virtually every election.

Yellow dog Democrats and rock ribbed Republicans are a declining force in American politics. Combined they now make up less than 30% of the electorate. The other 70% are either Independents or weak partisans. This larger group of voters are ticket splitters or party switchers who rarely if ever vote straight ticket Democratic or Republican.

The decrease in hard core committed Democrats and Republicans may be producing a less stable and more volatile electorate. Future voters—freed of partisan allegiences—may be more likely to shift from candidate to candidate during the campaign and they may remain undecided later. *See also: PARTY IDENTIFICATION*

6

VOTING AND POLITICAL BEHAVIOR

ABSENTEE BALLOT a ballot cast by an otherwise qualified voter unable to be physically present at the polls on election day. Absentee ballots are permitted in most states. Eligibility varies among the states, but generally voters who will be absent from home for military service or business reasons or who are severely ill may cast absentee ballots.

Voters who do not use absentee ballots usually must obtain a ballot within a prescribed period before the election, mark it, have it notarized, and mail it to the designated election officials.

Absentee voting in the United States is similar to what is known as postal voting in several other western democracies. Many of these countries have been far more aggressive than the United States in providing absentee voting opportunities. Several open their polling stations in advance of the date of the election for those who will not be present on election day.

Absentee voting is a relatively minor factor in the outcome of most American elections despite the fact that millions of voters would be disenfranchised every election for causes that would allow them to cast absentee ballots. Few voters seem inclined to make the effort to apply for and cast an absentee ballot. Even fewer political campaigns put any substantial effort into organizing absentee voters. *See also: BALLOTS.*

APATHETICS *See GLADIATORS*

ATTENTIVE PUBLICS the 15% or so of the population that consistently pays a good deal of attention to political matters, follows politics more or less regularly, and holds reasonably well informed views about public matters. Attentive politics is one of three broad categories used by political scientists to describe and classify people according to their political activity. The smallest of these three publics and the politically most involved are "political activists" who comprise not more than 5% of the population.

Political activists are people who participate regularly and intensely in politics. They include key government officials, politicians and leading citizens.

The next largest group is the attentive publics which make up perhaps 15% of the population. They are politically interested citizens who regularly and closely follow politics.

Attentive publics monitor the actions of government and generally let their opinions be known.

The largest public of all is the "general public" which consists of about 80% of the population. General publics pay very little direct attention to political affairs. They, in fact, get much of their information and derive most of their attitudes about politics from attentive publics. Because of their key role in opinion formation, a good deal of campaign strategy and political advertising is directed to attentive publics. This is especially so in primary elections and in elections where the turnout is expected to be low. *See also: GLADIATORS*

AUSTRALIAN BALLOT the generic name for the category of ballot that has been in general use throughout the United States since about 1890. The Australian ballot differs from earlier types of ballot in that it lists the names of all the candidates; it is produced and distributed only by election officials; and it is cast in secret.

The two major forms of the Australian ballot are the so-called "party column" or "Indiana ballot" and the office block or "Massachusetts" ballot. In the former the names of the candidates of each party are printed in separate columns under the party name. In the latter the names of the candidates and their party designations are printed in alphabetical order under each office.

Both the party column and office block formats can be used with paper ballot systems as well as voting machines. *See also: BALLOTS*

BALLOT BOX STUFFING the fraudulent addition of votes to those actually cast. Ballot box stuffing may well be the oldest form of voting fraud. It is surely one of the more obvious. In its most primitive form, ballot box stuffing is the overt act of putting illegal ballots into a ballot box.

Where voting machines are in use, the fraud involves multiple voting before the polls open or after they have closed. Both kinds of ballot box stuffing usually depend on the aid and abettance of election officials.

Ballot box stuffing probably doesn't occur as often today as it did in earlier times. This may be because it is fairly easy to detect and because there are now other less risky and more efficient ways to steal votes. *See also: CHAIN BALLOTS; VOTING FRAUD*

BALLOTS the formats in which voters cast votes. Various styles of ballots, including oral ballots, were used in the United States until the late 19th Century. Since then the Australian or secret ballot has been used almost exclusively.

It has two main forms. One of these, the "Indiana or party column" ballot lists all candidates for office in a single column under their party affiliation. The other, known as the Massachusetts or office block ballot, groups all candidates for office in blocks according to the office they seek. Both the party column and office block formats may be in paper ballot form or adapted to voting machines.

The type of ballot used in a jurisdiction is believed to have some influence on the outcome of elections. In those states using party column ballots, voters are more likely to vote straight tickets. And in these same party column ballot states, voters are more likely to resist voter falloff and to cast ballots for candidates running for the lesser offices, as well as those running for the major offices.

As a rule those states with stronger party organizations use the party column ballot while those with weaker party structures use the official block ballots. *See also: AUSTRALIAN BALLOT; ELECTORAL SYSTEM; LONG BALLOT; NON-PARTISAN ELECTION; STRAIGHT TICKET; VOTER FALLOFF*

BASE VOTE *See NORMAL VOTE*

BEDSHEET BALLOT *See LONG BALLOT*

BEHAVIORAL DEMOCRATS AND REPUBLICANS voters who are classified as either Democrat or Republican on the basis of some observed or self-reported behavior, such as voting a straight ticket or consistently voting for one or the other of the two parties. Voters are behaviorally classified as Independents on the basis of their ticket splitting or party switching. Behavioral Democrats, Republicans, or Independents are then voters whose partisan leaning or lack of it is inferred from their own past behavior.

The other major approach to determining the partisan orientation of voters is to ask them (usually during a poll) if they think of themselves as Democrats, Republicans, or what. These self-defined party identifications will sometimes classify a voter differently than the same voter would be classified using behavioral criteria. That is, voters will sometimes self-identify with one party or as Independents when this is inconsistent with their own past voting behavior.

There is controversy among public opinion experts as to which of the classification systems—behavorial based or self-defined party identification—is most reliable. The issue is an important one in politics because partisan orientation is known to be a major predicator of future voting behavior. In practice both systems of classifying voters are widely used. *See also: PARTY IDENTIFICATION; VOTING BEHAVIOR*

BIG LEVER the popular name for those voting machines that allow voters to enter the polling place, pull a single lever and vote automatically for all of the candidates of a political party. Big levers are found in some states which have adopted the "Indiana" or "party column ballot"—a format which lists all candidates in a single column under their party affiliation. Big levers are not used however in those states which provide the "Massachusetts" or "office block ballot"—a ballot style which lists all candidates for office in blocks according to the office sought. In these states voters must vote for each office individually rather than simply pull the Democratic or Republican lever.

States which do feature big levers actually give voters the option of voting straight ticket or parcelling out their vote among candidates of different parties. In Indiana for example a voter can simply ignore the party lever and plunk their way through each set of candidates and offices.

Not suprisingly, research suggests that the big lever encourages straight ticket voting while its absence produces more ticket splitting. Big levers probably also increase the coattail effects of popular candidates. When a candidate at the top of the ticket is a heavy vote getter, more people will pull the big lever for other candidates of the same party. *See also: BALLOTS; COATTAILS; STRAIGHT TICKET; TICKET SPLITTERS*

BLACK VOTERS the most conspicuous exception to the general rule that Americans do not vote in large solid blocs. Blacks do and it has important consequences for both major political parties.

Since about 1932 blacks have strongly supported Democrats. They have in fact been consistently the most cohesive constituency group in the Democratic Party, giving 80 to 90% of their vote to Democratic candidates. But before 1932 blacks tended to be overwhelmingly Republican. Traditionally then, black voting patterns have tended toward bloc voting.

This monolithic cast to black voting is one of two major differences between blacks and whites in overall voting behavior. The other is in registration and turnout rates which have been lower among blacks. Only about 10 million of the 17 million blacks eligible to register did so in 1982 and only 7 million of these actually voted.

Registration and turnout rates among white voters are about 20% higher than among blacks. This gap between white and black voting is usually explained in terms of the dissimilar socio-economic status of the two groups. Blacks are disproportionately low income and low education—characteristics that have been shown to be associated with low levels of political activity in the population as a whole.

In any case the differences between black and white registration and turnout may be disappearing. This is especially so among urban blacks who have recently been voting in very high numbers in support of black candidates. *See also: BLOC VOTING; DEMOCRATIC COALITION; ETHNIC GROUPS*

BLOC VOTING the tendency of some groups in the electorate to heavily support the same party or candidate. Several interest and ethnic groups are often classified as bloc voters. Thus it is said that there is a union vote, a farm vote, a black vote, a Polish vote, a Catholic vote, and so on.

These voting blocs are essentially the same as the constituency groups that make up the Democratic and Republican party coalitions. And like the two major parties, the voting blocs are heterogeneous collections of members, all of whom do not respond in the same way to candidates or issues. The relative importance of a voting bloc to a candidacy or party depends on three main factors: the size of the group, the strength of the group's commitment; and the group's voter turnout. For example, labor is a huge voting bloc, but its impact is diluted because it gives considerable support to both Democrats and Republicans. On the other hand, black voters are usually the most faithful supporters of any of the Democratic voting blocs, but their turnout rates are traditionally low. And Jewish voters comprise a relatively small proportion of the total electorate, but they are geographically concentrated and they turnout at a very high rate. *See also: BLACK VOTERS; DEMOCRATIC COALITION; ETHNIC GROUPS; JEWISH VOTERS; VOTERS*

BLUE COLLAR VOTE *See UNION HOUSEHOLDS*

CANDIDATE IMAGE the overall impression of a candidate or public figure held by the electorate. Scholars believe that candidate image is one of the three major influences—party identification and issue voting are the others—that determine voting behavior for the electorate as a whole.
Candidate image is made up of a complex of four distinct factors that mark out the mental picture voters have of their politicians. These factors include:

1. a personality factor—the personal qualities of a candidate such as warmth, intelligence, friendliness, integrity, etc.
2. an issue factor—the position of a candidate on issues important to the voter.
3. a job performance factor—the capability of a candidate to carry out the function of their office.
4. a political party factor—the political party or ideological label associated with a candidate.

Pollsters have developed a number of sophisticated ways to measure each of these components of the candidate image. For example a "thermometer scale" is used to determine how warm or cold voters feel about a candidate's personality. A job rating question is used to measure voters' evaluation of a candidate's job performance. And various "scales" and other techniques are employed to gauge the electorate's evaluation of a candidate's issue positions.
Many political observers believe that candidate voting is increasing in the United States—in more and more elections, voters are supporting candidates mainly because of their personal appeal. It is strongest where the political parties are weakest. It is also prominent in primary elections where voters must look beyond party affiliation for their cues. Candidate voting is normally highest in elections which feature well-known candidates or highly visible offices. It declines in elections which involve less recognized

candidates or less visible offices. Most ticket splitters—who make up from one-fourth to one-half of the electorate—are also candidate voters. *See also: COOL MEDIUM; ISSUE VOTING; PARTY IDENTIFICATION; POSITIONING; VOTING BEHAVIOR*

CATEGORIC GROUPS *See REFERENCE GROUPS*

CHALLENGES a charge by a poll watcher or other authorized election official that a potential voter is not qualified to vote. Challenges may be made if the identity of the prospective voter is questioned, if his residence is disputed, if he is not legally registered, or if fraud is alleged.

In some election districts a challenged voter may not vote until the challenge has been satisfied. In others, however, the voter may vote, but the vote is not counted until the challenge has been settled.

Usually a bipartisan panel of election judges or inspectors are designated to resolve challenges at the local polling place. If those officials cannot decide a challenge the question may be sent to the courts for a decision. *See also: ELECTION JUDGES; POLLWATCHER; VOTING FRAUD; VOTING QUALIFICATIONS*

CLEAVAGES the major divisions in the electorate. Cleavages are those factors which separate one group of voters from other groups.

Historically the most important cleavages in the United States have been regional (North, South and East, West), racial (black, white), religious (Catholic, Protestant), geographic (rural, urban), and ethnic (Polish, Italian, German, Irish, etc). Class based cleavages and language based cleavages—common in Europe—have never been major influences in America.

The notion of cleavages has some important applications in politics. Cleavages are the natural material of which coalitions are built. Knowing the important cleavages in an electorate allows analysts to predict how voters might behave and coalitions might be formed.

Pollsters also measure cleavages when they run their crosstabs. These analyses of polling data reveal the political differences among the electorate and suggest why they exist. *See also: COALITION; DEMOCRATIC COALITION*

COATTAILS the electoral appeal of a popular candidate that attracts voters to other candidates running on the same ticket. Coattails bring into office with the popular candidate some other candidates who would not have won on their own.

Coattail effects are seen most often in presidential elections and in those elections that feature a considerable amount of straight ticket voting.

There is good evidence that even very popular candidates have shorter coattails than was once the case. This is probably due to the frequency of ticket splitting among today's electorate as well as the rise in candidate voting. The modern American voter is less likely than earlier voters were to tie support for a favored candidate to other candidates of the same party. *See also: BALLOTS*

COMPULSORY VOTING legally compelled exercise of the franchise, enforced by sanctions or other penalties. The punishment for the failure to vote can range from a warning letter or small fine on through disenfranchisement of the non-voter.

Compulsory voting has been adopted in many European and South American nations. All together about thirty western democracies use some form of it. It has been seriously discussed in the United States, but never enacted into law.

The effects of compulsory voting have been studied extensively. It undoubtedly does increase voting if the law is enforced and the penalties are significant. Some studies indicate that it raises turnout an average of about 10%. It is less certain that compulsory voting alters the outcome of elections. Experience in several counties suggests that it does not, however, that might not hold if compulsory voting was used in this country.

In the United States a light turnout usually means a high proportion of those voting are loyalists of one or both of the major political parties. Conversely, a heavy turnout means that more Independents are voting. It follows then that the adoption of compulsory voting in the United States would probably produce a higher proportion of Independent voters.

It would also probably increase the proportion of Democrats voting since non voting is higher among Democratic identifiers than among Republican identifiers. Either or both of these changes in voting—an increase in Independent voting and an increase in Democratic voting—might shift the outcome of some American elections. *See also: NON VOTERS; TURNOUT*

CONSERVATIVE *See TRUE BELIEVER*

CONSERVATIVES an ideological cleavage in the American electorate who hold the political philosophy that free economic markets—those unburdened with government regulations or intervention—will produce the best possible social world. Conservatives stress individualism and they believe that change—when necessary at all—should come slowly. Conservative idealogues are found in both the Democratic and Republican parties.

Conservatism as a philosophy is often contrasted with liberalism. Most of the electorate however is probably neither liberal nor conservative. American voters by and large do not behave with great ideological consistency. Polls show for example that a majority of Americans believe that government should be smaller and spend less. But when the same polls ask specific questions about which programs should be cut, those polled reply that present spending is too low or about right.

This inconsistency has led political scientist Everett Carll Ladd, Jr. (1982), to suggest that Americans are "operational liberals" and "symbolic conservatives." They regularly support the symbolism of conservative rhetoric and values while they regularly oppose any actions that would actually reduce the role of government in society. *See also: CLEAVAGES; LIBERALS; TRUE BELIEVER*

CONVERSION shifting a voter's support from one candidate or party to another during the stages of a political campaign. Conversion is probably rare. The evidence from voting behavior studies is that when political attitudes change they do so slowly. Political scientists in fact estimate that only about 5% of those committed to a candidate become shifters, that is, change their mind during the campaign.
Arnold Steinberg in POLITICAL HANDBOOK (1976:171) expressed the conventional view about conversion:

> . . . the myth of conversion (is) an evangelical belief among diehard supporters that the more the candidate gets around before new audiences, the greater the support . . . public apathy, party loyalty, commitment to the opposition candidate, pre-conceptions and biases are all conveniently overlooked in this messianic strategy.

While conversion is not common, campaigns do have other similar affects on the electorate. Political scientists estimate that about 70% of those exposed to a campaign will eventually be "reinforced" or "activated" by the campaign—that is they will be motivated in the direction of their long standing predispositions for one party and its candidates.
Another 5% will be moved from their original partisan choice to Independent status. And about 15% will be unaffected by the campaign and essentially oblivious to it. Only 5% or one in twenty voters will be converted during the campaign. *See also: LAW OF MINIMAL CONSEQUENCES; VOTING BEHAVIOR*

CROSS PRESSURE conflicting social and political pressures which act on a voter in two different directions, one in a Republican direction and the other in a Democratic direction. The cross pressured voter might be a lifelong Republican who strongly favors one or more Democratic party policies—or a voter with deep roots in the Democratic Party who nevertheless is strongly attracted to Republican candidates. Independents are also subject to cross pressures.
The early voting behavior literature emphasized the importance of cross pressures in the outcome of elections. Voters who are cross pressured behave differently from those who are not. Cross pressured voters tend to be less interested in elections or who wins. They remain undecided longer and they are less likely to vote. If they do vote, they are more likely to be ticket splitters.
Voters who are not cross pressured—so called "consistently pressured" voters— are quite different. They tend to have high interest in elections and who wins. They make earlier decisions on voting. And they are more likely to vote and to be straight ticket voters.
Cross pressured voters are often heavily courted by both parties—especially during close elections where they may hold the balance of power. The effects of this attention are not clear. Earlier studies suggested that increas-

ing the cross pressures increased the chances that an individual would not vote. Some later studies have however reopened this issue. It may be that some types of cross pressure do spur political activity and increase turnout—while others have the opposite affect. *See also: VOTING BEHAVIOR*

CROSSOVERS voters who participate in the primary election of a political party other than their own, but then cross back over to support the candidate of their own party in the general election. Crossovers are possible only in those states that hold an open primary.

There is controversy among political analysts about both the extent and the effect of crossover voting. Some believe it is common and can determine the outcome of a close election because voters will tend to vote in the more exciting contests. Others discount the importance of crossover voting and argue that those voters who do vote for primary candidates of another party will also vote for them in the general election.

Democratic party rules prohibit crossover voting in presidential primaries, however there has been some difficulty enforcing this. Republicans permit it if it is allowed by state law. *See also: OPEN PRIMARY; RAIDING*

DISENFRANCHISE to deprive someone of their right to vote. Today the franchise or suffrage has been extended to almost every citizen 18 years or older. Nevertheless there are still several ways in which an individual voter can be disenfranchised.

The most common way to lose the right to vote is failure to register. Twenty to thirty percent of the potential electorate may not vote in any given election because they have not registered. Some voters are disenfranchised because they don't meet local residency requirements. These are however no longer important obstacles to voting since being reduced to 30 days or less in most states.

The other major legal sources of disenfranchisement are those disqualifications imposed on mental incompetents, persons convicted of serious crime, or citizens living on autonomous federal reservations such as military posts. Someone who gives up or loses their citizenship is also disenfranchised.

The term disenfranchisement is sometimes used loosely to describe voters who have been victims of some voting fraud. Voters who have not been given full representation under the doctrine of one man, one vote—or whose districts have been gerrymandered—are said to have been disenfranchised. Denial of the right to vote on the basis of race, color, or creed is also a form of disenfranchisement that still occasionally occurs in the United States.

Finally, pollsters inadvertently perform a kind of de-facto disenfranchisement on voters who seem poor prospects to vote. Screening questions used early in a poll measure a respondent's chances of actually casting a ballot. Those voters who do not pass the screen as likely voters are dropped from the poll—neither their opinions or their prospective vote is counted because they are unlikely to exercise the franchise on election day. *See also:*

ONE MAN, ONE VOTE; REGISTRATION; RESIDENCY REQUIREMENTS; VOTERS; VOTING QUALIFICATIONS; VOTING FRAUD

DONKEY VOTING the practice of purposefully and maliciously spoiling one's own ballot. Write in votes for Donald Duck or some other non candidate is donkey voting. So is marking ballots with nonsense symbols, numbers, or words, or simply leaving an entire ballot blank.
Donkey voting affects only 1—2% of the ballots cast in the United States. It is however considerably more common in those Western European and South American countries which have adopted compulsory voting. *See also: COMPULSORY VOTING; PROTEST VOTE.*

EARLY DECIDERS voters who make up their minds early in the campaign or even before the campaign begins. Early deciders then use the campaign to reinforce their original choice. Strong partisans—both Democrats and Republicans—tend to be early deciders. So do those voters who pay a lot of attention to politics and public affairs.
Political scientists once believed that a majority of voters were early deciders. The conventional wisdom was that about one-third of the electorate made their decision before the campaign started, another one-third decided very early in the campaign, and the remaining one-third made their choice sometime during the campaign.
Today more and more voters seem to be "late deciders" who make up their minds toward the end of the campaign, often in the last two to three weeks. Whereas early deciders are often strong partisans of one or another party, late deciders are more likely to be weak partisans or Independents.
The steady increase in the proportion of Independents and weak partisans in the electorate may in fact explain why late deciders are becoming more common in American elections. *See also: VOTING BEHAVIOR*

EFFICACY the sense of power and control individuals have about their ability to influence the political system. Efficacy also refers to the faith and trust people have in their government and elected officials.
Pollsters measure efficacy in several ways. Respondents are asked if government is honest, whether government is run for the benefit of all the people and how much of the time the government can be trusted. One standard question is often used by itself to gauge efficacy:

> Do you agree or disagree with the following? People like me don't have any say about what government does.

Political scientists have found that individuals vary considerably in the amount of efficacy they have. Not surprisingly, people with higher incomes, more education, and general self confidence are also people who score highly on indicators of efficacy.
Voting turn-out is known to be related to feelings of efficacy, i.e. people who have higher levels of trust in government and belief in their ability to influence it, are more likely to vote on election day. Scholars reason that

those who do vote are expressing faith in the system, as well as a belief that their own vote does count.

Republicans and their candidates probably benefit from the differences in efficacy levels found among various voting groups. Those groups in society with higher levels of efficacy tend to be disproportionately Republican while those groups with lower levels of efficacy tend to be disproportionately Democrats.

This pattern means that normally Republicans vote at a higher rate than do Democrats. This is why the Democratic Party and its candidates sometimes loses elections to Republicans despite having wide edges in numbers of registered voters. It is also the reason why Democrats usually put more effort into canvassing and GOTV programs than do Republicans. *See also: VOTING BEHAVIOR*

ELECTION FRAUD *See VOTING FRAUD*

ELECTION JUDGES officials who supervise balloting in each local voting district or precinct. Election judges are also known as election inspectors and election commissioners. These officials are responsible for the general operation of the polls on election day.

The exact duties of judges vary from place to place, but typically judges are charged with overseeing voting procedures, establishing the eligibility of individual voters, and tabulating and reporting election results. Before voting begins judges are required to insure that voting equipment is in good order and ready for operation. In paper ballot districts they unlock the ballot box; in voting machine districts they make ready the voting machine. During voting, judges process voters and administer the voting register which includes the names of eligible voters. Usually judges are also responsible for investigating and passing on the qualifications of prospective voters. After voting, judges count the ballots or record the totals from voting machines. These "tally sheets" are forwarded to municipal or county canvassing boards where they are eventually certified as the official returns.

Election judges are appointed in some jurisdictions and elected in others. Once selected they may designate one or more clerks to help them. These officials along with pollwatchers are the people that most voters encounter when they enter the official polling place on election day. *See also: CANVASSING BOARD; ELECTION DAY; POLLING PLACE; POLLWATCHERS; UNOFFICIAL RETURNS; VOTING FRAUD*

ELECTORATE *See VOTERS*

ETHNIC GROUPS classification of the electorate on the basis of race or national origin. Ethnic groups derive their political prominence from so called "ethnic voting"—the tendency of given members to vote for candidates who share their national or racial backgrounds. Italians vote for Italians, Poles vote for Poles, Irish for Irish, etc.

Political scientist Sandra Featherman explained the logic of ethnic voting in a 1984 interview with the PHILADELPHIA INQUIRER. According to her, familiar ethnic names provide some people with cues that influence their vote:

> people are looking for someone who would vote the way they would vote if they held a public office . . people make assumptions that a member of their own group will share their concerns. They are looking for someone raised as they were raised.

Political campaigns appeal to ethnic groups in several ways. One traditional approach is ticket balancing which slates candidates on party tickets so that each important ethnic group is represented. One version of this is the practice common in big cities of formally reserving legislative seats for particular ethnic groups. Thus, there might be a Jewish seat, a Black seat, a Hispanic seat and so on.

Another popular campaign tactic is to establish ethnic committees which promote specific candidates. These special groups carry names like Polish Americans for Hennessey or Italians for Ludwig. Sometimes special groups are mere letterhead committees, but often they actively raise money, sponsor campaign events, and provide volunteers.

Political scientists differ about the political importance of ethnic groups. Some believe that ethnic voting patterns will gradually disappear as assimilation continues. Others disagree, arguing that ethnic identification is a strong influence even after the 3rd, 4th, or 5th generations. Neither side to this dispute is likely to prevail soon since there is evidence supporting both points of view. *See also: BLOC VOTING; DEMOCRATIC COALITION; SPECIAL GROUPS*

ETHNIC VOTING *See ETHNIC GROUP*

EXPECTED VOTE *See NORMAL VOTE*

FLOATORS *See TICKET SPLITTER*

FULL CLEVELAND originally midwestern male attire consisting of a white tie, white belt, white patent leather shoes, double knit polyester maroon jacket and plaid pants. In political jargon full clevelands are middle American conservatives, home spun and basic in their views and their politics. Francis X. Clines and Warren Weaver Jr. staff writers for the NEW YORK TIMES attribute the term to Mark Shields, a Democratic political consultant. He first encountered the full cleveland in 1976 in Ohio while working for liberal presidential candidate Morris Udall of Arizona.

As Shields himself recalls that moment—"When I saw six full clevelands come out of the polls within two minutes, I knew we were dead."

There is no known sartorial equivalent to the full cleveland for other points on the political spectrum.

GENDER GAP the sex based differences in public opinion and voting behavior that apparently now exists within the American electorate. Women are more likely to identify with the Democratic party than the Republican party; they are more likely to vote for Democratic candidates; and they are likely to hold different opinions than men on a range of domestic and foreign issues. These differences, which are on the order of 5 to 10 percentage points, are especially clear among people under 45.

The gender gap is of recent origin. Until the late 1970's most polls showed public opinion to be undifferentiated by sex. Moreover, women did not vote significantly different from men. But beginning in 1980, consistent differences have been recorded in choice of candidate, party, and on issue positions.

Theories seeking to explain the gender gap abound. The most popular of these link the gender gap to the belief that women in general have been harshly affected by the economic turbulence of the last several years. According to this view, women are now simply voicing and voting their own best economic interest in the candidates they support and the issue positions they adopt. Whatever the cause of the gender gap, its continuation or even widening, would be a very serious problem for the Republican party and its candidates.

GENERAL PUBLICS *See ATTENTIVE PUBLICS*

GLADIATORS activists who perform the most demanding and absorbing political tasks. Gladiators are highly involved politically. The term was used by political scientist Lester Milbrath (1977) to describe people who undertake heavy duty political combat: things like working in a political party, volunteering for political campaigns, raising political money, and running for public office.

Milbrath contrasted gladiators with "spectators" and "apathetics". "Spectators" approach politics more as observers than as participants. They vote regularly, they often discuss politics with friends or family and they might wear a campaign button or paste a bumper sticker on their car. Apathetics are the least active politically. They generally ignore the political world. They are almost completely unaware and unconcerned about politics, candidates, or elections, and they don't vote. *See also: POLITICAL PARTICIPATION*

GRAY V. SANDERS *See ONE MAN, ONE VOTE*

HATCHED ineligible for most political activity other than voting because of one's civil service status. Virtually all federal government employees are hatched and subject to the restrictions of the Hatch Act. The exceptions are few and mostly limited to senior appointed officials, such as cabinet officers, their deputies, and assistants. State and local governments vary in the proportion of their employees that are hatched under civil service laws. The trend, however, is toward greater extension of civil service coverage.

The original purpose of hatching was to protect government employees from political pressure. In part this was a response to the abuses of patronage that had occurred under the "spoils system." Recently, there has been some interest in relaxing Hatch Act restrictions. Efforts to accomplish this have made the argument that hatching limits the expression of basic political rights, and it excludes many well qualified people from participation in the political process.

It could release a great amount of energy into American politics if government employees were generally exempted from Hatch Act provisions. On the other hand it is not clear what consequences this might have on the management of public affairs. In any case there is apparently no ground swell of support among government employees themselves for a general repeal of Hatch Act restrictions. *See also: PATRONAGE*

HIGH STIMULUS ELECTIONS elections that generate a lot of excitement and result in high voter turnout. High stimulus elections differ from low stimulus elections which stir less voter interest and lower turnout. Elections for federal and the major state offices are generally high stimulus while elections for other state and local offices are low stimulus.

Political scientists believe a number of factors determine whether a given election is high or low stimulus. These include: (1) the amount of media coverage received, (2) the prestige of the office sought, (3) the seriousness of the issues discussed, and (4) the attractiveness of the candidates running. High stimulus elections score high on most or all of these four factors while low stimulus elections score low on them. Low stimulus elections in fact place the burden on the political campaign to produce the voter interest that occurs more or less spontaneously in high stimulus elections. *See also: SURGE AND DECLINE THEORY; TURNOUT*

HIGH VISIBILITY ELECTIONS *See HIGH STIMULUS ELECTIONS*

HINGE EVENTS major incidents such as foreign interventions, economic crises, and notorious scandals that can change the basic direction and character of a campaign. Recent examples of hinge events include the Watergate scandals, Ford's pardon of Nixon, the Iranian crisis, and the Soviet invasion of Afghanistan.

Hinge events can also influence state and local politics. The closing of a large plant, natural disasters such as floods and fires, unexpected tax increases, and serious scandal can alter the outcome of these elections.

Hinge events of course don't occur in every campaign. When they are absent, elections tend to turn on what political scientists refer to as the long and short term forces in politics. *See also: SHORT TERM FORCES; VOTING BEHAVIOR*

HUSBANDS AND WIVES probably the most reliable predictor of voting behavior. Husbands and wives constitute what sociologists describe as a "primary group." They tend to be similar in their political outlook and orientation, and they tend to vote the same way.

Usually, about 90% of husbands and wives vote for the same party and candidates. This high degree of voting consistency is not found in any other social grouping. It remains to be seen if the recently uncovered gender gap will alter this relationship. *See also: GENDER GAP*

IDEOLOGUE *See TRUE BELIEVER*

IMAGE *See CANDIDATE IMAGE*

IMMUNIZATION resistance to new political ideas or rival political attachments. Immunization is the notion that repeated voting and other acts of support strengthen loyalty to a political party. The longer someone identifies with a party, votes for its candidates, or backs its policies, the more immune is that person to the blandishments of other parties.

This idea is consistent with what political science has learned about voting behavior. Voters are unlikely to convert from one party to another. When they do change it is usually in the intensity of their views—and not in their political party affiliation.

Immunization predicts long term stability in the electorate's choice of party. It explains realignment from one party to another as a process in which new non-immune voters come into the electorate. Some of these voters are newly eligible younger voters. Others are people who haven't voted much before. Immunization continues to protect older voters from newer ideas and changing partisan allegiances. Gradually realignment is brought about however as the newer voters assume majority status and replace the older electorate. *See also: CONVERSION; PARTY IDENTIFICATION; REALIGNING ELECTION*

INDEPENDENTS voters who describe themselves as non partisan—neither Democrats nor Republicans. Independents make up more than a third of the electorate. Moreover they are growing faster than either Democrats or Republicans. In 1937, the Gallup Poll reported that only 16% of the electorate considered themselves to be Independents. By 1980 that had increased to 36%.

Independents are not all alike. Pollsters divide them into three roughly equal groups based on how these voters describe themselves: Independents who "lean" Democratic; Independents who "lean" Republican; and "pure" Independents.

Leaners—both Democratic and Republican—are voters who tend to be informed and better educated. They are more influenced by issues and candidates than by party—and they are likely to vote.

But pure Independents—voters who don't even lean toward a political party—are very different. They tend to be uninterested in politics, less

informed and not well educated. Pures are more influenced by simple slogans and political advertising, and they are much less likely to vote.
Both types of Independents—the leaners and the pures—tend to be ticket splitters and party switchers. They make up their minds later than other voters and they are more likely to move back and forth between candidates or parties. This volatility along with their growing numbers has made Independents the critical swing vote in many elections. *See also: LEANERS; PARTY IDENTIFICATION; TICKET SPLITTERS*

INDIANA BALLOT *See BALLOTS*

ISSUE VOTING voting that is based mainly or exclusively on the voters' awareness and evaluation of campaign issues. Scholars believe that issues are one of the three major variables that determine voting behavior. The others are the party identification of the voter and the candidate image that voters hold.
The importance of issue voting compared to these other two factors is a continuing controversy in political science. Some scholars think that any influence that issues may have on voting is strongly colored by the voter's prior attitude toward the candidate and the political parties; in essence voters first make up their minds about the candidates and the political parties, then they think about the issues of the campaign.
Other political scientists believe it is issues and not the influence of party or candidate that motivates many voters; the nub of this argument is that voters use issues to help themselves make up their minds about candidates and parties.
In any case there is general agreement among political scientists that three conditions are necessary for issue voting to occur:

(1) voters must be aware of the issue and possess some understanding of it; (2) then voters must feel some intensity with regard to the issue; (3) finally voters must detect a difference among the candidates on the issue.

The best evidence is that this three part test can be met by only about 20% of the electorate for most elections. Furthermore there are convincing arguments that most Americans do not think in the kind of consistent ideological terms that encourages issue voting.
This does not mean however that issue voting is unimportant in American elections. There is no doubt that at least a few voters in every election are issue voters. Moreover, issue voting is often significant in primary elections and non-partisan elections where the influence of the political parties is less. Finally voters now entering the electorate are apparently more inclined to be issue oriented than older voters have been. *See also: CANDIDATE IMAGE; PARTY IDENTIFICATION; VOTING BEHAVIOR*

JEWISH VOTERS one of the smallest yet most influential ethnic groups in American politics. Jewish voters are arguably the single most important ethnic group in American politics, even though they make up only 2 and one half percent of the national population.

The political importance of Jewish voters owes to three main factors: they are geographically concentrated; they aggressively use their political resources; and they give most of their support to one of the two major parties.

GEOGRAPHIC CONCENTRATION—Jewish voters cluster in a relatively few large states. New York is about 11% Jewish; New Jersey 6%, Florida, Maryland, and Massachusetts, 5% and Pennsylvania, Connecticut and California, 3% to 4%. These are all nationally prominent states, rich in electoral votes and often swing areas in Presidential elections.

USE OF POLITICAL RESOURCES—Jewish voters turnout at rates considerably greater than most other groups. Moreover they tend to contribute more often to political campaigns and candidates and they become involved more in organized politics.

PARTISAN VOTING PATTERNS—Jewish voters are heavy supporters of the Democratic Party. Rarely do Jews give less than 75% of their vote to Democratic presidential candidates. In 1960, Jewish voters gave John Kennedy 80%, in 1964 Lyndon Johnson received 91% and in 1968 Hubert Humphrey got 89% Jewish support. Jewish weight within the Democratic party is such that no candidate can expect to win either the Democratic presidential nomination or the presidency itself without substantial Jewish support.

Ideologically Jews tend to be liberal which accounts for their strong pro-Democratic voting patterns. Their liberalism is unique among voting groups. It runs through all income levels, unlike the economic class based lines that prevail elsewhere in the electorate. *See also: BLOC VOTING; DEMOCRATIC COALITION; ETHNIC GROUPS; SPECIAL GROUPS*

JUDGE OF ELECTION *See ELECTION JUDGE*

LAW OF MINIMAL CONSEQUENCES the long prevalent belief among political scientists that campaigns convert few voters from one party or candidate to another. This is the so-called "limited effects hypothesis of campaigning" which holds that campaigns only reinforce or activate voters in the basic predisposition they have before the campaign starts.

This view of campaigns grew out of the early voting studies of the 1940s and 1950s which concluded that conversion during campaigns was rare. Most voters made their decisions before the campaign began, based on their party affiliation and then used media to selectively reinforce those decisions.

Some political scientists argue that this traditional view of the campaign is outdated. They stress that both the electorate and the nature of campaigning has changed substantially since the 1940s and 1950s. In particular, the breakdown in party loyalty, and the increased influence of the mass media have combined to produce a voter much more open to influence by the campaign. *See also: CONVERSION; UNCERTAINTY*

LEFT the popular political label for people and organizations that hold economic or political views that stress the need for institutional change and reform. In the United States, the left is associated with programs and policies that emphasize the use of government to solve problems and bring about a more equitable society.

Tradition is that the term evolved from the seating arrangements of the National Assembly in revolutionary France. The more radical members were seated to the left of the presiding officer, while the more conservative members were seated toward the right. Moderates were seated in the center of the assembly.

Today the left includes a wide swath of political spectrum ranging from liberals, socialists, and labor parties to communists, Marxists, Maoists. In fact, many political observers eschew use of either the terms left or right because they lack precision.

Extremes of the political left have never received broad support in the United States. Even the mild designation liberal is avoided by politicians and the term leftist is usually used disparagingly to label a person or group whose political views are considered radical and irresponsible. *See also: LIBERAL; RIGHT*

LIBERALS an ideological cleavage in the American electorate who hold the political philosophy that government is a legitimate tool for solving social problems. Liberals stress social equity, and they believe that change and reform can improve society. Liberal ideologues are found in both the Democratic and Republican parties. There are, however, substantially fewer of them among Republicans.

As a philosophy liberalism is often contrasted with conservatism. The bulk of the electorate, however, is neither liberal nor conservative. American voters by and large do not exhibit great ideological consistency. Polls show, for example, that most Americans believe that government should be smaller and spend less. But when the same polls ask specific questions about which programs should be cut, those polled say that present spending is too low or about right.

These contradictory attitudes have led political scientist Everett Carll Ladd, Jr. (1982) to suggest that Americans are "operational liberals" and "symbolic conservatives." They regularly support the symbolism of conservative values and rhetoric while they regularly oppose any actions that would actually reduce the role of government in society. *See also: CONSERVATIVES; TRUE BELIEVERS*

LIFE CYCLE EFFECTS the political differences among generations, especially those that may encourage people to become more conservative as they age. Life cycle effects include all of the various attitudinal changes—social, political, and economic—that are associated with an individual's age.

The evidence for life cycle effects is mixed. On the one hand there is very little evidence that people become more conservative as they get older, at least insofar as they switch their voting allegiance from one party to the other. On the other hand, young people are more likely to be Independents or liberals than are older people.

Some political scientists dismiss the idea of life cycle effects. They point out that each generation experiences a unique history that shapes their political attitudes. So if older people are more conservative, it is their life experiences and not their age that explains their conservatism. Life cycle effects and their causes remain an interesting controversy in political science today. *See also: VOTING BEHAVIOR*

LIMITED EFFECTS HYPOTHESIS *See LAW OF MINIMAL CONSEQUENCES*

LIMITED VOTING a system of voting intended to provide representation to minority parties. Limited voting can be used only in multi member districts in which there are several offices of the same type to be filled. Each elector is allowed to vote for at least one fewer candidates than there are offices to be filled. For example, if three legislators are to be elected, a voter may vote for only two candidates.

In the United States, limited voting is used mainly in local elections. Several major cities, including Boston, New York, and Philadelphia, have employed it at one time or another. One popular form of limited voting allows both of the major parties to nominate one fewer candidates than there are offices to be filled.

In Pennsylvania, where three county commissioners are elected, the Democratic party and the Republican party may nominate only two candidates. Voters then may vote for any three of the four nominated—insuring that at least one member of the minority party will be elected. *See also: AT LARGE ELECTIONS; PROPORTIONAL REPRESENTATION*

LIST SYSTEM: *See PROPORTIONAL REPRESENTATION*

LITERACY TEST a written or oral examination of prospective voters to ascertain their ability to read. Literacy tests were employed chiefly in the South. In principle they were designed to insure that a voter had the minimum qualifications necessary to vote intelligently.

In practice they were ruses to disenfranchise new immigrants and later blacks through discriminatory administration of the test. Literacy tests used to determine fitness to vote were outlawed by the 1970 amendments to the Voting Rights Act. *See also: VOTING RIGHTS ACT*

LOCAL ISSUES those topics and controversies discussed during a campaign that turn on local conditions and local interests. The nature and the scope of local issues differs widely from constituency to constituency.

In New York politics, Israel is a local issue; in the Midwest, farm price supports and interest rates are local issues; and in the Southwest, national immigration policy and oil are local issues. On the other hand some local issues are found almost everywhere. For example, utility rates, highways, tax increases, and crime are regularly discussed and debated in campaigns at every level across America.

It is a maxim among professional politicians that the electorate is not interested in broad abstract issues—unless there is a clear and explicit association between them and local concerns and situations. The only political issues that matter are ultimately local issues. *See also: ISSUE VOTING*

LOCAL RESIDENCY RULES a stipulation in election law that candidates must live in the jurisdiction in which they are running. Local residency is legally required for many state and local offices. And it is almost always a substantial political advantage for a politician to have long standing ties with the electoral district.

Local residency is, however, not required for all public offices. For example, a candidate for the United States Congress only must be an inhabitant of the state from which he or she is chosen. Although congressmen (and some other state and local officials) do not legally have to live in the district they represent, the custom of local residence is strong in most areas of the country. Candidates who flout it are open to the charge that they are carpetbaggers. *See also: CARPETBAGGER*

LONG TERM FORCES *See SHORT TERM FORCES*

LOW STIMULUS ELECTIONS *See HIGH STIMULUS ELECTIONS*

LOW VISIBILITY ELECTIONS *See HIGH STIMULUS ELECTIONS*

MAINTAINING ELECTION *See REALIGNING ELECTION*

MASSACHUSETTS BALLOT *See BALLOTS*

MINORITY PRESIDENT winning presidential candidates who receive less than 50% of the vote. Minority presidents stir some anxiety among those who believe presidents should be supported by a majority of voters. Since the presidency is the only office that includes the entire nation in its constituency, the occupant of that office should have received the votes of a majority of the electorate.

Actually minority presidents have been very common in American history. During this century alone, four presidents have received less than 50% of the votes cast—Wilson (1912, 1916); Truman (1948); Kennedy (1960); and Nixon (1968). And four other presidents have received only 51% of the votes cast—McKinley (1900); Taft (1908); Carter (1976); and Reagan (1980). Since 1828 a total of 14 presidents have been elected with less than 50% of the votes cast.

Calculating presidential margins in terms of the proportion of votes cast actually overstates the support any candidate has had among the voting age population. Since 35% to 45% of the eligible electorate don't vote, a majority of the eligible electorate has never voted for the winning candidate.

During the 19th Century the proportion of adult Americans voting for the winning candidate never exceeded 20%. Abraham Lincoln won his first term with support of 12% of adult Americans, Grover Cleveland won with 17% and William McKinley with 19%.

The winning presidential candidate's margin among the electorate has increased during the 20th Century as the suffrage has been expanded and various obstacles to voting have been removed or reduced. But no president has ever received more than 40% of the eligible electorate's votes. Even "landslides" have produced minority presidents. In 1964 Lyndon Johnson won 61% of the popular vote, but only 38% of the potential vote. Richard Nixon's landslide in 1968—61% of votes cast—represented only 33% of the voting age population.

The long tradition of minority American presidents is almost sure to continue unless some form of compulsory voting is adopted. Even then the presence of third party candidates on the ballot would probably prevent any candidate from receiving a majority of the vote. *See also: PLURALITY; POPULAR VOTE; TURNOUT; VOTERS; VOTING QUALIFICATIONS*

NEGATIVE VOTING *See NEGATIVE ADVERTISING*

NORMAL VOTE the proportion of the vote that is due to voters' party loyalty. Normal vote is also referred to as "base vote" and "expected vote." Most election analysis is grounded in assumptions about the normal vote. Basically analysts assume that voter loyalty to a particular party (the so called "long term force") determines how that person votes—unless he or she also comes under the influence of important campaign issues or feelings about a candidate. When these latter (so called short term) forces are present, one or both of them may affect voting.

Political science uses the notion of the normal vote to isolate the effects of short term forces in elections. For example, if the normal Republican vote in a national election is 48%, but the Republican presidential candidate receives 58%, some major factors beyond party influence are working. Apparently voters are being motivated by issues, candidates or both.

Normal vote analysis has different strategic implications depending on whether candidates are affiliated with the majority party or the minority party. Majority party candidates can expect to win an election as long as the short term forces are not strong. Their tactics should emphasize loyalty to party and avoidance of controversial issues. Minority party candidates however must bring short term forces into the campaign. They need to overcome their normal vote disadvantage by emphasizing candidate strengths or favorable issues.

Recent political experience suggests that high visibility, top of the ticket offices like president, U.S. senator, and governor, are less and less determined by the normal vote. Low visibility races however continue to be normal vote contests. Municipal offices, many state wide offices, and state legislative races are usually close to the expected normal vote. *See also: REPRESENTATIVE VOTE; SHORT TERM FORCES; VOTING BEHAVIOR*

OFFICE BLOCK BALLOT *See BALLOTS*

ONE MAN, ONE VOTE a legal principle enunciated in a series of U.S. Supreme Court cases which required the apportionment of voting districts strictly on the basis of population. One man, one vote means that each elected legislator must represent the same number of people as every other elected legislator of that same class—and each voter must be equal to every other voter in the weight given to their vote. Voting districts that do not conform to this rule are in violation of the 14th Amendment's equal protection clause.

The Supreme Court's policy on the issue was first expressed in Baker v. Carr (1962) which held that the question of the fairness of legislative apportionment was justifiable and could be heard by the courts. The principle of one man, one vote was applied to local elections in Gray v. Sanders (1963). It was extended to state legislative districts in Reynolds v. Sims (1963) and to Congressional districts in Wesberry v. Sanders (1964). *See also: APPORTIONMENT; ROTTEN BOROUGHS*

PARTY IDENTIFICATION a voter's attachment to a particular political party. Long term studies of voting behavior have examined the distribution of party identification among the electorate: voters have been asked if they thought of themselves as "strong Republicans," "strong Democrats," "weak Republicans," "weak Democrats," or Independents.

The result of these surveys indicate that almost 90% of the electorate identify to some extent with one of the two major political parties: about one in three people view themselves as strong or weak Democrats; about one in four people view themselves as strong or weak Republicans; and about one in three view themselves as Independent leaners who tilt Democratic or Republican.

Knowing the distribution of party identification in the electorate allows some predictions to be made about voting behavior. For example the known chances are eight out of ten that a "strong Democrat" or "strong Republican" will vote for the candidate of their party. And the known chances are six out of ten that a weak Democrat or a weak Republican will vote for the candidate of their party.

Party identification is also linked to turnout rates. Between the two major political parties, turnout is higher among Republicans than it is among Democrats. Both "strong Democrats" and "strong Republicans" vote at substantially higher rates than do less committed partisans. And Independents as a class turn out at the lowest rates of all.

Scholars have long believed that party identification was the key influence in voting. Today however many political observers are questioning the continuing importance of party attachment.

The number of Independents is increasing steadily—while the heavy use of television and radio in campaigns means that the mass media is disseminating more and more information about candidates and issues. These changes, it is argued are producing an electorate better informed about both candidates and issues—and more likely to make a voting decision on the basis of this information, than on the basis of party.

Despite these important changes in the electorate, knowledge of a voter's party identification continues to be the most reliable predictor of how he or she will actually vote. *See also: BEHAVIORAL DEMOCRATS AND REPUBLICANS; CANDIDATE IMAGE; ISSUE VOTING; NORMAL VOTE; VOTING BEHAVIOR*

PERMANENT REGISTRATION *See REGISTRATION*

POCKETBOOK INDEX an economic rule of thumb that has correctly identified the eventual winner of every presidential election since 1948. The pocketbook index measures what economists call disposable income or the amount of money people have after they account for inflation and pay their taxes.

When that disposable income exceeds 3.8% of the previous year's, the incumbent president or his party wins. When it falls at or below 3.8% the incumbent president or his party loses.

The pocketbook index is a gauge to the role economic factors will have in an election. the consistency of the measure—it has predicted 10 successive presidential elections—supports the common wisdom that American presidential elections area referenda on the economy.

There is however some controversy among scholars about why this is so. Do voters hold presidents accountable for their personal circumstances or do they judge presidents for the nation's economic health regardless of their personal circumstances? *See also: BELLWETHER*

POLITICAL ACTIVISTS *See ATTENTIVE PUBLICS*

POLITICAL PARTICIPATION a term used to describe a person's or group's political involvement. Political participation runs the gamut from occasional voting or displaying a campaign sticker to contributing money to a candidate, becoming an active member of a political party or even running for office.

People differ in the intensity of their political participation. On the basis of a large number of studies political scientists have developed a Socio-Economic Status (S.E.S.) profile of those who are most likely to participate in politics and those who are least likely.

The person most likely to be politically active in the United States is a white, upper income, college educated middle aged male who has a high status job, owns his home and lives in a metropolitan area. The person least likely to be politically involved is a black or minority, lower income, grade school educated, non-middle aged female who has a low status job, rents her home and lives in a small town or rural area.

These profiles suggest political participation is closely linked to how much money a person makes, how well educated a person is, and how much status is given by one's job. *See also: GLADIATORS*

POLL TAX a per capita tax on the privilege of voting. Poll taxes were nominally revenue raising devices levied on people registering to vote or showing up at the polls on election day. In practice however poll taxes became devices to discourage poor and blacks from trying to vote. If a prospective voter couldn't or wouldn't pay they were purged from the registration rolls.

Poll taxes were used in several states for both federal and state elections. But they are no longer legal. The 24th Amendment to the Constitution forbid them in federal elections in 1965. The following year the Supreme Court declared them to be unconstitutional in state elections.

Ironically poll taxes were originally designed to encourage wider voting by substituting a per capita tax for the more onerous property ownership requirements. Instead they became a major obstacle to black voting.

No poll tax as such exists today but many municipalities do levy per capita taxes of from 10 to 100 dollars. Voters are not tossed off the registration rolls for non-payment, but the registration rolls are often used to locate voters who owe the tax. Many voters are aware of this process and some may be inhibited from registering because of it. *See also: VOTING QUALIFICATIONS; VOTING RIGHTS ACT*

POLLING PLACE the physical location where votes are cast on election day. The typical polling place is a temporary site in a church, firehall, apartment building, store or private residence.

There are upwards of 175,000 polling places nationally, each of which serves as the voting location for from about 100 to 1000 voters. Polling places are located in precincts which are the basic administrative units for operating the electoral machinery in most states.

The states closely regulate the operation of their polling places, specifying in detail their hours, staffing, and procedures. Usually actual solicitation is prohibited in the immediate area of the polling place although literature distribution is sometimes permitted a prescribed distance from the actual voting. *See also: ELECTION DAY; ELECTION JUDGES; PRECINCTS; POLLWATCHER*

POLLWATCHERS election officials who monitor the voting process on election day. Pollwatchers are generally expected to observe the polling operation, detect any improper or illegal behavior; issue challenges to any ineligible voters, and witness the counting of ballots after the polls have closed.

Unlike other election officials pollwatchers are the representatives of specific candidates or political parties. Before primary elections individual candidates are entitled to appoint watchers in each local voting district. For general elections the competing political parties are authorized to appoint watchers to represent them.

The importance of pollwatching varies from place to place. In jurisdictions with long traditions of voting fraud pollwatchers are considered essential to honest elections. But in other jurisdictions, candidates and political parties may not even bother to appoint the pollwatchers to which they are entitled.

Usually pollwatchers must be registered voters of the local voting districts in which they work. They are volunteers in some cases, but in others they are paid for their services by a candidate or political party. Expenditures of this sort are one example of the uses of "street money" on election day. *See also: CHALLENGES; ELECTION DAY; ELECTION JUDGES; VOTING FRAUD*

POPULAR VOTE the ballots cast by eligible voters on election day. Popular vote is the direct vote. Today all American elections except the presidential are decided by the direct popular vote. General and most primary elections are determined by a plurality of the popular vote, while runoff primaries are settled by a majority of the popular vote.

Presidential elections of course are different because the final arbiter is not the popular vote, but the electoral vote. All but three times in the nation's history the winner of the popular vote and the winner of the electoral vote have been the same person. Nevertheless it remains possible for a candidate to lose the popular vote but win the electoral vote.

This can happen because electoral vote is awarded on a winner take all basis, state by state. For example a candidate might win a few large states rich in electoral votes while losing heavily in most other states.

One other circumstance in which the presidential popular vote might be frustrated is the situation in which three or more serious candidates are running. When this happens it becomes possible that no candidate will win the constitutionally required majority of electoral votes, throwing the election into the House of Representatives.

Political observers speculate every presidential election about these various contingencies. But they never do happen. Not since 1876 has a presidential election been thrown into the House and not once in this century has the winner of the popular vote failed to become president. *See also: BATTLEGROUND STATES; MINORITY PRESIDENT*

PREFERENTIAL VOTING a somewhat exotic election system which weighs votes according to whether they are first, second or third choices. Preferential voting is designed to produce elections decided by a majority rather than only a plurality of the electorate.

Two versions of preferential voting have been used in the United States. One, known as the Bucklin Plan adds first and second choices together (and third if necessary) to provide a winner. The other version, called the Ware Plan eliminates the weakest candidates and then assigns their second and third choices to surviving stronger candidates.

Some variations of both versions weigh votes so that second choice is worth (say) one-half of first and third is worth (say) one-third. Preferential voting has been tried on and off in the United States. At least 50 cities and counties have adopted it at one time, but very few continue to use it. *See also: MAJORITY; PLURALITY*

PSEPHOLOGY the study of voting and elections. Psephology is concerned primarily with voting behavior—how and why people vote as they do. According to columnist and author William Safire the term may have been coined by Michael Demarist writing in *Time* magazine in 1964 (Safire, 1978:576). At any rate it was popularized by Richard Scammon and Ben Wattenberg in their 1970 book, *The Real Majority*.

To paraphrase Scammon and Wattenberg, psephology asks three questions about American voters:

Who did they vote for?
Why did they vote that way?
How will they vote in the future?

Interest in voting is not new. Politicians, journalists and political scientists have always found the subject fascinating. But as a specialized field of systematic study psephology has been around for less than 50 years.

The earliest academic contribution—The People's Choice—appeared in 1944. It was followed with three now classical studies: Voting in 1948, The Voter Decides in 1954, and The American Voter (1960). Since these early works the literature on voting behavior has grown steadily—spurred on by developments in survey research and in quantitative data analysis. Today the field is one of the most highly developed in political science—and one of the most popular.

Psephology has an interesting derivation. The word comes from the Greek word for pebbles—psephos. Ancient Greeks used to vote by pitching pebbles. They employed different colored pebbles to designate their voting choices. After making their decision they would deposit the appropriate colored pebble in an urn which served as the ballot box. Reportedly Greek politicians would never leave a stone unturned on election day. *See also: VOTING BEHAVIOR*

QUALIFICATIONS *See VOTING QUALIFICATIONS*

REGISTRATION the legal procedure under which prospective voters establish their qualifications to vote in future elections. Most registration systems in the United States today are some form of so called "permanent registration." Eligible voters must sign up several weeks or months before election day. They then remain registered unless they move or fail to vote for some prescribed number of elections.

A handful of states still do maintain an alternate form of registration known as "periodic registration." Under it voters are required to register before each election or at other scheduled intervals.

Historically registration laws were a response to the wide spread voting frauds that existed in many places in the late 19th and early 20th Centuries. The original objective of registration—along with residency requirements and other strict election laws—was the prevention of ballot box stuffing, vote buying, multiple voting and other types of voting irregularities.

Today voting fraud has been considerably reduced. But many of the measures designed to combat it still survive to inhibit voting. Most observers believe that current registration laws reduce voter turnout more than does any other factor. Experts estimate that 20% to 30% of the potential electorate are ineligible to vote only because they are not registered. Some studies have in fact concluded that abolishing registration requirements or adopting some form of universal voter enrollment would raise average turnout 10% or more.

Momentum seems to be increasing in the United States to reform existing registration systems. Several states now have some form of election day registration which permits voters to fulfill requirements when they appear at the polls to vote. And half the states have supplemented their registration procedures with provisions that allow voters to register by mail. *See also: RESIDENCY REQUIREMENT; TURNOUT; UNIVERSAL VOTER ENROLLMENT; VOTERS; VOTING QUALIFICATIONS*

RESIDENCY REQUIREMENT the interval a citizen must reside within a jurisdiction before becoming eligible to vote. Residency requirements once provided a formidable barrier to registration and voting.

Most states used some version of a three layered residency qualification: a minimum residency in the state, a shorter residency in the country, and a still shorter residency in the voting district. In a typical state, a prospective voter might have been required to have lived within the state for at least one year, in the country for at least 6 months and in the voting district at least thirty days.

Pressures to reduce lengthy residence requirements built up after World War II as the electorate became more mobile—and many states did reduce their residency rules. Congress intervened in this area of traditional state responsibility in 1970 when it set a uniform in-state residency requirement of thirty days for presidential elections. Then in 1973 the U.S. Supreme Court ruled that a fifty day residency requirement was the legal maximum for State elections.

These congressional and judicial actions have virtually ended residency requirements as a serious barrier to registration and voting. About half the states now have no residency requirements at all. Most of those states that still do, have set them at 30 days. *See also: VOTING QUALIFICATIONS; VOTING RIGHTS ACT*

REYNOLDS v. SIMS *See ONE MAN, ONE VOTE*

RIGHT the popular political label for people and organizations that hold views that emphasize the importance of stability and continuity in society. In the United States the Right is associated with programs and policies that stress limited government, economic freedom, individualism, and the importance of established values.

Tradition is that the term Right evolved from the seating practice of the National Assembly in revolutionary France: the more conservative members were seated to the right of the presiding officer while the more radical members were seated toward the left; political moderates were seated in the center of the assembly.

Today the Right includes a wide band of the political spectrum ranging from conservatives and neo conservatives to reactionary extremist groups such as the American Nazi Party, and the John Birchers. Many political observers in fact eschew use of either the terms Right or Left because they lack precision.

Extremes of the political right have never received broad support in the United States. Nevertheless the designation conservative is almost never used disparagingly in political dialogue, while the term liberal almost always is. *See also: CONSERVATIVE; LEFT*

ROLL OFF *See VOTER FALL OFF*

SECRET BALLOT *See AUSTRALIAN BALLOT*

SHIFTERS voters who change their mind during a campaign. Shifters make a choice to support a party or candidate but then shift to another candidate or party before election day.

Shifters are usually Independents, or weak partisans. Since their attachment to a political party is not strong, they are vulnerable to opposition blandishments based on issue appeals or candidate personality.

Shifters are distinguished from "swtichers" and "swing voters." Switchers are voters who support one political party in one election, but a different party in another. A switcher might vote the Republican ticket in this election, then switch to the Democratic ticket in the next.

Swing voters are voters who hold the balance of power in an election because they are undecideds or leaners. They can swing either way. Swing voters might be concentrated in a particular ethnic group, geographic region or other demographic classification. Often in fact the same groups are the swing vote in election after election. *See also: CONVERSION; STANDPATTERS; TICKET SPLITTING*

SHORT BALLOT *See LONG BALLOT*

SHORT TERM FORCES influences on voting behavior that are brief in duration, lasting only for a single election cycle. Short term forces include two main influences that can get factored into electorate decision making.

One of these is collectively referred to as candidate image. It includes the overall impressions voters form of politicians. The other factor is issue voting which is made up of the electorate's awareness and evaluation of specific campaign issues.

Scholars distinguish these short term forces from "long term forces." The main long term force in voting is the tendency of the electorate to support the prevailing majority party in election after election.

Political scientists often explain the outcome of particular elections in terms of the conflict played out in them between long term forces and short term forces. Basically scholars believe most elections are determined by the long term force of voter loyalty and identification for the majority party. Elections that conform to this pattern are called "maintaining elections."

Only when the long term partisan loyalists are permanently shifted to another political party is the existing order of things really changed. Then a realigning election is said to have occurred—resulting in a new set of both long and short term forces which themselves continue until the next realignment takes place. *See also: CANDIDATE IMAGE; ISSUE VOTING; PARTY IDENTIFICATION; REALIGNING ELECTION; VOTING BEHAVIOR*

SPECTATORS *See GLADIATORS*

SPLIT—TICKET *See TICKET SPLITTING*

STANDPATTERS voters who vote for the candidate of the same party in two or more successive elections. Standpatters differ from both "switchers" and "swing voters."

Switchers support one party in one election, but a different party in the next election. Swing voters are those who hold the balance of power in a particular election because they are undecideds or leaners.

Some examples illustrate these differences. A voter who supported Jimmy Carter in 1980 and Walter Mondale in 1984 would be a standpatter. So would someone who voted for Ronald Reagan in both 1980 and 1984. These voters support the same party in both elections.

Switchers on the other hand changed parties between 1980 and 1984. They may have been for Carter in 1980 but for Reagan in 1984—or Reagan in 1980 before switching to Mondale in 1984.

Swing voters in these two elections would be anyone not firmly committed to a candidate early in the campaign. The election of 1980 produced a large swing note which broke for Ronald Reagan late in the campaign. The election of 1984 however generated no sizable swing vote since there were few undecided voters during that campaign. *See also: SHIFTERS; TICKET SPLITTERS*

STRAIGHT TICKET a vote for all the candidates of a single political party for every office listed on the ballot. Straight ticket voting differs from ticket splitting in which voters divide their ballot among candidates of two (or more) parties.

Straight ticket voting is a steadily decreasing factor in American politics. In 1900 about 95% of all voters pulled the big lever in presidential elections—this is voted straight Democratic or Republican. By 1970 the proportion of the electorate casting straight tickets had dropped below 50%. Today straight ticket voting is less than 35%. Moreover only about 15% of the electorate always votes straight ticket.

Straight ticket voting is probably encouraged somewhat where the "party column" ballot is used, and discouraged somewhat where the "office block" ballot is employed. The highest incidence of ticket splitting is among non-whites, grade school educated, older voters and Southerners. Among partisans the highest concentration of straight ticket voting comes from strong Republicans and strong Democrats.

The decrease in straight ticket voting has paralleled the decline of strong party identification within the electorate. As voters come more and more to think of themselves as Independents or only weak partisans they are less and less likely to consistently support the candidates of either party. *See also: BALLOTS; TICKET SPLITTER*

SUFFRAGE *See VOTING QUALIFICATIONS*

SURGE AND DECLINE a theory first advanced by political scientist Angus Campbell to explain why voter turnout rises in presidential elections, but declines in the subsequent mid-term election (Campbell, 1966).

Surge and decline theory holds that turnout does go down in the off years (on average about 15%) because voters are less interested. Presidential contests are high stimulus elections while off year elections may be low stimulus.

Surge and decline theory has a corollary: many voters who come out only to vote for president, stay home in off years—meanwhile those voters who do turnout tend to vote along party lines or in support of familiar incumbents.

Not all political scientists subscribe to the surge and decline view of mid-term elections. Many believe these contests are governed instead by the condition of the economy. In good economic times voters turnout in smaller numbers, but they tend to support the president's party. If times are bad however voters will turnout in larger numbers to vote against the president's party. *See also: HIGH STIMULUS ELECTION; MID-TERM ELECTION; TURNOUT*

SWING VOTERS *See TICKET SPLITTER*

SWITCHERS *See TICKET SPLITTER*

TICKET SPLITTER a voter who votes for the candidate of one party for the top of the ticket office like president, governor, or U.S. senator but candidate(s) of a different party for other offices. Ticket splitters are voters who don't vote straight tickets.

Ticket splitting is usually measured at the precinct level. For example if the Republican candidate for governor received 52 percent of the vote while the Republican candidate for Congress received only 47% of the vote—the ticket splitting index would be (52-47 or) 5%. An even simpler technique to gauge ticket splitting is to calculate the percentage difference between the highest and lowest vote getters on a party's ticket.

Ticket splitters are a steadily increasing proportion of the electorate. At least 80% of the electorate are ticket splitters some of the time. The highest incidence of them is among the affluent, college educated, younger voters, and Westerners. Among partisans the highest concentration is from Independents followed by weak Democrats and then weak Republicans.

Ticket splitters are distinguished from both "switchers" and "swing voters." Switchers (also known as floaters) are voters who support one party in one election, but a different party in another election. Switchers may vote straight tickets, but they float back and forth between the major parties.

Swing voters are voters who hold the balance of power in a given election because they are undecideds or leaners. They are often concentrated in one or more pockets of an electoral jurisdiction. Switchers are usually not ticket splitters while swing voters usually are. *See also: INDEPENDENTS; STRAIGHT TICKET*

TRUE BELIEVER a voter who is strongly oriented to a particular political philosophy. True believers are ideologues whose view of political life rests on some clearly enunciated principles and assumptions—about who holds power in society, the important values, and in what direction change should occur.

The term true believer is usually applied to conservatives, especially those well toward the right on the political spectrum. These true believers stress the benefits of capitalism, limited government, free enterprise, unrestricted competition, and the importance of private property. They are likely to be supply-siders or monetarists in economic matters, and traditionalists on social and moral questions. And they are often willing to apply a "litmus test" to discover if others are also true believers.

Most Americans, are not true believers—either of the right or the left. The evidence from voting studies is persuasive. Voters simply do not evaluate parties, candidates, or issues according to any coherent consistent system of ideological thought. Americans are liberal on some issues, conservative on others, and moderate on most. Both major political parties in fact include substantial representation from all shades of the political spectrum.

This non-ideological cast to American politics may be due to the low level of class consciousness in society. In any case it stands as one of the most enduring qualities found across the long span of American political history. *See also: CONSERVATIVES; LIBERALS*

TURNOUT the proportion of eligible voters who actually come to the polls and cast ballots. Turnouts are usually reported as a percentage of the total electorate, including those who are not registered.

Turnout rates in the United States are low relative to that achieved in other western democracies—and they have been steadily declining for several years. Presidential elections now turnout less than 55% of the vote. State elections often bring out less than 50% of the electorate, while local elections and primary elections sometimes record 25% or less participation.

Several factors seem to influence turnout. It is higher in general elections than in primary elections—higher in close competitive elections than one sided elections—and higher in "top of the ticket" races than for minor offices. Turnout also varies among demographic groupings. It is higher among the more affluent and better educated—higher among whites than blacks—higher among older voters than youth—higher among Catholics and Jews than Protestants and higher among Republicans than Democrats.

Political scientists have speculated considerably about the causes of the low and declining turnout in the United States. All of the following have been proposed and investigated: the demise of strong political organizations who got out the vote on election day; the increase in Independents who vote much less regularly than the committed partisans they are replacing; restrictive registration laws which continue to exclude 20% to 30% of the potential electorate; and rising cynicism about government in the aftermath of Vietnam and Watergate.

Professional politicians also worry about turnout because it can determine the outcome of a close election. An increase or decrease of 1% in a national election can mean the difference of almost one million votes. In a state the size of Ohio the same 1% would mean about 60,000 votes and in a city the size of Philadelphia it would be equal to about 10,000 votes. Elections today are often won or lost by much less. *See also: CHLOROFORMING; HIGH STIMULUS ELECTION; NEGATIVE ADVERTISING; REGISTRATION; SURGE AND DECLINE; VOTER ENROLLMENT; VOTERS*

UNIVERSAL VOTER ENROLLMENT a frequently suggested system of voter registration which would enroll virtually every citizen 18 years or older. Universal voter enrollment would require wholesale reform of the hodgepodge of complicated registration laws that now exist at state and local levels. The objective of universal enrollment would be to substantially increase voter turnout in the United States which is 10 to 20% lower than those of most western European democracies.

Scholars who have studied American practices believe that cumbersome registration laws account for the greatest amount of non-voting. One study indicated that 80% of the difference in turnout between the United States and European countries was caused by American registration laws.

Universal enrollment could affect the balance of electoral strength between the two major parties. Under current registration practices, those disenfranchised tend to be disproportionately young, poor, less educated, black, and residents of large cities. On the whole, these groups register Democratic much more heavily than Republican. *See also: REGISTRATION; TURNOUT*

UPSTATE AND DOWNSTATE popular political shorthand for the geographic cleavage that exists in many states between the Democratic urban areas and the Republican small towns and rural areas. Sometimes upstate demarcates an urban area, such as in Illinois' Cook County, while the downstate small towns and rural areas make up much of the rest of the state. Other times it is the downstate urban areas, such as New York City pitted against the upstate New York small towns and rural areas.

Especially in many northern states, elections are often battles between the Democratic urban areas and the Republican small towns and rural areas. The suburbs frequently hold the balance of power in these contests between city and countryside. Steady population growth since World War II has produced suburban and ex-urban areas as large or larger than their original core cities. These areas tend to register Republican, but they usually contain a high proportion of Independents and ticket splitters. As a consequence, the suburbs are the swing vote in many political struggles between upstate and downstate. *See also: DEMOCRATIC COALITION; COALITION*

VOTER FALL OFF the drop in the voting participation rate that can occur after voters have cast ballots for the more prominent offices at the top of the ticket. Voters make their choices for candidates for governor, United States senator, and mayor, but then fail to vote for the lesser offices further down the ticket like state legislator, country commissioner, or school board official.

Voter fall off, or "roll off" as it is called, is measured as a percentage of the highest votes cast for any office. For example, if 97% of those voting actually voted for the office of governor, but only 90% voted in the state legislative race, the fall off rate would be 7% in the latter contest.

Political scientists distinguish between two kinds of voter fall off: fatigue fall off and partisan fall off. The former is a drop off in voting in which voters simply fail to vote for any of the candidates for a given office. Fatigue fall off is often attributed to the seemingly endless lists of offices to be filled on long ballots. Partisan fall off on the other hand is a drop off in voting between races on the same party ticket. It is the vote differential between candidates of the same party. Political professionals consider it to be a more serious problem because it usually reveals weaknesses in individual candidates.

Some studies have shown that voter fall off is higher with the "office block ballot" than with the "party column ballot." Almost certainly, ticket splitting increases voter fall off since voters who do not vote a straight ticket must vote separately for each candidate or office. *See also: BALLOTS; LONG BALLOT*

VOTERS those eligible to vote who exercise their franchise, who register, and actually cast ballots. Today the suffrage has been extended to virtually all citizens who are age 18 or older; the only exceptions are resident aliens, those who are institutionalized, and those unable to meet minimum residence requirements.

According to the United States Census Bureau, the composite voter in the United States is a white, married woman, in her late 50's to early 60's who lives in her own home, works for some level of government, and has a family income of at least $25,000. The electorate in the United States is a dynamic one; 15 to 20% are new voters every four years.

Whether one is or is not a voter is associated with four main socio-economic factors.

(1)Education: About 80% of college graduates vote while only 43% of those with only an elementary school education do;

(2) Race: Whites vote twice as heavy as Hispanics and over 20% greater than blacks;

(3) Income: Families with incomes of $25,000 or more vote twice as frequently as those with incomes below $5,000;

(4) Occupation: People in white collar occupations vote almost 50% heavier than blue collar workers.

The number of people who actually vote is usually reported in terms of eligibles rather than in terms of those registered. In 1980 about 53% of those eligible to vote did so. But when actual registration is taken into account, the voting rate goes up substantially. In that same year (1980) for example, only about 77% of all eligibles were registered to vote, meaning 23% of the potential electorate could not legally vote in election day had they wanted to do so. So, about 80% of those who were registered to vote did vote—in contrast to the 53% of the overall electorate who did so.

Studies have suggested that universal voter enrollment would increase overall voting turnout by 10%. Highly represented in this additional voting would be the groups who now register and vote at low rates: Hispanics, black, poor, blue collar, and those with less education. *See also: REGISTRATION; TURNOUT; VOTING BEHAVIOR*

VOTING the casting of a ballot on election day. Procedures for voting are similar in most jurisdictions. A voter enters the polling place and signs a voter's certificate or affidavit which is then given to an election judge. The election judge compares the signature with the signature of eligible voters in the precinct binder. If the signature is determined to be valid, the voter is allowed to proceed into the voting booth where he or she will cast his or her ballot.

Poll watchers or other election officials have the right to challenge a voter's registration or identity. When this happens, the challenged voter may not vote until they have produced identification or other proof required by law of their right to vote. A voter usually has from 2–5 minutes to actually vote after they have been given a ballot or entered the voting machine.

Where voting machines are used, voters may receive instructions in their use if they request it. Voting assistance is also available to disabled voters. The election laws however, are usually strict in stipulating the conditions and manner in which voting assistance may be rendered. *See also: CHALLENGE; POLLING PLACE; POLLWATCHERS*

VOTING BEHAVIOR survey research and political science nomenclature for the study of how and why people vote as they do. Voting behavior studies go back to 1944 when the eminent political scientist Paul Lazersfeld produced the PEOPLES CHOICE—a survey based analysis of voter decision making in Erie County, Ohio, during the 1940 presidential campaign. This groundbreaking work was followed by VOTING, a 1948 study of Elmira, New York, and by THE VOTER DECIDES (1954) and THE AMERICAN VOTER (1960).

Since these early studies, the literature on voting behavior has grown steadily. Political scientists have examined the influence on voting of a great number of possible factors including age, income, education, sex, political affiliation, occupation, and residence. These scholars have come to believe that of all the possible influences on electoral decision making, three are the most important. They are:

(1)party identification, or the strength with which voters associate themselves with a particular political party;

(2) candidate image, or the quality and intensity of a voter's feelings about a candidate;

(3) issue orientations, or the saliency, and importance of issues in the campaign.

Most of the academic and professional analysis of voting that goes on is grounded in the assumption that voters' behavior can be explained by these three factors. Basically, political scientists believe that the three are hierarchical: voter identification with a particular political party controls the voting decision—unless either candidate feelings or important issues are introduced. When they are, one or both of them may control the voting decision. Voting can also turn on the complicated interaction of all three factors.

Many political observers believe that party identification is becoming less important to the outcome of today's elections. The number of Independents is increasing steadily and the heavy use of television and radio in campaigns means that the mass media is disseminating more and more information about both candidates and issues. These changes may be producing an electorate more influenced by their evaluation of candidates or their attitude toward campaign issues. Even so, knowledge of a voter's partisan affiliation continues to be the most reliable predictor of how he or she will actually vote. *See also: CANDIDATE IMAGE; ISSUE VOTING; NORMAL VOTE; PARTY IDENTIFICATION*

VOTING FRAUD consists of ballot box stuffing, chain ballots, short counting, vote buying, and a good deal more. Voting fraud may have been more common in earlier times, but it is certainly not unknown in modern politics. In the nature of things, nobody knows for sure how much voting fraud goes on today. An educated guess is that there is still a considerable amount of it—in both urban and rural areas—and perhaps especially in the closer elections.

Most voting fraud is some version of four basic techniques: (1) stuffing ballot boxes (or voting machines); (2) buying votes and bribing voters; (3) miscounting and misreporting vote results; and (4) influencing voters improperly in the polling place. All of these have an almost infinite number of variations.

The best defense against voting fraud is a strong election day organization, one with the capability to monitor voting irregularities and man each election district with poll watchers and election judges. *See also: BALLOT BOX STUFFING; CHAIN BALLOT; CHALLENGES; DIRTY TRICKS; ELECTION DAY; ELECTION JUDGES; POLLWATCHER; SHORT COUNTING; VOTE BUYING*

VOTING QUALIFICATIONS the legal requirements that must be met in order to register and vote. The Constitution left the formulation of voting qualifications to the individual states. The states have been constrained, however, by four constitutional amendments—the fifteenth, nineteenth, twenty-fourth, and twenty-sixth. These prohibited the states from denying suffrage on grounds of race, sex, failure to pay a poll tax, or to any citizen age eighteen or more. The Voting Rights Act (1965) also restrains the states in the administration of their electoral systems where discriminatory practices are at issue. Beyond these limitations, the states are free to establish their own legal definitions of suffrage.

During the 19th and early 20th Centuries, the states did show considerable diversity in the qualifications they set. More recently, however, the legal standards used by the various states don't vary a great deal.

About half of the states have residency requirements of not more than fifty days. The other half have no residency rules at all. The only disqualifications remaining are those imposed on institutionalized mental incompetents, those convicted of a serious crime, or those citizens living on autonomous federal reservations, such as national parks and military posts. With the exception of these, the suffrage today has been extended to virtually all citizens age eighteen or older. *See also: CHALLENGES; POLL TAX; REGISTRATION; RESIDENCY REQUIREMENT; VOTING RIGHTS ACT*

VOTING RIGHTS ACT landmark civil rights legislation designed to end the barriers to black registration and voting that had grown up in some states. The original Voting Rights Act was passed in 1965. It was amended and extended in 1970, in 1975, and in 1982.

The major provisions of the Voting Rights Act were aimed at preventing future discrimination and curing some of the consequences of past discrimination. The Act gave the federal government a substantial amount of power to move against those states where a pattern of discrimination could be shown: Federal registrars were empowered to protect and enforce voting rights in counties and states where discrimination had occurred; election law changes in those countries and states had to be submitted to the United States Attorney General for approval; literacy tests were banned; and residence requirements for federal elections were limited to a maximum of thirty days.

The Voting Rights Act has been a major factor in the expansion of the black electorate that has occurred since 1965. There have been dramatic increases in black registration and voting in that period of time. For example, in 1960 black registration in Mississippi was 5%; by 1976 it was 61%. In South Carolina it was 14% in 1960 and 57% by 1976. In Alabama it was 15% in 1960, but 58% by 1976. Similar increases in registration were recorded in Georgia, North Carolina, Louisiana, and Virginia.

Despite the impact of the Voting Rights Act, millions of blacks in the South today are still not registered. The civil rights movement, in fact, has begun to focus much of its energies on voting registration. Still, much has been accomplished, and the older patterns of gross systematic discriminations have been ended. *See also: BLACK VOTERS; POLL TAX; RESIDENCY REQUIREMENT; VOTING QUALIFICATIONS*

YOUNG VOTERS 18–24 year olds who are registered and regularly vote. Since passage of the 26th Amendment in 1971, 18 year old voters have been able to vote in both federal and state elections. Young voters have not, however, voted in large numbers.

The 18–24 year old segment makes up the largest age cohort of the voting age population, yet they have the lowest turnout. In 1984 only 40% of them actually voted, while the national turnout was 53%. This age group in fact accounts for almost 35% of all the unregistered voters in the country.

There are lots of hypotheses about the reasons 18–24 year olds don't vote: absenteeism, apathy, mobility, lack of a perceived stake in the political system, too busy getting established, and so on. Political scientists have found that young people are much less inclined to participate in any kind of political activity. They are not only less likely to register and vote, but they are less likely to support a particular candidate, contribute to a campaign, or get involved in their local government.

The conventional assumption is that an increase in voting and other kind of political participation by 18–24 year olds would favor the Democratic party. This may not be so. There is no evidence that 18–24 year old voters are homogeneous in their political attitudes or loyalties. Moreover there is some evidence that Republican candidates are receiving increasing support from younger voters. It seems likely then that an increase in political participation by 18–24 year olds would benefit both political parties. *See also: VOTERS; VOTING BEHAVIOR*

7

MONEY AND POLITICS

AUTHORIZED COMMITTEES legalese used by the Federal Elections Commission (FEC) in connection with the administration and enforcement of the Federal Elections Campaign Act (FECA). Authorized committees in FEC parlance are any campaign committees that have been authorized by a candidate to receive contributions or make expenditures.

An operating committee that is not disavowed by a candidate is also said to be an authorized committee. But any committee which has not been authorized by the candidate or a committee which has been disavowed is said to be an unauthorized committee. Expenditures on behalf of a candidate by any unauthorized committee are defined as independent expenditures. *See also: FEDERAL ELECTIONS CAMPAIGN ACT (FECA); INDEPENDENT EXPENDITURES*

BAGMAN the intermediary who transports illegal campaign contributions from their source to their destination. The term bagman is also sometimes applied to the middleman in any corrupt transaction involving a bribe or payoff to a politician.

The working bagman might be an employee or agent of the local political organization, who derives his income from skimming a percentage off the top of any delivery. When very large sums or very important people are involved, the bagman himself might be a major public figure. Bagmen exist because of the pressure in political campaigns to hide the source of some contributions.

The incidence of illegal cash contributions has probably been minimized in federal elections as a consequence of the reforms of the 1970's. After Watergate, some states also tightened up their campaign financing laws. It is generally believed however that many state and local campaigns continue to be the beneficiaries of large amounts of unreported cash. *See also: BLACK MONEY; LAUNDERED MONEY*

BLACK MONEY funds that have been contributed to campaigns or given to politicians from illicit sources, especially organized crime. Black money comes from bribes or payoffs and is graft. It is almost always in cash that must be laundered before it can be used.

Opinion varies considerably about the significance of black money in campaign financing. Some estimates make it as high as 15% of the money spent in state and local campaigns—close to 100 million dollars. If these are accurate, black money plays a substantial role in American state and local politics. *See also: BOODLE; LAUNDERED MONEY*

BOODLE money paid as a bribe, a fix, or graft for the improper use of political influence. Boodle is loot or a payoff received by public officials or political leaders who use their positions to illegally favor or enrich their patrons and supporters.

Those who receive boodle are said to be corrupt. The term originated in the late 19th Century during the heyday of the large urban political machine. This kind of systematic corruption was probably more common in the pre-reform eras of American politics, but it has by no means been eliminated from politics today. *See also: BLACK MONEY; LAUNDERED MONEY*

BUCKLEY V. VALEO (1976) an important United States Supreme Court decision which validated in principle most of the campaign finance reforms enacted in the post Watergate period. Buckley was actually brought before the court as a challenge to the Federal Elections Campaign Act (FECA) of 1974.

This landmark reform legislation had established spending and contribution limits for federal elections and had required that all federal campaigns conform to strict disclosure provisions. It had also provided for public financing of presidential elections and for a Federal Elections Commission (FEC) which would administer and enforce the law.

In Buckley the Supreme Court struck down expenditure limitations as a substantial restraint on free speech. The court also ruled that it was unconstitutional to limit the amount individuals could spend on their own behalf. But much more important, the new enforcement principles were affirmed, the limits on contributions were upheld, and the strict disclosure requirements were sustained.

The Buckley decision legitimatized a substantial federal role in overseeing the raising and spending of money in election campaigns. Indirectly it also influenced the direction of campaign finance reform in the states. After Buckley, many states rewrote their election laws to conform to the guidelines enunciated by the Supreme Court. *See also: CAMPAIGN FINANCE LAWS; FEDERAL ELECTIONS CAMPAIGN ACT (FECA)*

CAMPAIGN EXPENDITURES *See GROSS POLITICAL PRODUCT*

CAMPAIGN FINANCE LAWS the rules and regulations that govern the raising and spending of money in political campaigns. There are five basic mechanisms which a jurisdiction may use to regulate the financial operation of a political campaign:

1. The size or source of contributions can be limited.
2. Overall expenditure levels can be set.
3. Disclosure of the source of contributions and the purpose of expenditures can be required.
4. Public financing of campaigns can be provided.
5. Enforcement mechanisms can be established to ensure the laws are observed.

Campaign finance laws in the United States vary considerably in their mix of these five mechanisms and in the emphasis they place on each. Federal election campaigns are regulated by the Federal Elections Campaign Act (FECA) and its amendments. State and local campaigns are regulated by those laws prevailing in the individual states.

The FECA has become the model for much of the campaign finance law reform that has been enacted in the states since the 1970's. It limits contributions to $1000 for individuals and $5000 for PAC's, requires strict disclosure of campaign expenditures and contributions, and provides public financing for presidential candidates. It also establishes the Federal Elections Commission (FEC) to administer and enforce the act.

Few states have enacted laws as stringent as those of the federal government. But most states now require extensive disclosure of contributions and expenditures. Many have also enacted limitations on the sources and amounts of contributions that can be made (labor unions and corporations for example usually may not contribute directly to a campaign). And a few states have adopted limited public financing (New Jersey for example provides public funds for gubernatorial elections).

In general, however, few states have enacted any serious limits on overall spending or provided for public financing of elections. In most states a campaign can spend as much money as it is possible to raise and there are few limitations on the amount of money an individual or PAC can contribute. *See also: FEDERAL ELECTIONS CAMPAIGN ACT (FECA); GROSS POLITICAL PRODUCT; PUBLIC FINANCING*

CATTLE SHOW early presidential election campaign events which feature joint appearances by several presidential contenders. Cattle show formats usually includes an introduction of all candidates, followed by a ten minute after dinner speech and questions from the audience. Sometimes candidates provide receptions before the dinner and most will "work the crowd" during the evening.

Candidates attend these multi-candidate forums to gain wider exposure, to meet party activists, and recruit supporters. The media pay attention to them because they provide an early opportunity to size up candidates and to hear them speak. And political organizations hold them because they can raise large sums for their sponsors—as much as a quarter of a million dollars for the evening.

Many cattle shows also include straw polls taken after all of the candidates have performed. These surveys are widely dismissed as meaningless, but candidates do put effort and resources into doing well in them—and reporters spend a good deal of time analyzing and reporting the results.

The emergence of the cattle show format may reflect some deeper changes in American politics—"less individual running and more comparative showing" as columnist William Safire puts it. Or it may simply become one more way that candidates campaign and that campaigns raise money. *See also: STRAW POLL*

CHECKOFF a provision in the Federal Revenue Act (1971) which permits taxpayers to designate or checkoff one dollar of their tax payment for the Presidential Election Campaign Fund. This fund is then used to provide public financing to eligible presidential candidates for the pre-convention, convention and post-convention periods of presidential election years.

About 30% of all federal taxpayers elect the checkoff provision each year. The recipient Presidential Election Campaign Fund however pays out only during presidential election years.

Thirteen states also use checkoffs in connection with their public financing programs. These include Michigan, Oregon, North Carolina, Kentucky and New Jersey. The latter is the only state to provide public financing for both the primary and general elections in gubernatorial contests. *See also: PUBLIC FINANCING*

C.O.B. cash on the barrelhead. In political campaigns most purchases of goods and services are C.O.B. Partly this is simply an extension of a practice that vendors and other providers also apply to non-political customers. Media time buying for example is generally done with up front cash regardless of whether purchases are being made for a political account or a non-political account.

But the prepaid policy also exists because many businesses consider political campaigns to be poor credit risks. Some campaigns are managed irresponsibly and many campaigns become over budgeted in the closing days when spending is most frenzied and fund raising most unpredictable.

The C.O.B. stipulation places a serious handicap on campaign planning because the money to pay in advance is rarely available early in the campaign. Usually contributions come in slowly until the last three to four weeks before the election. By this time it is late to make many kinds of expenditures.

Some campaigns solve this problem by arranging loans or lines of credit guaranteed by the candidate or a supporter. Other campaigns simply forego those goods and services that cannot be paid for in advance. *See also: EARLY MONEY; LATE MONEY*

CONTRIBUTION LIMITS *See FEDERAL ELECTIONS CAMPAIGN ACT (FECA)*

DELEGATE COMMITTEES legalese used by the Federal Elections Commission (FEC) in connection with the administration and enforcement of the Federal Elections Campaign Act (FECA). Delegate committees are made up of people working autonomously to get elected as delegates to the national convention of one of the major political parties. In principle they are independent of the presidential candidate whose nomination they support.

Under FEC regulations a delegate committee can raise and spend money free of a candidate's legal spending limits. This characteristic makes them attractive to presidential candidates short of cash. It also makes them vulnerable to charges that they are merely convenient loopholes in the campaign finance law.

Democratic candidate Walter Mondale encountered political controversy in 1984 when his delegate committees were challenged by opponent Gary Hart on the ground that they were not really independent of the Mondale campaign. The Mondale committees were later disbanded, however many of the issues raised regarding them remain to be resolved. *See also: FEDERAL ELECTIONS CAMPAIGN ACT (FECA)*

DISCLOSURE *See CAMPAIGN FINANCE LAWS*

EARLY MONEY contributions made during the first days and weeks of a campaign. Early money is highly valued in electoral politics. Receipt of it permits the campaign to efficiently organize, staff, and achieve exposure for the candidate. Where media is to be part of political advertising early money permits planning and budgeting for an expensive and scarce resource.

Many political professionals consider early contributions to be a barometer to the support a candidate has. Large givers particularly tend to handicap races. If they contribute it indicates that the candidate is viable and the campaign is to be taken seriously.

Early money can also give a candidate an important psychological advantage. It sends would be opponents a message that the campaign is strong and substantial. In fact some political observers now believe that early money is more important than endorsements in revealing the depth and breadth of support for a candidate.

Early money given before the formal campaign begins is known as "seed money." It is used to set up the campaign organization and begin formal fund raising. Seed money ordinarily comes from a few well heeled friends of the prospective candidate, who contribute the money themselves or who raise it from among their own friends. Candidates without such supporters provide their own seed money or perhaps forego running for office. *See also: HANDICAPPING; LATE MONEY*

EVENTS *See SPECIAL EVENTS*

FAT CATS wealthy contributors who have the resources to give large sums of money to a political party or candidate. According to author George Thayer (1973) most American fat cats are not members of old established families as is commonly supposed. Instead they are mostly self made men and women who have either personally accumulated or are actively managing their wealth.

Fat cats were once important sources of funds in American politics. Well known fat cats like C. Clement Stone and Richard Mellon Scaife were legendary for their willingness to write out checks for as much as a million dollars. A handful of these wealthy contributors could bankroll an entire campaign.

Today fat cats have declined in prominence. Campaign finance laws—especially limits on the amount of money that individuals may contribute—have diminished the role of the big givers. More and more the emphasis in campaigns is on raising money in small amounts from a large number of contributors. Now it is the "moneyman" rather than the fat cat who is the focus of attention.

Nevertheless fat cats remain important in American politics. Their influence is still felt even at the national level. Loopholes in the Federal Elections Campaign Act (FECA) allows large unlimited contributions if they are made as so called independent expenditures. Fat cats may also contribute up to $25,000 to both national political parties, and they may contribute up to $1000 per election to individual federal candidates.

State and local elections too continue to provide opportunities for large contributors. Most states still do not limit the amount of money that an individual can contribute. In these states fat cats still may and do contribute heavily to both candidates and political parties. *See also: CAMPAIGN FINANCE LAW; INDEPENDENT EXPENDITURES; MONEYMAN*

FEDERAL ELECTIONS COMMISSION *See FEDERAL ELECTIONS CAMPAIGN ACT (FECA)*

FEDERAL ELECTIONS CAMPAIGN ACT (FECA) landmark reform legislation that radically changed the financing of federal election campaigns. The Federal Elections Campaign Act (FECA) was initially passed in 1971. In 1974—in the aftermath of the Watergate revelations—the FECA provisions were amended.

Then in 1976 Congress again rewrote the FECA to conform to the Supreme Court specification enunciated in BUCKLEY v. VALEO. The present act includes the following four key provisions:

1. Disclosure—strict detailed accounting and reporting of all campaign contributors and expenditures is required; donors must be identified by name, address and occupation.
2. Contribution limits—individual givers are limited to $1000 per candidate per election; PAC's are limited to $5000.
3. Public Financing—presidential primary candidates qualify for federal matching funds after they raise at least $5000 in each of 20 states; major party nominees are

entitled to public monies to finance their general election campaigns; minor party candidates may also qualify for public financing if they receive 5% or more of the vote.
4. Enforcement—the Federal Elections Commission (FEC) was established to administer, interpret, and enforce the new legislation.

The FECA has become the model for much of the campaign finance reforms enacted by individual states since the mid 1970's. After Buckley many states rewrote their election laws to meet the guidelines established by the Supreme Court.
Political observers differ in their assessment of FECA. Some fault the law because it hasn't actually ended the influence of large contributors. Affluent givers can still make independent expenditures, channel money to those state parties which have no restrictions, or even run themselves as candidates. Critics also argue that the FECA has actually weakened political parties by shifting the source of contributions to individuals and PAC's.
Many however praise the FECA. They point out that the influence of fat cats and other big contributors has been reduced if not eliminated. And the stringent disclosure regulations in the legislation have eliminated the type of fraud and deception practiced before 1974.
Supporters also argue that the contribution base has been significantly expanded. Limits on contributions have encouraged more grass roots fund raising efforts such as direct mail—and the check off provision has allowed millions of taxpayers to participate in the financing of presidential elections.
See also: AUTHORIZED COMMITTEES; BUCKLEY v. VALEO; CAMPAIGN FINANCE LAW; DELEGATE COMMITTEES; INDEPENDENT EXPENDITURES; MULTI-CANDIDATE COMMITTEES; PRINCIPAL CAMPAIGN COMMITTEES; PUBLIC FINANCING

FUND RAISING *See SPECIAL EVENTS*

GROSS POLITICAL PRODUCT the amount of money spent overall in American elections. Gross political product was about 2 billion dollars in 1984—about 1 billion dollars in 1980—and about one-half billion in 1976. Critics allege that American campaign spending is extravagant, but these charges don't hold up under careful examination. American spending for campaigns is just about average when compared to spending in other democratic countries.
According to Howard Penninan (1984) of the American Enterprise Institute, U.S. federal elections cost $3.25 per eligible voter. By contrast, Canadian elections cost $1.83 per eligible voter, West German elections $3.20, Irish elections $3.93, Israeli elections $4.34 and Venezuelan elections $26. Moreover the reported cost of foreign elections often doesn't include the expenditures of corporations, labor unions and other interest groups. Nor do they include the value of government subsidized television available in some countries.
Authorities on campaign financing mostly agree that—American campaigns do not spend too much—and probably spend too little. Herbert

Alexander (1980) the executive director of the Citizens Foundation points out that campaigns spend less than 1/10 of one percent of all government spending and less than 3/100 of one percent of the Gross National Product. Overall campaign spending is actually only about equal to the advertising budget of the Proctor & Gamble Company.

Experts also argue that the current level of expenditure doesn't buy that much. Television commercials can cost $10,000 or more to produce, and thousands more to air. A poll can cost $20 to $30 thousand and many campaigns commission several of them. Direct mail is also expensive. A single mailing in a congressional district can cost $20,000 or more. And there is much more. Telephone banks, radio and newspaper advertising, legal costs, staff salaries, and travel all add substantially to the campaign spending that makes up the gross political product. *See also: CAMPAIGN FINANCE LAWS*

HARD MONEY *See SOFT MONEY*

HONEST GRAFT a semantic inconsistency that seems to have presented little confusion to its most famous 19th Century practitioner, one George Plunkett of Tammany Hall. The original example of honest graft—attributed to Plunkett by author William Riordan—was the inside buying of land about to be made more valuable by a public taking.

Honest graft is any financial gain achieved through access to political power or confidential information. The term is archaic. When used today it usually refers to money made or employment gained through political connections. Honest graft is usually unethical but never illegal. *See also: CONNECTIONS*

INDEPENDENT EXPENDITURES campaign spending in a federal election made free of any involvement with the benefitting candidate. The Federal Elections Commission (FEC) defines independent expenditures this way:

> an expenditure for a communication especially advocating the defeat of a clearly identified candidate that is not made with the cooperation or prior consent of, or in consultation with, or at the request or suggestion of any candidate or his/her authorized committees or agents.

Independent expenditures are a major loophole in the FEC's regulations that generally limit political candidates to $1000 for individuals and $5000 for PAC's. The U.S. Supreme Court has upheld these limits but ruled that an independent individual or organization may spend freely to support or oppose federal candidates. These expenditures may not be coordinated in any way with the favored campaign—otherwise they are unrestricted.

Independent expenditures give PAC's an enormous opportunity to influence campaigns beyond the $5000 they may contribute. Non-connected PAC's particularly have moved aggressively to exploit the opportunity to make independent expenditures. The bulk of independent expenditures made by the non-connected's go for negative advertising—which is designed to weaken and undermine support for opposition candidates rather than to strengthen and promote favored candidates. Negative advertising is preferred because it is believed to be more effective. *See also: HIT LIST; NCPAC; NON CONNECTED PAC'S*

IN KIND CONTRIBUTION contributions of goods or services to campaigns in lieu of cash. In kind contributions have a long, if somewhat spotted record in American politics. They have always been favored by would be contributors short of cash, as well as those contributors whose cash was of questionable origin. And they are known as an effective way to conceal both the source and the value of a political contribution.

The Federal Elections Commission (FEC) defines in kind contributions as "services, goods or property offered free or at less than the usual charge to a political committee." Traditionally these goods and services have included things like use of office space, free transportation, and equipment. Even regular corporation or union employees—assigned to the campaign while remaining on the employer's payroll—have been counted as in kind contributions.

Until recent changes in the law and enforcement policy, in kind goods and services have not usually been reported. They were rarely accounted for or disclosed in official campaign documents. When they were acknowledged their actual value was likely to be understated.

Today the federal government and most of the states have tightened disclosure requirements. They treat in kinds as gifts that must be reported with their value reasonably estimated. Furthermore that value may not exceed existing contribution limits—in federal elections $1000 for individuals and $5000 for PAC's.

The Federal Elections Commission (FEC) has probably reduced substantially the incidence of unaccounted for in kind contributions in federal elections. The record in the states is less clear. But there is probably still a large amount of unreported in kind contributions in state and local elections. *See also: CAMPAIGN FINANCE LAWS; LAUNDERED MONEY; SOFT MONEY*

LABOR MONEY an important and often decisive factor in political spending at all three levels of government. The Taft-Hartley Act (1947) outlawed both corporate and union contributions in federal campaigns. Some states do continue to allow direct contributions, but a large proportion of labor money is now spent indirectly.

Labor has evolved three principle ways to pump money into political campaigns. The newest of these is the establishment of political action committees. PAC's have no overall expenditure limits and can contribute up to $5,000 to a candidate for federal office. Unions may also spend money from their treasuries for so-called "nonpolitical educational expenditures" such as voter registration drives and get out the vote (GOTV) efforts. And unions may lawfully spend money for "public service activities" like sponsorship of radio and television programs that promote labor interests.

In addition to these indirect spending techniques, unions also may spend directly in those states which allow it. Several studies have concluded that labor contributes 10–20% of the campaign funds received by Democratic candidates in some states.

In spite of the financial support that labor can bring to bear, some analysts believe that labor's greatest political resource is its ability to turn out legions of volunteers to man phone banks, organize voter registration drives, coordinate GOTV efforts and even run campaigns. These immense manpower resources become more valuable as finance laws are passed limiting the amount of money that can be spent or contributed in campaigns. *See also: IN KIND CONTRIBUTIONS; FEDERAL ELECTIONS CAMPAIGN ACT (FECA); SOFT MONEY*

LATE MONEY contributions that come in during the final days and weeks of the campaign. A high proportion of late money is common in political fund raising—the rising activity of the campaign creates excitement in the electorate which stimulates contributions.

Campaign contributions are normally barometers of how well a candidate is doing. A winning campaign can usually raise money and a losing campaign usually can't. A surge of late money is a particularly reliable indicator of campaign momentum. Conversely, a sharp falloff in contributions may indicate a decline in popular support. *See also: EARLY MONEY*

LAUNDERED MONEY campaign contributions whose origin has been concealed because they were received from illegal or embarrassing sources. Labor unions, large corporations, and organized crime are believed to be the major sources of laundered money. No one knows for certain how much laundered money finds its way into political campaigns, but there are some estimates that organized crime alone accounts for up to 15% of all campaign expenditures.

There are a number of established schemes by which illegal campaign contributions are laundered. The use of slush funds or unaccounted for cash is a common tactic. Another is the payment of employee bonuses given with the understanding that part or all of the money would be passed on to a campaign. Keeping campaign "volunteers" on company or union payrolls or providing free equipment or services, are in kind efforts to obscure the source of a campaign contribution. A method especially suited to media campaigns is to pay as a business expense the advertising agency fees for services actually provided to a political campaign.

The passage of the Federal Election Campaign Act (FECA) has made it difficult to hide illegal contributions made for federal office, however, there is still probably a substantial flow of laundered money to state and local campaigns. *See also: BLACK MONEY; BOODLE*

MACING systematic dunning of government employees for contributions to the incumbent political party. Macing refers to the specific practice of soliciting funds from patronage job holders under the implied threat of dismissal or other retaliation. Three near synonyms are "assessment," "tollgating," and "kickback."

Assessments are levies imposed on elected officials by the political party to which they belong. Often assessments are set at a percentage of the politician's salary. Tollgating is the practice of requiring holders of government licenses or permits to make regular contributions to a political party. A utility operator for example might be expected to give money to the political party in power. Kickbacks are payments based on a percentage of the value of a government contract. A road builder for instance might kickback ten percent of a contract's worth to the incumbent political party.

The working distinctions between these four kinds of fund raising are important. Macing is used only with government employees, usually non-civil service workers; assessment is practiced on elected officials; kickbacks are a one time arrangement tied to a specific government contract; while tollgating is a more systematic and regularized method of raising money from government suppliers.

Macing is historically associated with patronage systems. It flourished before civil service and merit systems were widely introduced. Federal law now prohibits macing of federal employees or state-local employees paid with federal monies.

Most states have also outlawed macing, although the practice persists in some places. The best known surviving system is Indiana's "two percent club." There state employees are expected to give 2% of their wages to the political party in power. *See also: PATRONAGE*

MONEYMAN a political fund raiser, especially one who raises substantial sums of money for a candidate or party. There are two main types of moneyman. One type raises a lot of money for one or two candidates. These moneymen are often friends or close associates of the politician they support. But their interest and involvement in politics doesn't extend beyond this personal relationship.

The second type of moneyman raises some funds for many candidates. These moneymen are frequently long time supporters of either the Democratic or Republican parties. They work in many campaigns and their interest and involvement in politics is more or less continuous.

Both types operate similarly. They are usually members of extensive networks of affluent (mostly male) businessmen, bankers, lawyers, investors and entrepreneurs—people who are able and often willing to contribute $5000 or more to a political party or candidate. Moneymen raise funds by using social, business, and family connections to tap into these networks. Federal Elections Campaign Act (FECA) limits on the amount of money an individual may contribute have increased the prominance of moneymen in modern politics. Fat cats—wealthy individuals who can easily contribute $5,000, $10,000 or even more—are not so important today. Instead the emphasis is on the well connected moneyman who can raise $500 or $1,000 from friends, acquaintances and business associates.

Moneymen sometimes play an even larger role than simply raising money. They are also top advisors and key strategists in many campaigns. These moneymen have special access to the candidate and enjoy special perquisites when a campaign is successful. *See also: CAMPAIGN FINANCE LAWS; FAT CATS; FUNDRAISING*

MULTI CANDIDATE COMMITTEES legalese used by the Federal Elections Commission (FEC) in connection with administration and enforcement of the Federal Elections Campaign Act (FECA). Multi-candidate committees are political action committees (PAC's) which have received contributions for federal elections from more than 50 persons and have made contributions to at least 5 candidates.

These committees may not contribute more than $5000 to a single candidate in any election. However, they may contribute up to $15,000 each to the Democratic and Republican National Committees and an additional $15,000 each to both parties' Senate and House Campaign Committees. Multi-Candidate Committees have no limitation on the overall amount of money they can receive as contributions or on the overall amount of money they can spend. *See also: FEDERAL ELECTIONS CAMPAIGN ACT (FECA); PAC's*

NON-CONNECTED PAC's political action committees that are not tied to any sponsoring parent organization such as a corporation, a labor union or a trade association. Non-connected PAC's cut across the political spectrum. The most prominent of them however, have been markedly conservative in orientation.

The non-connecteds differ from other categories of PAC's—corporate PAC's, labor PAC's, trade association PAC's, etc.—in some important ways: unlike most others the non-connected PAC's stress ideological concerns rather than economic interests; they also tend to support challengers and oppose incumbents much more regularly than do other PAC's.

But the most important characteristic of the non-connecteds is their use of independent expenditures in support of favored candidates. Since independent expenditures are not subject to the $5000 contributions limit that governs most federal campaign contributions, PAC's can spend an unlimited amount of money in federal elections as long as there is no communication or coordination with the benefitting campaign. The bulk of these expenditures go for negative advertising intended to undermine and weaken opposition candidates rather than to promote favored candidates.

Federal level non-connected PAC's number about 500. These include many large and well know organizations such as NCPAC, Fund For A Conservative Majority, National Committee For An Effective Congress, National Women's Caucus and The National Rifle Association. *See also: HIT LIST; INDEPENDENT EXPENDITURES; PAC's*

PRINCIPLE CAMPAIGN COMMITTEE legalese used by the Federal Elections Commission (FEC) in connection with the administration and enforcement of the Federal Elections Campaign Act (FECA). Principle campaign committees must be designated by an individual within 15 days of becoming an official candidate.

They are legally the candidate's principle committee to receive contributions and make expenditures. Principle committees must register with the FEC, designate a depository for the receipt and disbursement of funds, and submit the various reports required by the Federal Elections Campaign Act (FECA).

Candidates are not limited by the law to a single committee. They may designate additional campaign committees to also serve as "Authorized Committees." All authorized committees are permitted to accept contributions or make expenditures on behalf of the candidate. *See also: AUTHORIZED COMMITTEES; FEDERAL ELECTIONS CAMPAIGN ACT (FECA)*

PROSPECTING LIST *See HOUSE LISTS*

PUBLIC FINANCING a method of financing political campaigns that provides partial or full public funding for campaign operations. Public financing was enacted for presidential campaigns beginning in 1976.

The objective of public financing is to limit or exclude the (allegedly) malign influence of private contributions in American politics. The federal law allows presidential primary candidates to qualify for matching funds after they raise at least $5,000 in each of 20 states. Both major political parties receive subsides for their conventions and major party nominees are entitled to public monies to run their general election campaigns.

Thirteen states also provide some form of public financing—many for gubernatorial elections and other major state offices. About half the states distribute public finance funds to the political parties, who can spend them as they wish. In the other states the funds are distributed directly to candidates or given to the parties with restrictions on expenditures.

Most observers believe that the three presidential elections held under public financing have been freer of the taint of corruption than earlier elections. Whether public financing favors one party over another is not clear, but Republicans have recently had much more success than Democrats in raising private funds. This suggests Democrats may gain more from the public subsidy.

Experience in states with public financing reveals a couple of patterns. The availability of public financing in primaries probably encourages more candidates to run than otherwise would. Public financing may also benefit incumbents because it limits expenditures. This restricts challengers who often spend more to be competitive. *See also: CAMPAIGNING FINANCE LAW; CHECKOFF; FEDERAL ELECTIONS CAMPAIGN ACT (FECA)*

SEED MONEY *See EARLY MONEY*

SLACK the notion that future political prospects can be measured by the excess money a candidate raises over current election needs. Slack is political capital.

The basic idea is that a politician with slack has room to grow—to seek more power, enlarge his constituency or run for higher office. Political money flows to winners and those who look like winners. The ability to raise more money than needed indicates how far one can go in politics.

Financial slack has a parallel in the slack that a candidate receives in running up large winning margins over opponents. Winning big may also reveal a politician's potential for higher office. Both financial slack and voting slack represent surplus political resources which a politician may invest in his career.

Slack finds some empirical support in political experience. Candidates who do win by large margins are often encouraged to run for higher office. And politicians with bursting campaign treasuries frequently aspire to headier political challenges.

Not all politicians with slack use it. Nor do those who use it always win. Nevertheless the accumulation of slack is one of the better predictors of who will eventually run for and win high office. *See also: CANDIDATE*

SOFT MONEY money that supports a campaign indirectly by being spent by state political parties for "party building" activities like voter registration, GOTV, telephone banks, and the like. Soft money has two main sources. Some of it comes from the national parties who are not limited in the amounts they can give to their state units for "party building activities." Other soft money comes from corporations, unions, PAC's and other large givers. Most of these contributors have either given the federal legal maximum or are not legal sources of funds for federal elections.

Soft money circumvents federal law limits on the amount national parties can spend or the maximum an individual or PAC may give. Both national parties—DNC and RNC, plus their respective House and Senate campaign committees—are limited in the sources of money they receive and the amounts they themselves can spend.

But state political parties have few if any of these constraints. Most can raise as much as they are able from anyone willing to give; and few state parties are limited in the amounts they can contribute to state and local candidates.

The converse of soft money is "hard money"—contributions made directly by individuals or PAC's. Hard money is the hard cash that flows into a campaign. It may be made by any legal source and used for any legal expenditures. Usually campaigns must account in detail for the income and outgo of hard money. *See also: INDEPENDENT EXPENDITURES; IN-KIND CONTRIBUTIONS*

SPECIAL EVENTS campaign functions intended to combine some electioneering with fund raising. Special events are often gala activities organized to showcase the candidate. Originally the term referred to any major promotion that put the campaign into contact with large numbers of voters: rallys; parades; major speeches, and so on. But now a special event is usually tied to fund raising.

Dinners, receptions, and cocktail parties are the most frequent special events. Other examples are testimonials, picnics, kaffeeklatches and headquarter openings. These events can raise substantial portions of a campaign budget while affording a candidate additional exposure before important voter groups. *See also: SCHEDULING*

STREET MONEY cash distributed to campaign workers and other supporters on election day. Street money or "walking around money" is a traditional election day perk in big cities—especially those like New York, Chicago, Philadelphia or Detroit which still have functioning political organizations. Street money comes from candidates or their campaigns. Sometimes it is channeled through political parties while other times it is paid directly to ward and precinct level officials. The term conveys an air of shabbyness and indeed street money is sometimes associated with corrupt electoral behavior and voting fraud.

Author David Chagall describes the seamier side of street money:

> (its) a traditional tool for picking up votes from minority bloc's . . . a candidate simply hands a packet of greenbacks to brokers who merchandise and deliver bloc votes. In the South the brokers are white men . . . connected with the state Democratic Party. There the customary payoffs are to black schoolteachers and ministers, who in turn distribute ten—or twenty dollar bills to voters they claim to represent. (Chagall, 1981:59)

But not all street money is used to buy votes. In many places it instead pays the expenses of election day. Ward leaders use it to reimburse volunteers, purchase supplies, buy gas, print sample ballots, and take voters to the polls. Many candidates, especially those who are well known or who lack their own campaign staff, think of street money as a way to acquire an election day organization.

Street money is a stronger tradition in poorer urban areas where Democratic constituencies predominate. And Democratic candidates probably rely on street money more than do Republicans, although Republicans have not been loath to use it when the occasion arose. *See also: ELECTION DAY ACTIVITIES*

TOLL GATING *See MACING*

BIBLIOGRAPHY

Abranson, Paul R., John H. Aldrich, and David W. Rhodes. *Change and Continuity in the 1980 Elections.* Washington, D.C.: CQ Press, 1982.

Agranoff, Robert. *The Management of Election Campaigns.* Boston: Holbrook Press, 1976.

Agranoff, Robert. *The New Style in Election Campaigns.* Rev. ed. Boston: Holbrook, 1976.

Alexander, Herbert E., *Financing Politics: Money, Elections, and Political Reform.* 3rd ed. Washington, D.C.: CQ Press, 1984.

Alexander, Herbert. In *Political Parties in America.* Robert J. Huckshorn, ed. North Scituate Mass: Duxbury, 1980.

Asher, Herbert. *Presidential Elections and American Politics: Voters, Candidates and Campaigns Since 1952.* 3rd ed. Homewood, Ill.: Dorsey Press, 1984.

Barber, James. *Pulse of Politics: Electing Presidents in the Media Age.* New York: W. W. Norton, 1980.

Barber, James D. ed. *Race for the Presidency.* Englewood Cliffs, N.J.: Prentice-Hall 1978.

Barone, Michael, and Grant Ujifusa. *Almanac of American Politics.* Washington, D.C.: National Journal, 1984.

Baus, Herbert M., and William B. Ross. *Politics Battle Plan.* New York: Macmillan, 1968.

Backstrom, Charles H., and Gerald Hursh-Cesar. *Survey Research* 2nd ed. New York: John Wiley and Sons, 1981.

Benjamin, Gerald. *The Communications Revolution in Politics.* New York: Academy of Political Science, 1982.

Benson, George. *Political Campaigns in America.* Lexington, Mass.: Lexington Books. 1978.

Berelson, Bernard R., Paul F. Lazarsfeld and William N. McPhee. *Voting: A Study of Opinion Formation in a Presidential Campaign.* Chicago: University of Chicago Press, 1954.

Blevins, Leon W. *The Young Voters Manual: A Topical Dictionary of American Government and Politics.* Totowa, N.J.: Littlefield, Adams, 1973.

Blumenthal, Sidney. *The Permanent Campaign: Inside the World of Elite Political Operatives.* Boston: Beacon Press, 1980.
Bone, Hugh A., and Austin Ranney. *Politics and Voters.* 5th ed. New York: McGraw-Hill, 1981.
Brams, Steven, J. *The Presidential Election Game.* New Haven, Conn.: Yale University Press, 1978.
Burnham, Walter. In *Electoral Behavior: A Comparative Handbook.* Richard Rose, ed. New York: Free Press, 1974.
Butler, David, et al. *Democracy at the Polls: A Comparative Study of Competitive National Elections.* Washington, D.C.: American Enterprise Institute, 1981.
Campbell, Angus, Philip E. Converse, Warren E. Miller, and Donald E. Stokes. *The American Voter.* New York: John Wiley & Sons, 1960.
Campbell, Angus. "Surge and Decline: A Story of Electoral Change" in *Elections and the Political Order,* edited by Campbell et al. New York: John Wiley & Sons, 1966.
Cantril, Albert H. ed. *Polling on the Issues.* Cabin John, M.D.: Seven Locks Press, 1980.
Chagall, David. *The New Kingmakers.* New York: Harcourt, Brace Jovanovich, 1981.
Clendenin, Dudley. "Dilemma of Voter Polls: Suspense of Knowledge." *New York Times* Nov. 7, 1984.
Davis, James W. *National Conventions In An Age of Party Reform.* Westport, Conn.: Greenwood Press, 1983.
deGrazia, Alfred. *Political Behavior.* rev. ed. New York: The Free Press, 1962.
DeVries, Walter and Lance Tarrance, Jr. *The Ticket Splitter.* Grand Rapids, Michigan: Eerdmans, 1972.
Drew, Elizabeth. *Portrait of An Election: The 1980 Presidential Campaign.* New York: Simon & Schuster, 1981.
Edelman, Murray, *The Symbolic Use of Politics.* Urbana: University of Illinois Press, 1964.
Eldersveld, Samuel P. *Political Parties in American Society.* New York: Basic Books, 1982.
Featherman, Sandra. "In Philadelphia Ethnic Voting Remains Alive and Well." *Philadelphia Inquirer.* Oct. 18, 1984.
Fenno, Richard F., Jr. *Homestyle: House Members in their Districts.* Boston: Little, Brown, 1978.
Fishel, Jeff. *Parties and Elections in an Anti-Party Age.* Bloomington: Indiana University Press, 1978.
Flanigan, William H., and Nancy H. Zingale. *Political Behavior of the American Electorate.* Boston: Allyn and Bacon, 1979.
Gallup, George. "The Quintamensional Plan of Question Design." *Public Opinion Quarterly.* Fall, 1947. p. 385.
Gallup, George. *The Sophisticated Pollwatcher's Guide.* Princeton, N.J.: Princeton Opinion Press, 1972.
Graber, Doris. *Mass Media and American Politics.* Washington, D.C.: CQ Press, 1980.
Greenfield, Jeff. *Running to Win.* Simon and Schuster, 1980.

Grove, Masloff. *After Daley*. Champaign, Ill: University of Illinois Press, 1982.
Heimanson, Rudolf. *Dictionary of Political Science and Law*. Dobbs Ferry, NY: Oceana, 1967.
Hershey, Marjorie R. *The Making of Campaign Strategy*. Lexington, Mass.: D.C. Heath, 1974.
Hess, Stephen. *The Government—Press Connection*. Washington, D.C.: The Brookings Institute, 1984.
Hiebert, Ray, et al. *Political Image Merchants: Strategies in the New Politics*. Washington, D.C.: Acropolis Books, 1971.
Hinckley, Barbara. *Congressional Elections*. Washington, D.C.: CQ Press, 1981.
Huckshorn, Robert J., *Political Parties In America*. North Scituate, Mass.: Duxbury, 1980.
Huckshorn, Robert J., and Robert C. Spenser. *The Politics of Defeat*. Amherst: University of Massachusetts Press, 1971.
Hudson, Kenneth. *Language of Modern Politics*. Atlantic Highlands, NJ: Humanities Press, 1978.
Jacobson, Gary C., *The Politics of Congressional Elections*. Boston: Little, Brown, 1983.
Jacobson, Gary C., and Samuel Kernell. *Strategy and Choice in Congressional Elections*. New Haven: Yale University Press, 1981.
Jewel, Malcolm E., and David M. Olson. *American State Political Parties and Elections*. Homewood, Ill.: Dorsey Press, 1982.
Johnson, Haynes. "What does Jim Rowe's Party Stand for Today? Not Much" *Washington Post National Weekly Edition*. July 9, 1984, p. 25.
Joslyn, Richard. *Mass Media and Elections*. Reading, Mass.: Addison-Wesley, 1984.
Kay, Beatrice. *Victory in the Voting Booth*. Palm Springs, CA.: ETC Publishers, 1981.
Kayden, Xandra. *Campaign Organization*. Lexington, Mass.: D.C. Heath, 1978.
Keefe, William J. *Parties, Politics and Public Policy in America*. 4th ed. New York: Holt, Rinehart, and Winston, 1984.
Kelley, Stanley, Jr. *Interpreting Elections*. Princeton, N.J.: Princeton University Press, 1983.
Kelley, Stanley, Jr. *Professional Public Relations and Political Power*. Baltimore: Johns Hopkins University Press, 1956.
Ladd, Everett Carll. *Where Have all the Voters Gone? The Fracturing of American Political Parties*. 2nd ed. New York: W.W. Norton, 1982.
Lazarsfeld, Paul, Bernard Berelson, and Hazel Gaudet: *The People's Choice*. New York: Columbia University Press, 1944.
Lengle, James I., *Representation and Presidential Primaries: The Democratic Party in the Post-Reform Era*. Westwood, Conn.: Greenwood, 1981.
Leuthold, David A. *Electioneering in a Democracy: Campaigns for Congress*. New York: John Wiley & Sons, 1968.
Luttbeg, Norman R. *Public Opinion and Public Policy*. New York: Bantam Books, 1981.
Mandrel, Ruth B. *In the Running: The New Woman Candidate*. New York: Ticknor and Fields, 1981.

McCleskey H. Clifton. *American Political Journal: An Introductory Reader.* Homewood, Ill.: Dorsey, 1982.

McLean, Iain. *Dealing in Votes.* New York: St. Martins Press, 1982.

Milbrath, Lester W., and M. L. Goel. *Political Participation: How and Why do People get Involved in Politics.* 2nd ed. Rand McNally, 1977.

Moore, Jonathon, ed. *Campaign for President: 1980 In Retrospect.* Cambridge, Mass.: Ballinger Publishing Co., 1981.

Nie, Norman H., Sidney Verba, and John R. Petrocik. *The Changing American Voter.* Cambridge, Mass.: Harvard University Press, 1976.

Nimmo, Dan D. *Popular Images of Politics.* Englewood Cliffs, N.J.: Prentice Hall, 1974.

Nimmo, Dan D., and Keith R. Sanders. *Handbook of Political Communications.* Beverly Hills, CA: Sage, 1981.

Nimmo, Dan D., and William L. Rivers. *Watching American Politics.* New York: Longman, 1981.

Paletz, David L., and Robert M. Entman. *Media Power Politics.* New York: The Free Press, 1981.

Parkinson, Hank. *Winning Your Campaign: A Nuts-and-Bolts Guide to Political Victory.* Englewood Cliffs, N.J.: Prentice-Hall, 1970.

Parkinson, Hank. *Winning Political Campaigns with Publicity.* Wichita, Kansas: Campaign Associates Press, 1973.

Patterson, Thomas E. *The Mass Media Election: How Americans Choose Their President.* New York: Praeger, 1980.

Patterson, Thomas E., and Robert D. McClure. *The Unseeing Eye: The Myth of Television Power in National Politics.* New York: G. P. Putnam's Sons, 1976.

Payne, Stanley. *Art of Asking Questions.* rev. ed. Princeton: Princeton University Press, 1980.

Penninan, Howard. In "Politicians Should Spend More Money Not Less On Campaigns." *Washington Post National Weekly Edition.* Sept. 24, 1984, p. 25.

Perry, James. "Liberal Incumbents Are Main Targets of T.V. Ads as Political Action Groups Exploit Court Ruling." *Wall Street Journal.* January 25, 1980, p. 38.

Phillips, Kevin P. *The Emerging Republican Majority.* New Rochelle, N.Y.: Arlington House, 1969.

Plano, Jack C., and Milton Greenberg. *The American Political Dictionary.* 5th ed. New York: Holt, Rinehart and Winston, 1979.

Polsby, Nelson W., and Aaron Wildavsky. *Presidential Elections: Strategies of American Electoral Politics.* 6th ed. New York: Schribner's Sons, 1984.

Pomper, Gerald, and Susan Lederman. *Elections in America.* 2nd ed. New York: Longman, 1980.

Ranney, Austin. "Parties in State Politics" in *Politics in the American States: A Comparative Analysis.* 2nd ed. Herbert Jacob and Kenneth N. Vines, eds. Boston: Little, Brown, 1971.

Roberts, G. K. *A Dictionary of Political Analysis.* New York: St. Martins, 1971.

Robinson John, and Robert Meadows. *Polls Apart.* Cabin John, M.D., Seven Locks Press, 1983.

Rose, Richard. *Electoral Behavior: A Comparative Handbook.* New York: The Free Press, 1974.

Rosenbloom, David. *The Election Men.* New York: Quadrangle, 1973.

Sabato, Larry J. "Dirty Tricks in Politics—How Insiders See It." *U.S. News and World Reports.* July 18, 1983.

Sabato, Larry J. *Pac Power: Inside the World of Political Action Committees.* New York: W.W. Norton, 1984.

Sabato, Larry J. *The Rise of Political Consultants.* New York: Basic Books, 1981.

Safire, William. *Safire's Political Dictionary: The New Language of Politics.* New York: Random House, 1978.

Salmore, Stephen A., and Barbara G. Salmore. *Candidates, Parties and Campaigns: Electoral Politics in America.* Washington, D.C.: CQ Press, 1985.

Scammom, Richard, and Ben Wattenberg. *The Real Majority.* New York: Coward, McCann and Geoghegan, 1970.

Schwartz, Tony. *The Responsive Chord.* Garden City, N.Y.: Doubleday, 1973.

Scrotan, Roger. *Dictionary of Political Thought.* New York: Harper and Row, 1982.

Simpson, Dick. *Winning Elections: A Handbook of Participatory Politics.* rev. ed. Athens, OH: Ohio University Press, 1982.

Smith, Edward C., and Arnold J. Zurcher. *Dictionary of American Politics.* 2nd ed. New York: Barnes & Noble, 1981.

Sorauf, Frank J. *Party Politics in America.* 3rd ed. Boston: Little, Brown, 1972.

Sperber, Hans, and Travis Trittschuh. *American Political Terms.* Detroit: Wayne State University Press, 1962.

Steinberg, Arnold. *The Political Campaign Handbook: Media, Scheduling and Advance.* Lexington, Mass.: D.C. Heath, 1976.

Thayer, George. *Who Shakes the Money Tree? American Campaign Finance Practices from 1789 to the Present.* New York: Simon and Schuster, 1973.

Vermeer, Jan Pon. *For Immediate Release: Candidate Press Releases in American Political Campaigns.* Westport, Conn.: Greenwood, 1982.

Wheeler, Michael. *Lies, Damm Lies, and Statistics: The Manipulation of Public Opinion in America.* New York: Norton, 1976.

Whisker, James B. *Dictionary of Concepts on American Politics.* New York: John Wiley & Sons, 1980.

White, Theodore. *American In Search of Itself: The Making of the President 1956–80. New York: Harper and Row,* 1982.

Wolfinger, Raymond, and Steven J. Rosenstone. *Who Votes.* New Haven: Yale University Press, 1980.

INDEX

A

B

C

D

E

F

G

H

I

J

K

L

M

Q

R

S

T

U

V

W

X-Y-Z

Yellow Dog Democrat	(5)
Young Voters	(6)
Zero Sum Game	(4)
Zone Coverage	(2)
Zoo	(2)